Third Edition

Building Strength and Stamina

Wayne L. Westcott, Ph.D.

HEALTHY LEARNING™

ISBN: 978-1-60679-361-9
Library of Congress Control Number: 2016942408
Book layout: Cheery Sugabo
Cover design: Cheery Sugabo
Cover photo: Jupiterimages/liquidlibrary/Thinkstock
Illustrations: Cheery Sugabo
Text photos: Daniela Huynh and Brian Doherty

Healthy Learning
P.O. Box 1828
Monterey, CA 93942
www.healthylearning.com

DEDICATION

I am honored to dedicate this book to the most important person in my life, my wonderful wife, Claudia.

ACKNOWLEDGMENTS

I appreciate the privilege of publishing the 3rd edition of *Building Strength and Stamina*, and express my sincere thanks to my excellent Healthy Learning editorial/production team of Dr. James Peterson, Kristi Huelsing, Ginger Bryant, Jacob Gustafson, and Ryan Rudd. I am equally grateful to my photographers Daniela Huynh and Brian Doherty for taking and developing outstanding photos of the exercise demonstrations. The exercise models were amazing, and I am pleased to acknowledge each of these special individuals—Michelle Anzalone, Diana Belanger, Susan Bossa, Robert Cobbett, Patty Churchill, Daniel Davis, Sarah Dolan, Julian Dorvil, Kim Driscoll, Stephanie Freedman, Jarred Gaines, Kendra Hanson (who also modeled the exercise video), Kristen Jones, Heather Keen, Rita La Rosa Loud, Blerina Mance, Brendon O'Brien, Karen Peterson, Dick Raymond, Christiana Marques, Deborah Stockbridge, Amanda Sullivan, Annie Tsaffaras, Peter Tsaffaras, Vincent Van Joolen, and Claudia Westcott.

I also genuinely appreciate the assistance and support from my college president, Dr. Peter Tsaffaras, my college dean, Dr. Vincent Van Joolen, and my exercise science associate, Rita La Rosa Loud, in almost every aspect of my work on this project. Most of all, I am thankful for the love, patience, and prayers of my wife, Claudia, and for God's enabling grace in writing this book.

CONTENTS

INTRODUCTION

Many people think of strength training as an activity for genetically gifted individuals who have inherited large muscles, such as weight lifters, bodybuilders, and football players. Similarly, many people believe that endurance exercise belongs to genetically gifted individuals who have inherited relatively large hearts, such as distance runners, cyclists, and rowers. As such, it is true that at the higher levels of competitive sports, genetics plays a major role in elite physical performance and outstanding athletic achievement.

With respect to participation sports, recreational activities, physical fitness, and general health, however, few factors are as helpful as an increased level of muscular strength and an enhanced degree of cardiovascular endurance. Equally encouraging, essentially everyone can attain greater muscular strength and cardiovascular endurance through appropriately designed exercise programs. It is critically important for adults, particularly older adults, to realize that they can reverse many of the debilitating physical processes and health risk factors associated with aging through sensible strength and endurance training.

Most adults do not know that they may lose up to 10 percent of their muscle mass and up to 30 percent of their bone mass every decade of their life, unless they perform regular resistance exercise. Even worse, they may assume that muscle loss, bone loss, metabolic slowdown, and fat gain are inevitable consequences of the aging process. Fortunately, this assumption is not true.

In fact, research clearly demonstrates that men and women of all ages can add muscle, rebuild bone, recharge metabolism, and reduce fat by performing strength training regularly and properly. The combination of resistance exercise and aerobic activity effectively reduces the risk of many degenerative diseases and disabilities, including sarcopenia, osteopenia, osteoporosis, obesity, metabolic syndrome, diabetes, heart disease, stroke, low back pain, arthritis, fibromyalgia, various types of cancer, depression, and all-cause mortality.

Equally impressive, the health and fitness benefits of exercise can be attained in a time-efficient manner. The American College of Sports Medicine and the American Heart Association endurance exercise guidelines call for 20 minutes of vigorous aerobic activity performed three days a week. Their strength training guidelines call for performing 8 to 10 resistance exercises that cumulatively address the major muscle groups performed two or three non-consecutive days a week. As such, doing one set of 10 exercises typically requires approximately 20 minutes.

Accordingly, one hour a week of endurance exercise and 40 minutes a week of strength training should be sufficient to increase physical fitness and decrease health risks. Based on our research with the United States Air Force, a 20-minute circuit training program, with combined strength and endurance exercise, performed three days a week, proved highly effective for improving all categories of the Air Force physical fitness assessment battery. In other words, just one hour of exercise a week can enable an individual to attain significant improvements in muscular strength and cardiovascular endurance.

There are almost unlimited strength training programs and aerobic exercise protocols that have worked well for different people and various purposes. For example, strength and conditioning coaches provide highly specialized workouts for essentially all professional sports, particularly with respect to strength athletes, endurance athletes, and power athletes. The typically high-volume training sessions that can be successfully sustained by elite athletes, however, are not usually well-tolerated by the vast majority of men and women who are not as physically gifted.

The primary focus of *Building Strength and Stamina*, 3rd edition, is to present research-based exercise principles, training protocols, and conditioning programs that are safe, practical, and productive for increasing muscular strength and cardiovascular endurance in men and women of various ages and fitness levels. The secondary intent of this book is to provide research-based training recommendations for advanced exercisers and high-level athletes. Although this book is not a nutrition textbook, recent research findings regarding the muscle and bone building benefits of higher protein consumption will be presented, along with specific guidelines for optimally increasing protein intake.

This edition of *Building Strength and Stamina* also features practical information on warm-ups, cool-downs, and stretching exercises, that is designed to provide a more complete context for experiencing safe and effective exercise sessions. With regard to correct exercise execution, Chapter 5 offers detailed descriptions and precise photographs of properly performed resistance exercises, using free-weights, resistance machines, and bodyweight. Chapter 6 presents properly performed aerobic activity, using cycles, treadmills, rowers, and steppers.

Among the things that you will learn by reading this book are the following:
- A basic and brief program of strength and endurance exercise can increase overall muscle strength by more than 50 percent in 10 weeks, while concurrently adding three pounds of muscle and reducing four pounds of fat.
- An advanced and brief program of resistance exercise can further increase muscle strength by more than 20 percent and muscle mass by more than two pounds after 10 weeks of higher intensity training.
- Beginning exercisers can enhance their strength gains by approximately 20 percent by performing static stretching exercises in conjunction with their resistance training.

- Beginning exercisers can enhance their muscle gains by more than 30 percent by consuming appropriate amounts of protein just before or just after their training sessions.
- Overweight exercisers can enhance their fat loss by more than 40 percent by consuming appropriate amounts of protein just before or just after their training sessions.

The 3rd edition of *Building Strength and Stamina* is divided into two complementary sections. The first section (Chapters 1 through 6) presents relevant, research-based information on strength training. The second section (Chapters 7 through 9) provides equally important information on endurance exercise, with a final chapter on nutritional recommendations.

Chapter 1 addresses the physiological and psychological benefits of resistance training. Chapter 2 presents basic information on muscle make-up and strength-building potential. Chapter 3 summarizes the essentials of muscle contraction and movement mechanics principles and provides research-based recommendations for maximizing strength training results. Chapter 4 presents the research-based recommendations for safe, sensible, and successful strength training experiences. Chapter 5 offers precise descriptions and focused photographs for properly performing a variety of free-weight, resistance machine, and bodyweight exercises. Chapter 6 details appropriate strength training programs for basic and advanced exercisers, as well as highly effective circuit strength training protocols based on our U.S. Air Force study. Chapter 7 discusses the health and fitness benefits of aerobic training, and presents the guidelines for performing effective endurance exercise. Chapter 8 provides practical information for selecting endurance exercise equipment and using each training mode properly. Chapter 9 outlines specific training protocols for performing basic endurance exercise, interval training, circuit training, and cross-training. Finally, Chapter 10 offers nutritional information for enhancing training results, with special attention to protein intake and calorie consumption.

This book is intended to provide all the information you need to perform sensible and successful exercise programs that enable you to attain higher levels of muscular strength and cardiovascular endurance in a safe, effective, and time-efficient manner. Furthermore, the accompanying training video offers model demonstrations of the most productive resistance machine and free-weight exercises, with concurrent performance guidelines. I hope that you will find the text and illustrations educational, motivational, practical, and applicable, and that the training programs will provide reinforcing results for attaining and maintaining a healthy and fit lifestyle.

CHAPTER 1
Strength Training Benefits: Physiological and Psychological

Muscles serve many functions. Most importantly, however, they are the engines of the body. Muscles are where combustion takes place, where energy is released, where power is produced, and where movement occurs. Muscles are essential for human movement, but they also play a major role in metabolism and weight management.

In reality, poor muscular fitness is associated with a variety of health risk factors, injuries, infirmities, diseases, and even all-cause mortality (Westcott 2012). In fact, recent research reveals that muscles produce hormone-like substances called myokines that exert a positive effect on other body tissues and systems. This chapter documents some of the impressive physiological adaptations and psychological benefits that result from strengthening the muscles of the body through resistance exercise on a regular basis.

Body Fat

Based on body mass index (BMI) calculations, approximately 70 percent of American adults have too much body fat (Hedley et al. 2004). Most people also realize that excess fat is associated with high blood sugar levels, elevated blood pressure readings, undesirable blood lipid profiles, insulin resistance, type 2 diabetes, cardiovascular disease, and certain types of cancer. Unfortunately, most people do not realize that dieting alone has never proven to be an effective intervention for permanent weight loss and sustained weight management.

Research demonstrates that almost all successful dieters regain all of the weight they lost within one or two years (Mann et al. 2007). Even more problematic is the fact that at least 25 percent of the weight lost on most diet plans is muscle tissue (Ballor and Poehlman 1994). Essentially, dieting alone produces temporary fat loss and permanent muscle loss, both of which are undesirable outcomes with respect to health, fitness, and physical appearance.

Dieting with exercise is a more successful and sustainable approach to weight management. However, the exercise program should not be limited to aerobic activity (e.g., walking, running, cycling). In order to maximize fat loss and minimize muscle loss, the exercise program should include regular resistance training. In fact, a sensible combination of diet, aerobic activity, and strength training can produce concurrent fat loss and muscle gain. For example, in a recent study, participants who reduced their calorie intake while performing both strength and endurance exercise experienced more than seven pounds of fat loss and almost two pounds of muscle gain over a 10-week training period (Westcott et al. 2013).

Even without calorie restriction, standard strength and endurance exercise typically results in significant fat loss, as well as muscle gain. As an example, research with over 1600 study participants demonstrated a three-pound increase in lean (muscle) weight and a four-pound decrease in fat weight after 10 weeks of training (Westcott et al. 2009). As will be explained in a following section, three relatively brief weekly weight workouts may be responsible for burning approximately 5,400 additional calories every month.

Although combined strength and endurance exercise can cause concurrent fat loss and muscle gain, fat loss is enhanced with dieting whereas muscle gain is enhanced without dieting. For example, in identical training programs, the group that reduced caloric intake significantly decreased body fat, but did not significantly increase lean (muscle) weight. Conversely, the group that did not reduce caloric intake significantly increased lean (muscle) weight, but did not significantly decrease body fat (Westcott et al. 2013).

Muscle

Most people assume that the heart is the engine of the body, but the heart actually functions as the fuel pump of the body. Although the heart is arguably the most important organ in the body, its primary purpose is to pump oxygen-rich blood to all body tissues. Muscles make up more than half of our lean weight, with bones, blood, organs, and skin comprising the other half.

As mentioned previously, muscles are the engines that provide combustion chambers for energy to be released and power to be produced. As muscles contract, they move the bones to which they attach, enabling an almost unlimited number of physical actions. As our human engines, muscles use large amounts of energy during physical activity and moderate amounts of energy 24 hours a day for ongoing tissue repair and remodeling processes.

Because muscle is very active tissue, it plays a major role in our metabolism, even when we are at rest. For people who do not perform strength training, each pound of skeletal muscle uses between five and six calories a day for tissue maintenance (Wolfe 2006). Even more impressive, for people who do regular resistance exercise, each pound of skeletal muscle uses approximately nine calories a day for tissue remodeling (Strasser and Schobersberger 2011). In other words, strength trained muscle burns about 50 percent more calories a day than non-strength trained muscle. Consider the impact that a full-body weight workout has on metabolic rate, energy use, and fat loss.

Metabolism

Muscle plays a major role in our resting metabolism, which is responsible for approximately 70 percent of daily calorie use in sedentary men and women (Wolfe 2006). Among inactive adults, muscle loss (atrophy) averages 2 to 3 percent per decade (Keys et al. 1973), and is the largest factor in the age-related reduction in resting metabolic rate (Phillips 2007). Unfortunately, a decrease in resting metabolism is generally accompanied by an increase in fat storage.

The good news is that regular resistance exercise can reverse both muscle loss and metabolic decline. As indicated in the previous section, strength training can significantly increase muscle mass in adults and older adults (Campbell et al. 1994; Fiatorone et al. 1990; Hagerman et al. 2000; Hunter et al. 2000; Nelson et al. 1994; Pratley et al. 1994; Westcott 2009; Westcott et al. 2009). Equally impressive, strength training can significantly increase resting metabolic rate in adults and older adults

(Broeder et al. 1992; Campbell et al. 1994; Hunter et al. 2000; Lemmer et al. 2001; Pratley et al. 1994; Van Etten et al. 1997).

One effect of resistance exercise on resting metabolism is the addition of new muscle tissue. Assuming an at-rest energy requirement of nine calories per pound, a three-pound muscle gain would increase resting energy use by almost 30 calories per day (Strasser and Schobersberger 2011).

An even greater effect of resistance exercise on resting metabolism is the increased protein turnover required for muscle remodeling. The tissue microtrauma caused by strength training activates relatively large amounts of energy for muscle rebuilding and building processes that continue for three or more days following the exercise session (Hackney et al. 2008; Heden et al. 2011). Both high-volume strength training and high-intensity strength training have been shown to significantly increase resting energy expenditure for 72 hours after the workout.

Hackney and associates examined the effects of a high-volume strength training session on resting energy expenditure using a single workout protocol of eight sets of eight exercises (Hackney et al. 2008). Over the following three days, the advanced exercisers averaged an 8-percent increase in resting energy expenditure, while the new exercisers averaged a 9-percent increase in resting energy expenditure. Heden and colleagues conducted a similar study with beginning strength trainers who performed either three sets of 10 resistance exercises or one set of 10 resistance exercises (Heden et al. 2011). Both high intensity training protocols produced a 5-percent increase in resting energy expenditure for three days following the relatively brief workouts. The results of these and other studies (Campbell et al.1994; Pratley et al.1994; Hunter et al. 2000; Broeder et al. 1992; Lemmer et al. 2001; Van Etten et al.1997) indicate that regular resistance exercise may increase resting energy expenditure by more than 100 calories per day.

As discussed in a previous section, three weekly strength training sessions may use more than 5,000 calories per month, due largely to the effects of enhanced resting energy expenditure. Consider that a short-rest circuit strength training program may burn about 200 calories during a 20 to 25 minute exercise session. Performing 12 weight workouts a month would therefore utilize approximately 2,400 calories (12 x 200 calories).

Assuming a 100-calorie per day increase in resting energy expenditure for muscle remodeling processes, a secondary benefit of the 12 weight workouts would be an additional 3000 calories burned every month (30 x 100 calories). Therefore, the total energy utilization associated with 12 brief strength training sessions is approximately 5,400 calories per month (2,400 calories + 3,000 calories), which is roughly equivalent to 1.5 pounds of body fat. Although the direct effect of resistance exercise on calorie use is similar to that of light-to-moderate aerobic activity (walking, jogging, etc.), the indirect effect is a significant elevation in resting energy expenditure (5 to 9 percent) that may more than double the rate of fat loss.

Type 2 Diabetes

Muscle, metabolism, and fat have a lot to do with risk of developing type 2 diabetes, a very serious disease that is predicted to affect more than 30 percent of adults by the middle of this century (Boyle 2010). The cascade of undesirable events proceeds from sedentary lifestyle to muscle loss, muscle loss to metabolic rate reduction, metabolic rate reduction to fat gain, fat gain to elevated blood glucose levels, and elevated blood glucose levels to type 2 diabetes. Diabetes is associated with excessive body fat, especially with the accumulation of fat in the abdominal area (Coon et al.1992; Kohrt et al.1993). High levels of body fat have a negative influence on insulin sensitivity, which interferes with glycemic (glucose) control, and predisposes type 2 diabetes.

Resistance exercise may be the most effective intervention for preventing and managing type 2 diabetes (Flack et al. 2001; Strasser et al. 2010). Strength training has been shown to reduce the risk of type 2 diabetes by decreasing abdominal fat (Hunter et al. 2002; Ibanez et al. 2005; Treuth et al.1994; Treuth et al.1995), increasing insulin sensitivity (Phillips and Winett 2010; Holten et al. 2004), improving glycemic control (Casteneda et al. 2002; Dunstan et al. 2002) and metabolic health (Gordan et al. 2004; Cauza et al. 2005; Strasser et al. 2010; Phillips and Winett 2010).

Although aerobic activity is advisable for people with diabetes, there is evidence that resistance exercise is even more effective for increasing insulin sensitivity (Eves 2006) and for decreasing blood sugar levels (HbA1c) (Bweir et al. 2009). Flack and colleagues (2011) review of the existing research on diabetes intervention led them to suggest that strength training programs should incorporate higher-intensity and higher-volume protocols for best results. This recommendation is in agreement with the American Diabetes Association guidelines that call for resistance exercises involving all major muscle groups, training three days a week, progressing to three sets of 8 to 10 repetitions, and performed at a high level of intensity (Standards 2006). When we realize that our muscles function as the engines of our body, that our muscles are the largest storage source of glycogen in our body, that our muscles play a major role in resting metabolic rate, and that resting metabolism has a significant influence on body fat, it becomes evident that regular resistance exercise is an essential element in the prevention and management of type 2 diabetes.

Cardiovascular Disease

Cardiovascular disease is the leading cause of death in the United States. There are many predisposing factors that increase the risk of cardiovascular disease, and associated life-threatening events, such as heart attacks and strokes. In addition to high body-fat percentage and high blood-sugar levels previously discussed, major coronary risk factors include high resting blood pressure readings, undesirable blood lipid profiles (i.e., high LDL cholesterol, low HDL cholesterol, high triglycerides), and poor vascular condition.

Fortunately, both aerobic activity and strength training have been shown to be effective for improving cardiovascular health and fitness, as well as for reducing coronary risk factors. A comprehensive research review by Strasser and Schobersberger (2011) revealed that resistance exercise was beneficial for improving body composition (decreasing fat weight and increasing muscle mass), reducing abdominal fat, lowering resting blood pressure, improving blood lipid profiles, and enhancing glycemic control. The reviewers concluded that strength training was as effective as endurance training for reducing some of the major cardiovascular disease risk factors. Consider the evidence-based effects of resistance exercise on resting blood pressure, blood lipid profiles and vascular condition.

Blood Pressure

Elevated blood pressure is essentially epidemic in the United States, with approximately 35 percent of American adults classified as hypertensive (Ong et al. 2007). A number of studies have shown significant reductions in resting blood pressure (systolic and diastolic), as a result of regular or circuit-style strength training (Cauza et al. 2005; Hurley et al.1995; Kelley 1997; Smutok et al.1993).

Two large research reviews (meta-analyses) have determined that resistance exercise is effective for lowering resting blood pressure readings (Kelley and Kelley 2000; Cornelissen and Fagard 2005). The most recent meta-analysis by Cornelissen and Fagard (2005) revealed that resistance training was associated with average resting blood pressure reductions of -6.0 mmHg systolic and -4.7 mmHg diastolic. These findings represented impressive improvements in resting blood pressure readings that were comparable with resting blood pressure reductions associated with endurance training (Cornelissen and Fagard 2005).

Even relatively brief programs of strength and endurance exercise have demonstrated significant reductions in resting blood pressure (Kelemen and Effran 1990; Westcott et al. 2009). A study by Westcott and colleagues (2009) examined the effects of 10 weeks of combined strength and endurance exercise of blood pressure readings in more than 1,600 men and women between the ages of 21 and 80 years. All of the program participants performed 20 minutes of strength training and 20 minutes of endurance training, two or three days each week, throughout the study period.

Individuals who exercised three days a week experienced a 4.6 mmHg reduction in resting systolic blood pressure and a 2.2 mmHg reduction in resting diastolic blood pressure. Those who exercised two days a week experienced a 3.2 mmHg decrease in resting systolic blood pressure and a 1.4 mmHg decrease in resting diastolic blood pressure.

Based on the results of these studies and research analyses, it appears that properly performed resistance exercise is a productive means for lowering resting blood pressure in adults and older adults. Properly performed strength training is characterized by continuous movement of the resistance (lifting and lowering actions) and continuous breathing (no breath holding) throughout every exercise repetition.

Blood Lipids

The American Heart Association reports that almost one of every two Americans has an increased risk of cardiovascular disease due to undesirable blood lipid profiles (Lloyd-Jones et al. 2009). Blood lipid profiles that raise cardiovascular disease risk include high LDL (bad) cholesterol levels, low HDL (good) cholesterol levels, and high triglyceride levels.

Although some studies have not shown significant effects of resistance exercise on blood lipids (Kokkinos et al. 1998; Smutok et al. 1993), several studies have demonstrated significant improvements in blood lipid profiles following participation in a strength training program (Boyden et al. 1993; Hagerman et al. 2000; Kelley and Kelley 2009; Tambalis et al. 2009; Tucker and Silvester 1996; Ulrich et al. 1987). In fact, research indicates that resistance training and aerobic activity are about equally effective for improving blood lipid levels (Kokkinos et al. 1998; Smutok et al. 1993).

Although a research review by Kelley and Kelley (2009) reported only modest changes in blood lipid profiles following participation in strength training programs, the American College of Sports Medicine position stand on Exercise and Physical Activity for Older Adults (2009) presents more impressive blood lipid improvements resulting from resistance exercise. This report reveals higher HDL cholesterol readings (range of 8 to 21 percent), lower LDL cholesterol readings (range of 13 to 23 percent), and reduced triglyceride levels (range of 11 to 18 percent) associated with resistance training.

These beneficial changes in blood lipid profiles are consistent with those reported in older women who experienced significant improvements in HDL cholesterol, LDL cholesterol, and triglycerides after completing an age-appropriate program of resistance exercise (Fahlman et al. 2002). Although it appears that strength training is an effective means for improving blood lipid profiles, research indicates that performing both strength and endurance exercise provides greater blood lipid benefits than doing either physical activity independently (Pitsavos et al. 2009).

Vascular Condition

One of the physiological factors that directly affect blood pressure is the ability of the arteries to accommodate blood flow. This blood vessel compliance is referred to as vascular condition. Some studies indicate that resistance exercise has a negative effect on arterial compliance (Cortez-Cooper et al. 2005; Miyachi et al. 2004). Other studies show no effect of resistance exercise on arterial compliance (Maeda et al. 2006; Rakobowchuk et al. 2005). Still other studies reveal that resistance exercise has a positive effect on arterial compliance (Anton et al. 2006; Fahs et al. 2010; Olson et al. 2006). While more research on this topic is clearly warranted, it appears that appropriately designed strength training programs may have the potential to enhance vascular condition.

Based on the research reviewed, resistance exercise may improve cardiovascular health and reduce the risk of coronary disease by reducing resting blood pressure, increasing HDL cholesterol, decreasing LDL cholesterol, and lowering triglycerides. As a result, vascular condition is enhanced, body weight and abdominal fat are reduced, and insulin sensitivity and glycemic control are improved.

In addition to its preventive benefits, strength training has proven useful for persons who have previously experienced coronary problems. Several studies have shown that resistance exercise is effective for attaining/maintaining desirable body weight, increasing muscular strength, improving physical performance, and enhancing self-efficacy/self-concept in cardiac patients (Faigenbaum et al. 1990; Marzolini et al. 2008; Pollock et al. 2000; Stewart et al. 1988).

Bone Density

The age-related reduction in muscle mass called sarcopenia, is closely associated with the loss of bone mass, known as osteopenia. Approximately 35 million Americans have insufficient bone mass, while another 10 million are living with frail bones (osteoporosis), which increases their risk of experiencing bone fractures (National Osteoporosis Foundation 2009). According to the U.S. Department of Health and Human Services (2004), approximately one of three women and one of six men will suffer from an osteoporosis-related bone fracture.

The average bone loss for adults who do not strength train is 1 to 3 percent per year, which is equivalent to a 10 to 30 percent decrease in bone mineral density every decade of life (Kemmler et al. 2005; Nelson et al. 1994; Warren et al. 2008). Fortunately, the same resistance training programs that increase muscle mass also increase bone mass. Although a few studies have not shown significant gains in bone mineral density following resistance exercise (Chilibeck et al. 1996; Nichols et al. 2007; Sinaki et al. 1996; Vuori et al. 1994; Warren et al. 2008), most of the related research has demonstrated significant increases in bone mass after several months of strength training (Cussler et al. 2003; Dornemann et al. 2002; Going et al. 2003; Judge et al. 2005; Kerr et al. 1996; Kerr et al. 2001; Lohman et al. 1995; Miliken et al. 2003; Nelson et al. 1994; Nichols-Richardson et al. 2007; Von Stengel et al. 2007; Yarasheski et al. 1997).

A comprehensive research review and meta-analysis by Wolfe and associates (1999) revealed that appropriate physical activity programs prevented or reversed bone loss by approximately 1 percent each year in pre- and post-menopausal women. Ten years later, an updated research review by Going and Laudermilk (2009) documented bone mineral density increases between 1 percent and 3 percent resulting from resistance exercise.

A classic study by Kerr and colleagues (2001) demonstrated more than 3 percent increase in bone mineral density after two years of strength training. A nine-month strength training study by Westcott and colleagues (2011) showed a similar rate of bone mineral density improvement for participants who consumed supplemental protein, calcium, and vitamin D, all of which have positively influenced bone development in other research studies (Cooper et al. 1996; Thorpe et al. 2008; Dawson-Hughes and Harris 2002; Kelley et al. 2002).

Although the majority of bone density studies have involved women, research has revealed that men can also significantly increase their bone density by performing resistance exercise (Almstedt et al. 2011). One study (Morris et al. 1997) shared that preadolescents (nine years old) who performed a basic and brief strength training program experienced approximately four times as much bone density development as their non-training peers over a 10-month period.

Without question, the bulk of research on strength training and bone density indicates that regular resistance exercise is an effective means for increasing bone density in males and females of all ages (Layne and Nelson 1999). Furthermore, strength training has been shown to enhance bone density more than other types of physical activity including aerobic and weight bearing exercise (Gutin and Kasper 1992).

Mental and Emotional Health

Numerous studies have shown that exercise is an effective means for enhancing both mental and emotional health (O'Connor et al. 2010). While much of this research has included aerobic activity, several studies have demonstrated significant improvements in mental and emotional parameters with strength training alone. For example, resistance exercise has been associated with increased cognitive performance in older adults with memory impairment (Busse et al. 2008), improved cognitive function in elderly individuals (Cassilhas et al. 2007), and memory enhancement in older adults (Lackmann et al. 2006). A meta-analysis of research on exercise and mental health revealed that endurance exercise, combined with strength training, improved cognitive abilities in inactive older adults significantly more than endurance exercise alone (Colcombe and Kramer 2003).

Emotional health involves a variety of psychological factors that are generally related to self-esteem and personal perceptions. For example, Annessi and Westcott (2004; 2007) examined the effects of combined strength and endurance exercise on the psychological components of physical self-concept, total mood disturbance, depression, fatigue, positive engagement, revitalization, tranquility, and tension in middle-aged and older women. Ten weeks of supervised training resulted in significant improvements in all of these emotional health parameters.

Several studies have reported enhanced self-esteem resulting from resistance exercise alone (O'Connor et al. 2010). For example, strength training has been associated with positive self-esteem changes in younger adults (Trujillo 1983), older adults (Tsutsumi et al. 1998), women (Brown and Harrison 1986), cardiac rehabilitation patients (Beniamini et al. 1997), and cancer patients (Courneya et al. 2007).

Research on depression, a major mental health problem that can adversely affect functionality, reveals that resistance exercise may significantly improve symptoms in depressed adults (O'Connor et al. 2010; Singh et al. 2005). In one study (Singh et al. 1997), older adults with clinical depression participated in a three-days-per-week strength training program. Following 10 weeks of regular resistance exercise, more than 80 percent of the elderly participants no longer showed symptoms of clinical depression.

Chronic Pain

Chronic pain represents another factor that can have a negative impact on mental and emotional health (O'Connor et al. 2010). Fortunately, strength training has been shown to have a positive effect on at least three conditions associated with chronic pain. With respect to the pervasive problem of low back pain, several studies have demonstrated significant reductions in lumbar discomfort following a few months of resistance exercise (Hayden et al. 2005; Liddle et al. 2004, Risch et al. 1993). Similar results have been attained with people who suffer from arthritis. Studies by Focht (2006), Jan et al. (2008), and Lange et al. (2008) have reported significantly less discomfort in arthritic patients who performed strength training. Likewise, resistance exercise has been associated with pain reduction in people who have fibromyalgia (Bircan et al. 2008; Brosseau et al. 2008; Hakkinen et al. 2001).

Mitochondrial Characteristics

Mitochondria, generally known as the power source for muscular contraction, control a number of cell functions that are associated with energy production. Several studies have shown that circuit-style strength training can significantly increase the mitochondrial content and oxidative capacity of skeletal muscle tissue (Parise et al. 2005; Phillips 2007; Tang et al. 2006).

In fact, evidence exists that standard strength training may reverse the mitochondrial deterioration that is associated with aging by actually altering gene expression (Melov et al. 2007). In this study, older adults (average age 68 years) who performed six months of regular resistance exercise experienced reversal in gene expression that resulted in mitochondrial characteristics similar to those in younger adults (average age 24 years). The beneficial changes observed in almost 180 mitochondrial genes indicated that strength training may be an effective means for reversing specific aging factors in skeletal muscle.

Myokines

A relative new area of research has revealed that our skeletal muscles produce hormone-like substances called myokines that have a positive effect on other body tissues (Pedersen 2007, 2011). Although additional study is clearly warranted, it appears that resistance training may facilitate myokine production, which may, in turn, enhance a variety of physiological functions.

Summary

Based on the numerous research studies detailed in this chapter, strength training may have important physiological and psychological applications for enhancing physical and mental health. The beneficial role of resistance exercise may be especially relevant for middle-aged and older adults who typically experience muscle loss of 5 to 10 percent per decade and bone loss of 10 to 30 percent per decade.

Strength training appears to be effective for increasing muscle mass, raising resting metabolic rate, reducing body fat, increasing bone density, enhancing insulin sensitivity and glycemic control, reducing resting blood pressure, improving blood lipid profiles, enhancing vascular condition, improving cognitive function, increasing self-esteem, reducing depression, decreasing musculoskeletal discomfort, reversing specific aging factors, and facilitating physical function. As a result of these beneficial physiological adaptations, strength training may reduce the risk of experiencing a variety of degenerative problems, including sarcopenia, osteopenia, obesity, type 2 diabetes, cardiovascular disease, stroke, low back pain, arthritic pain, cognitive impairment, depression, and premature aging.

References

1. Almstedt HC, Canepa JA, Ramirez DA, Shoepe TC. (2011). Changes in bone mineral density in response to 24 weeks of resistance training in college-age men and women. *J. Strength Cond. Res.* 25(4): 1098-1103.
2. American College of Sports Medicine Position Stand. (2009). Exercise and physical activity for older adults. *Med. Sci. Sports Exerc.* 41:1510-1530.
3. Annesi J, Westcott W. (2004). Relationship of feeling states after exercise and total mood disturbance over 10 weeks in formerly sedentary women. *Percept. Mot. Skills.* 99:107-115.
4. Annesi J, Westcott W. (2007). Relations of physical self-concept and muscular strength with resistance exercise-induced feeling states in older women. *Percept. Mot. Skills.* 104:183-190.
5. Anton M, Cortez-Cooper M, Devan A, et al. (2006). Resistance training increases basal limb blood flow and vascular conductance in aging humans. *J. Appl. Physiol.* 101(5): 1351-1355.
6. Ballor D, Poehlman E. (1994). Exercise training enhances fat-free mass preservation during diet-induced weight loss: A meta analytic finding. *Int. J. Obesity.* 18:35-40.
7. Beniamini Y, Rubenstein JJ, Zaichowsky LO, Crim MC. (1997). Effects of high intensity strength training on quality of life parameters in cardiac rehabilitation patients. *Am. J. Cardiol.* 80:841- 846.
8. Bircan C, Karasel SA, Akgun B, et al. (2008). Effects of muscle strengthening versus aerobic exercise program in fibromyalgia. *Rheumatol.* Int. 28:527-532.
9. Boyden T, Pamenter R, Going S, et al. (1993). Resistance exercise training is associated with decreases in serum low-density lipoprotein cholesterol levels in pre-menopausal women. *Arch. Inter. Med.* 153:97-100.
10. Boyle JP. (2010). Projection of the year 2050 burden of diabetes in the US adult population: Dynamic modeling of incidence, mortality, and prediabetes prevalence. *Population Health Metrics.* 8(1):29.
11. Broeder C, Burrhus K, Svanevik L, Wilmore J. (1992). The effects of either high-intensity resistance or endurance training on resting metabolic rate. *Am. J. Clin. Nutr.* 55:802-810.
12. Brosseau I, Wells GA, Tugwell P, et al. (2008). Ottawa panel evidence-based clinical practical guidelines for strengthening exercises in the management of fibromyalgia: Part 2. *Phy. Ther.* 88:873-886.
13. Brown RD, Harrison JM. (1986). The effects of a strength training program on the strength and self-concept of two female age groups. *Res. Q. Exerc. Sport.* 57: 315-320.
14. Busse AL, Filo WJ, Magaldi RM, et al. (2008). Effects of resistance training exercise on cognitive performance in elderly individuals with memory impairment: Results of a controlled trial. *Einstein.* 6: 402-407.

15. Bweir S, Al-Jarrah M, Almalty AM, et al. (2009). Resistance exercise training lowers HbA1c more than aerobic training in adults with type 2 diabetes. *Diab. Metab. Syndr.* 1:27.
16. Campbell WW, Crim MC, Young VR, Evans WJ. (1994). Increased energy requirements and changes in body composition with resistance training in older adults. *Am. J. Clin. Nutr.* 60(2):167-175.
17. Cassilhas RC, Viana VAR, Grasmann V, et al. (2007). The impact of resistance exercise on the cognitive function of the elderly. *Med. Sci. Sports Exerc.* 39: 1401-1407.
18. Castaneda C, Layne JE, Munez-Orians L, et al. (2002). A randomized controlled trial of resistance exercise training to improve glycemic control in older adults with type 2 diabetes. *Diab. Care.* 25(12):2335-2341.
19. Cauza E, Strasser B, Haber P, et al. (2005). The relative benefits of endurance and strength training on metabolic factors and muscle function of people with type 2 diabetes. *Arch. Phys. Med. Rehab.* 86:1527-1533.
20. Chilibeck P, Calder A, Sale D, Webber C. (1996). Twenty weeks of weight training increases lean tissue mass but not bone mineral mass or density in healthy, active women. *Can. J. Physiol. Pharmocol.* 74(10):1180-1185.
21. Colcombe S, Kramer AF. (2003). Fitness effects on the cognitive function of older adults: A meta-analytic study. *Phychol. Sci.* 14:125-130.
22. Coon PJ, Rogus EM, Drinkwater D, et al. (1992). Role of body fat distribution in the decline in insulin sensitivity and glucose tolerance with age. *J. Clin. Endocrin. Metab.* 75(4):1125-1132.
23. Cooper C, Atkinson E, Hensuid R, et al. (1996). Dietary protein intake and bone mass in women. *Calcif.* 58:320-325.
24. Cornelissen VA, Fagard RH. (2005). Effect of resistance training on resting blood pressure: A meta-analysis of randomized controlled trials. *J. Hypertens.* 23(2):251-259.
25. Cortez-Cooper MY, Devan AE, Anton MM, et al. (2005). Effects of high-intensity resistance training on arterial stiffness and wave reflection in women. Am. *J. Hypertens.* 18:930-934.
26. Courneya KS, Segal RJ, Mackey JR, et al. (2007). Effects of aerobic and resistance exercise in breast cancer patients receiving adjuvant chemotherapy: A multicenter randomized controlled trial. *J. Clin. Oncol.* 25:4396-4404.
27. Cussler E, Lohman T, Going S, et al. (2003). Weight lifted in strength training predicts bone change in postmenopausal women. *Med. Sci. Sports Exerc.* 35:10-17.
28. Dawson-Hughes B, Harris S. (2002). Calcium intake influences the association of protein intake with rates of bone loss in elderly men and women. *Am. J. Clin. Nutr.* 75:773-779.
29. Dornemann T, Mc Murray R, Renner J, Anderson J. (1997). Effects of high intensity resistance exercise on bone mineral density and muscle strength of 40-50 year-old women. *J. Sports Med. Physi. Fitness.* 37(4):246-251.
30. Dunstan DW, Daly RM, Owen N, et al. (2002). High-intensity resistance training improves glycemic control in older patients with type 2 diabetes. *Diab. Care.* 25(10): 1729-1736.
31. Eves ND, Plotnikoff RC. (2006). Resistance training and type 2 diabetes: Considerations for implementation at the population level. *Diab. Care.* 29:1933-1941.
32. Fahlman MM, Boardly D, Lambert CP, Flynn MG. (2002). Effects of endurance training and resistance training on plasma lipoprotein profiles in elderly women. *J. Gerontol. A: Biol. Sci. Med. Sci.* 57A(2):B54-60.
33. Fahs C, Heffernan K, Ranadive S, et al. (2010). Muscular strength is inversely associated with aortic stiffness in young men. *Med. Sci. Sports Exerc.* 42(9):1619-1624.
34. Faigenbaum A, Skrinar G, Cesare W, et al. (1990). Physiologic and symptomatic responses of cardiac patients to resistance exercise. *Arch. Physic. Med. Rehab.* 70:395-398.

35. Fiatarone MA, Marks E, Ryan N, et al. (1990). High-intensity strength training in nonagenarians. *JAMA.* 263(22):3029-3034.
36. Flack KD, Davy KP, Huber MAW, et al. (2011). Aging, resistance training, and diabetes prevention. *J. Aging Res.* doi:10.4061/2011/127315.
37. Focht BC. (2006). Effectiveness of exercise interventions in reducing pain symptoms among older adults with knee osteoarthritis: A review. *J. Aging Phys. Act.* 14:212-235.
38. Going S, Laudermilk M. (2009). Osteoporosis and strength training. *Am. J. Lifestyle Med.* 3:310-319.
39. Going S, Lohman T, Houtkooper L, et al. (2003). Effects of exercise on BMD in calcium replete postmenopausal women with and without hormone replacement therapy. *Osteoporo. Int.* 14:637-643.
40. Gordon B, Benson A, Bird S, Fraser S. (2009). Resistance training improves metabolic health in type 2 diabetes: A systematic review. *Diab. Res. Clin. Pract.* 83:157-175.
41. Gutin B, Kasper MJ. (1992). Can exercise play a role in osteoporosis prevention? A review. *Osteopor. Int.* 2:55-69.
42. Hackney KJ, Engels HJ, Gretebeck RJ. (2008). Resting energy expenditure and delayed-onset muscle soreness after full-body resistance training with an eccentric concentration. *J. Strength Cond. Res.* 22(5):1602-1609.
43. Hagerman F, Walsh S, Staron R, et al. (2000). Effects of high-intensity resistance training on untrained older men: Strength, cardiovascular, and metabolic responses. *J. Gerontol. A: Biol. Sci. Med. Sci.* 55:8336-8346.
44. Hakkinen A, Hakkinen K, Hannonen P, Alen M. (2001). Strength training induced adaptations in neuromuscular function of premenopausal women and fibromyalgia: Comparison with healthy women. *Ann. Rheum. Res.* 60:21-26.
45. Hayden JA, van Tulder MW, Tomlinson G. (2005). Systematic review: Strategies for using exercise therapy to improve outcomes in chronic low back *pain. Ann. Intern. Med.* 142:776-785.
46. Heden T, Lox C, Rose P, et al. (2011). One-set resistance training elevates energy expenditure for 72 hours similar to three sets. *Eur. J. App. Physiol.* 111:477-484.
47. Hedley AA, Ogden CL, Johnson CL, et al. (2004). Obesity among U.S. children, adolescents, and adults. (1999-2002). *J. Am. Med. Assoc.* 291:2847-2850.
48. Holten MK, Zacho M, Gaster C, et al. (2004). Strength training increases insulin-mediated glucose uptake, GLUT4 content, and insulin signaling in skeletal muscle in patients with type 2 diabetes. *Diabetes.* 53(2):294-305.
49. Hunter GR, Wetzstein CJ, Fields DA, et al. (2000). Resistance training increases total energy expenditure and free-living physical activity in older adults. *J. Appl. Physiol.* 89(3):977-984.
50. Hunter GR, Bryan DR, Wetzstein CJ, et al. (2002). Resistance training and intra-abdominal adipose tissue in older men and women. *Med. Sci. Sports Exerc.* 34:1025-1028.
51. Hurley B. (1995). Strength training in the elderly to enhance health status. *Med. Exerc. Nutr. Health.* 4:217-229.
52. Ibanez J, Izquierdo M, Arguelles I, et al. (2005). Twice weekly progressive resistance training decreases abdominal fat and improves insulin sensitivity in older men with type 2 diabetes. *Diab. Care.* 28:662-667.
53. Jan M, Lin J, Liau J, et al. (2008). Investigation of clinical effects of high- and low-resistance training for patients with knee osteoarthritis: A randomized controlled trial. *Phys. Ther.* 88:427-436.
54. Judge J, Kleppinger A, Kenny A, et al. (2005). Home-based resistance training improves femoral bone mineral density in women on hormone therapy. *Osteoporo. Int.* 16(9):1096-1108.

55. Kelemen MH, Effron MB. (1990). Exercise training combined with antihypertensive drug therapy. *JAMA.* 263:2766-2771.
56. Kelley G. (1997). Dynamic resistance exercise and resting blood pressure in healthy adults: A meta-analysis. *J. Appl. Physiol.* 82:1559-1565.
57. Kelley G, Kelley K. (2000). Progressive resistance exercise and resting blood pressure: A meta-analysis of randomized controlled trials. *Hypertension.* 35:838-843.
58. Kelley G, Kelley K, Tran Z. (2002). Exercise and lumbar spine bone mineral density in postmenopausal women: A meta-analysis of individual patient data. *J. Gerontol. A: Biol. Sci. Med. Sci.* 57:M599-M604.
59. Kelley G, Kelley K. (2009). Impact of progressive resistance training on lipids and lipoproteins in adults: A meta-analysis of randomized controlled trials. *Prev. Med.* 48:9-19.
60. Kemmler WS, Von Stengel S, Weineck J, et al. (2005). Exercise effects on menopausal risk factors of early postmenopausal women: three-yr Erlangen fitness osteoporosis prevention study results. *Med. Sci. Sports Exerc.* 37:194-203.
61. Kerr D, Morton A, Dick I, Prince R. (1996). Exercise effects on bone mass in post-menopausal women are site-specific and load-dependent. *J. Bone Miner. Res.* 11:218-225.
62. Kerr D, Ackland T, Masten B, et al. (2001). Resistance training over two years increases bone mass in calcium-replete postmenopausal women. *J. Bone Miner. Res.* 16:175-181.
63. Keys A, Taylor HL, Grande F. (1973). Basal metabolism and age of adult man. *Metabolism.* 22:579-587.
64. Kohrt WM, Kirwan JP, Staten MA, et al. (1993). Insulin resistance in aging is related to abdominal obesity. *Diabetes.* 42(2):273-281.
65. Kokkinos P, Hurley B, Vaccaro P. (1998). Effects of low and high repetition resistive training on lipoprotein-lipid profiles. *Med. Sci. Sports Excer.* 29:50-54.
66. Lackmann ME, Neupert SD, Betrand R, Jette AM. (2006). The effects of strength training on memory of older adults. *J. Aging Phys. Act.* 14:59-73.
67. Lange A, Vanwanseele B, Fiatarone Singh M. (2008). Strength training for treatment of osteoarthritis of the knee: A systematic review. *Arthritis and Rheum.* 59:1488-1494.
68. Layne J, Nelson M. (1999). The effects of progressive resistance training on bone density: A review. *Med. Sci. Sports Exerc.* 31:25-30.
69. Lemmer J, Ivey F, Ryan A, et al. (2001). Effect of strength training on resting metabolic rate and physical activity. *Med. Sci. Sports Exerc.* 33:532-541.
70. Liddle SD, Baxter GD, Gracey JI. (2004). Exercise and chronic low back pain: What works? *Pain.* 107:176-190.
71. Lloyd-Jones D, Adams R, Carnethon M, et al. (2009). Heart disease and stroke statistics: 2009 update. A report from the American Heart Association Statistics Committee and Stroke Statistics Subcommittee. *Circulation.* 119:480-486.
72. Lohman T, Going S, Pamenter R, et al. (1995). Effects of resistance training on regional and total BMD in premenopausal women: A randomized prospective study. *J. Bone Miner. Res.* 10:1015-1024.
73. Maeda S, Otsuki T, Iemitsu M, et al. (2006). Effects of leg resistance training on arterial function in older men. *Brit. J. Sports Med.* 40:867-869.
74. Mann T, Tomiyama J, Westling E, et al. (2007). Medicare's search for effective obesity treatments: diets are not the answer. *Am. Psychol.* 62:220-233.
75. Marzolini S, Oh P, Thomas S, Goodman J. (2008). Aerobic and resistance training in coronary disease: Single versus multiple sets. *Med. Sci. Sports Exerc.* 40:1557-1564.
76. Melov S, Tarnopolsky M, Beckman K, et al. (2007). Resistance exercise reverses aging in human skeletal muscle. *PLoS ONE.* 2:e465.
77. Milliken L, Going S, Houtkooper L, et al. (2003). Effects of exercise training on bone remodeling, insulin-like growth factors, and BMD in post-menopausal women with and without hormone replacement therapy. *Calcif. Tissue Int.* 72:478-484.

78. Miyachi M, Kawano H, Sugawara J, et al. (2004). Unfavorable effects of resistance training on central arterial compliance: A randomized intervention study. *Circulation.* 110:2858-2863.

79. Morris F, Naughton G, Gibbs J, et al. (1997). Prospective ten-month exercise intervention in premenarcheal girls: Positive effects on bone and lean mass. *J. Bone Min. Research.* 12(9):1453-1462.

80. National Osteoporosis Foundation. Fast Facts. 23 Nove. (2009). www.nof.org/osteoporosis/diseasefacts.htm.

81. Nelson ME, Fiatarone M, Morganti C., et al. (1994). Effects of high-intensity strength training on multiple risk factors for osteoporotic fractures. *JAMA.* 272: 1909-1914.

82. Nichols J, Nelson K, Peterson K, Sartoris D. (1995). BMD responses to high intensity strength training in active older women. *J. Aging Physical Activ.* 3:26-28.

83. Nichols-Richardson S, Miller L, Wootten D, et al. (2007). Concentric and eccentric isokinetic resistance training similarly increases muscular strength, fat-free soft tissue mass, and specific bone mineral measurements in young women. *Osteoporo. Int.* 18(6):789-796.

84. O'Connor PJ, Herring MP, Caravalho A. (2010). Mental health benefits of strength training in adults. *Am. J. Lifestyle Med.* doi: 10.1177/1559827610368771.

85. Olson J, Dengel D, Leon A., Schmitz K. (2006). Moderate resistance training and vascular health in overweight women. *Med. Sci. Sports Exerc.* 38:1558-1564.

86. Ong KL, Cheung BMY, Man YB, et al. (2007). Hypertension treatment and control: Prevalence, awareness, treatment, and control of hypertension among United States adults 1999-2004. *Hypertension.* 49:69-75.

87. Parise G, Brose A, Tarnopolsky M. (2005). Resistance exercise training decreases oxidative damage to DNA and increases cytochrome oxidase activity in older adults. *Exper. Gerontol.* 40:173-180.

88. Pederson B. (2011). Muscles and their myokines. *J. Exper. Biol.* 214(2):337-346.

89. Pederson B, Thorbjom C, Nielsen A, Fischer C. (2007). Role of myokines in exercise and *metabolism. J. Appl. Physiol.* 103:1093-1098.

90. Phillips SM. (2007). Resistance exercise: Good for more than just Grandma and Grandpa's muscles. *Appl. Physiol. Nutr. Metab.* 32:1198-1205.

91. Phillips SM, Winett RA. (2010). Uncomplicated resistance training and health-related outcomes: Evidence for a public health mandate. *Current Sports Med. Reports.* 9(4):208-213.

92. Pitsavos C, Panagiotakos DB, Tambalis KD, et al. (2009). Resistance exercise plus aerobic activities is associated with better lipids profile among healthy individuals: The ATTIICA study. *QJM.* 102:609-616.

93. Pollock ML, Franklin BA, Balady GL, et al. (2000). AHA Science Advisory. Resistance exercise in individuals with and without cardiovascular disease: Benefits, rationale, safety, and prescription: An advisory from the Committee on Exercise Rehabilitation, and Prevention, Council on Clinical Cardiology, American Heart Association; Position paper endorsed by the American College of Sports Medicine. *Circulation.* 101(7):828-833.

94. Pratley R, Nicklas B, Rubin M, et al. (1994). Strength training increases resting metabolic rate and norepinephrine levels in healthy 50- to 65-year-old men. *J. Appl. Physiol.* 76(1):133-137.

95. Rakobowchuk M, McGowan CL, DeGroot PC, et al. (2005). Effect of whole body resistance training on arterial compliance in young men. *Exp. Physiol.* 90:645-651.

96. Risch S, Norvell N, Polock M, et al. (1993). Lumbar strengthening in chronic low back pain patients. *Spine.* 18:232-238.

97. Sinaki M, Wahner H, Bergstralh E, et al. (1996). Three-year controlled, randomized trial of the effect of dose-specified loading and strengthening exercises on BMD on spine and femur in non-athletic, physically active women. *Bone.* 19:233-244.

98. Singh NA, Clements KM, Fiatarone MA. (1997). A randomized controlled trial of progressive resistance exercise in depressed elders. *J. Gerontol. A: Biol. Sci. Med. Sci.* 52:M27-M35.

99. Singh NA, Stavrinos TM, Scarbek Y, et al. (2005). A randomized controlled trial of high vs low intensity weight training versus general practitioner care for clinical depression in older adults. *J. Gerontol. A: Bio. Sci. Med. Sci.* 60:768-776.

100. Smutok M, Reece C, Kokkinos P, et al. (1993). Aerobic vs. strength training for risk factor intervention in middle-aged men at high risk for coronary heart disease. *Metabolism.* 42:177-184.

101. Standards of medical care in *diabetes.* (2006). *Diab. Care.* 29(1):S4-S42.

102. Stewart K, Mason, Kelemen M. (1988). Three-year participation in circuit weight training improves muscular strength and self-efficacy in cardiac patients. *J. Cardiopulm. Rehabil.* 8:292-296.

103. Strasser B, Siebert U, Schobersberger W. (2010). Resistance training in the treatment of metabolic syndrome. *Sports Med.* 40(5):397-415.

104. Strasser B, Schobersberger W. (2011). Evidence of resistance training as a treatment therapy in obesity. *J. Obesity.* doi:1155/2011/482564.

105. Tambalis K, Panagiotakos D, Kavouras S, Sidossis L. (2009). Responses of blood lipids to aerobic, resistance and combined aerobic with resistance exercise training: A systematic review of current evidence. *Angiology.* 60:614-632.

106. Tang J, Hartman J, Phillips S. (2006). Increased muscle oxidative potential following resistance training induced fiber hypertrophy in young men. *Appl. Physiol. Nutr. Metab.* 31:495-501.

107. Thorpe M, Jacobson E, Layman D., et al. (2008). A diet high in protein, dairy, and calcium attenuates bone loss over 12 months of weight loss and maintenance relative to a conventional high-carbohydrate diet in adults. *J. Nutr.* 138(6):1096-1100.

108. Treuth MS, Ryan AS, Pratley RE, et al. (1994). Effects of strength training on total and regional body composition in older men. *J. Appl. Physiol.* 77(2):614-620.

109. Treuth MS, Hunter GR, Kekes-Szabo T, et al. (1995). Reduction in intra-abdominal adipose tissue after strength training in older women. *J. Appl. Physiol.* 78(4):1425-1431.

110. Trujillo CM. (1983). The effect of weight training and running intervention programs on the self-esteem of college women. *Int. J. Sport Psychol.* 14:162-173.

111. Tsutsumi T, Don BM, Zaichkowsky LD, et al. (1998). Comparison of high and moderate intensity of strength training on mood and anxiety in older adults. *Percept. Mot. Skills.* 87(pt1):1003-1011.

112. Tucker LA, Silvester LJ. (1996). Strength training and hypercholesterolemia: An epidemiologic study of 8499 employed men. *Am. J. Health Promot.* 11(1):35-41.

113. Ulrich I, Reid C, Yeater R. (1987). Increased HDL-cholesterol levels with a weight training program. *Southern Med. J.* 80:328-331.

114. U.S. Department of Health and Human Services. (2004). *Bone Health and Osteoporosis: A Report of the Surgeon General.* Rockville, MD. U.S. Department of Health and Human Services, Public Health Service, Office of the Surgeon General.

115. Van Etten L, Westerterp K, Verstappen F, et al. (1997). Effect of an 18-week weight-training program on energy expenditure and physical activity. *J. Appl. Physiol.* 82(1):298-304.

116. Von Stengel S, Kemmler W, Kalender W, et al. (2007). Differential effects of strength versus power training on bone mineral density in postmenopausal women: A two-year longitudinal study. *Br. J. Sports Med.* 41(10):649-655.

117. Vuori I, Heinonen A, Sievanen H, et al. (1994). Effects of unilateral strength training and detraining on BMD and content in young women: A study of mechanical loading and deloading on human bones. *Calcif. Tissue Int.* 54-67.

118. Warren M, Petit A, Hannan P, Schmitz K. (2008). Strength training effects on bone mineral content and density in premenopausal women. *Med. Sci. Sports Exerc.* 40(7):1282-1288. 140.

119. Westcott WL. (2009). Strength training for frail older adults. *J Active Aging.* 8(4): 52-59.
120. Westcott WL. (2012). Resistance training is medicine: effects of strength training on health. *Curr. Sports Med. Rep.* 11(4):209-216.
121. Westcott WL, Apovian C, Puhala K, et al. (2013). Nutrition programs enhance exercise effects on body composition and resting blood pressure. *Physician Sportsmed.* 41(3): 85-91.
122. Westcott WL, Varghese J, DiNubile N, et al. (2011). Exercise and nutrition more effective than exercise alone for increasing lean weight and reducing resting blood pressure. J. Exerc. Physiol. 14(4):120-133.
123. Westcott WL, Winett RA, Annesi JJ, et al. (2009). Prescribing physical activity: Applying the ACSM protocols for exercise type, intensity, and duration across three training frequencies. *Physician Sportsmed.* 2(37):51-58.
124. Wolfe I, Van Cronenbourg J, Kemper H, et al. (1999). The effect of exercise training programs on bone mass: A meta-analysis of published controlled trials in pre and post-menopausal women. *Osteoporo. Int.* 9:1-12.
125. Wolfe RR. (2006). The unappreciated role of muscle in health and disease. *Am. J. Clin. Nutr.* 84:475-482.
126. Yarasheski K, Campbell J, Kohrt W. (1997). Effect of resistance exercise and growth hormone on bone density in older men. *Clin. Endocrino.* 47:223-229.

CHAPTER 2:
Strength Training Performance Factors

There are several factors besides the physiological properties of muscle tissue that influence a person's effective muscle strength. These include biomechanical factors, size factors, sex factors, age factors, training experience, training technique, and training specificity. It is important to understand how each of these factors may affect a person's strength potential, and to use this information in designing and evaluating individualized strength training programs.

Biomechanical Factors

It is quite possible for two persons who can produce equal amounts of muscle force to differ significantly in the amount of weight they can lift. Human movement is dependent upon muscle force applied to bones that comprise a lever system. The long bones act as levers, the joints serve as axes of rotation, and the skeletal muscles produce forces of sufficient magnitude to overcome resistance and control movement.

First-Class Levers

In a first-class lever, the axis of rotation is between the movement force and the resistive force. As shown in Figure 2-1, the triceps muscle operates as a first-class lever, because the elbow (axis of rotation) is between the triceps insertion (movement force) and the weight stack cable (resistance force).

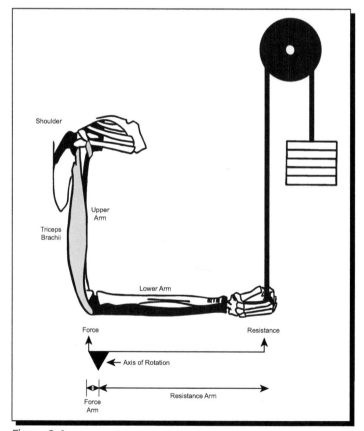

Figure 2-1

Second-Class Levers

In a second-class lever, the resistance force occurs between the axis of rotation and the movement force. Most muscles that cross two joints function as second-class levers at the first joint. For example, the quadriceps muscles cross both the hip joint (hip flexion) and the knee joint (knee extension). Because a resistance force applied to the thigh is between the first joint axis (hip) and the movement force (quadriceps insertion in leg), the quadriceps function as a second-class lever with respect to hip flexion.

Third-Class Levers

In a third-class lever, the movement force is between the axis of rotation and the resistance force. As illustrated in Figure 2-2, the biceps muscle serves as a third-class lever because the biceps insertion (movement force) is between the elbow (axis of rotation) and the dumbbell (resistance force).

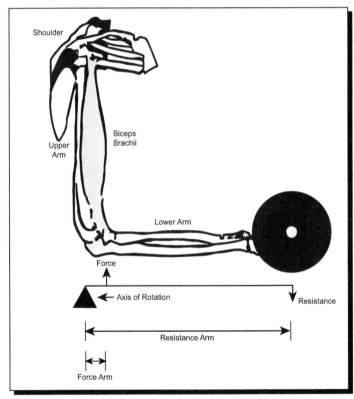

Figure 2-2

The distance between the axis of rotation and the movement force is called the force arm, and the distance between the axis of rotation and the resistance force is called the resistance arm. The product of the resistance times the resistance arm is equal to the product of the force times the force arm, when the lever is held in a static position (R X RA = F X FA). Of course, the effective force varies throughout the range of movement due to leverage factors, such as the perpendicular distance to the line of pull. Disregarding the angle of tendon insertion and the weight of the forearm, consider how the point of tendon insertion can provide leverage advantages that profoundly influence a person's effective strength in the following examples involving the biceps muscle (see Figures 2-3 and 2-4).

❑   Example #1:

John has a 10-inch forearm with a biceps insertion 1.0 inches from the elbow joint. If John can produce 300 pounds of force in his biceps muscle, how heavy a dumbbell can he hold at 90-degrees elbow flexion?

$$R \times RA = F \times FA \qquad\qquad R = \frac{F \times FA}{RA}$$

$$R = \frac{300 \text{ Pounds} \times 1.0 \text{ Inches}}{10 \text{ Inches}} \qquad\qquad R = 30 \text{ Pounds}$$

Figure 2-3

❑   Example #2:

Bob also has a 10-inch forearm, but his biceps insertion is 1.2 inches from the elbow joint. If Bob can likewise produce 300 pounds of force in his biceps muscle, how heavy a dumbbell can he hold at 90-degrees elbow flexion?

$$R \times RA = F \times FA \qquad\qquad R = \frac{F \times FA}{RA}$$

$$R = \frac{300 \text{ Pounds} \times 1.2 \text{ Inches}}{10 \text{ Inches}} \qquad\qquad R = 36 \text{ Pounds}$$

Figure 2-4

In these examples, both John and Bob produce a maximum biceps force of 300 pounds. However, due to a biceps tendon insertion that is farther from the joint axis of rotation, Bob can hold a heavier dumbbell than John (36 pounds versus 30 pounds) at 90 degrees of elbow flexion.

Another leverage factor that has a major influence on effective strength is the length of the long bones. Other things being equal, individuals who have shorter levers (arms and legs) have a strength advantage over individuals who have longer levers. The following examples demonstrate the difference in effective strength due to longer or shorter resistance levers (see Figures 2-5 and 2-6).

In these examples, both Nancy and Susan produce a maximum biceps force of 300 pounds. However, due to a shorter forearm, Susan can hold a heavier dumbbell than Nancy (30 pounds versus 25 pounds) at 90 degrees of elbow flexion.

These examples also demonstrate that third-class lever systems require relatively large amounts of muscle force to overcome relatively small amounts of resistance force. Although this factor is a disadvantage with respect to movement force, it is an advantage with respect to movement speed.

❑ Example #3:

Nancy has a 12-inch forearm with a biceps insertion 1.0 inches from the elbow joint. If she can produce 300 pounds of force in her biceps muscle, how heavy a dumbbell can she hold at 90 degrees of elbow flexion?

$$R \times RA = F \times FA \qquad\qquad R = \frac{F \times FA}{RA}$$

$$R = \frac{300 \text{ Pounds} \times 1.0 \text{ Inches}}{12 \text{ Inches}} \qquad\qquad R = 25 \text{ Pounds}$$

Figure 2-5

❑ Example #4:

Susan has a 10-inch forearm with a biceps insertion 1.0 inches from the elbow joint. If she can likewise produce 300 pounds of force in her biceps muscle, how heavy a dumbbell can she hold at 90 degrees of elbow flexion?

$$R \times RA = F \times FA \qquad\qquad R = \frac{F \times FA}{RA}$$

$$R = \frac{300 \text{ Pounds} \times 1.0 \text{ Inches}}{10 \text{ Inches}} \qquad\qquad R = 30 \text{ Pounds}$$

Figure 2-6

Size Factors

While biomechanical factors have an influence on a person's ability to lift heavy weights, the contractile strength of a muscle is most clearly related to its cross-sectional size. Although considerable variation exists due to fiber type and fiber arrangement, most muscles produce about two to four pounds of contractile force per square centimeter of cross-sectional area (Lamb 1978). Accordingly, it stands to reason that the larger the cross-sectional area, the greater total force the muscle can exert.

The cross-sectional area of a person's muscle is initially determined by heredity. As such, a large-framed individual is likely to have larger muscles than a small-framed person. Strength training, however, can increase the cross-sectional size of a muscle by adding contractile proteins, actin and myosin. Because there is little evidence that strength training can produce new muscle fibers in humans, it is generally agreed that greater muscle size results from enlargement (not proliferation) of individual muscle fibers (Atherton et al. 1981; MacDougal 1985b). The increase in muscle size that results from strength training is called hypertrophy. Conversely, the decrease in muscle size that occurs when strength training is discontinued is known as atrophy. The reduction in muscle mass that accompanies inactive aging is called sarcopenia.

The length of the muscle belly may also be an important factor with respect to muscle size (see Figure 2-7). The muscle belly represents the actual muscle length between the tendon attachments. Other things being equal, it is assumed that the person with a longer muscle belly has the potential to develop greater muscle size and strength than an individual with a shorter muscle belly. The length of the muscle belly appears to be an inherited characteristic that cannot be changed through training. Most people have a mixture of long-bellied muscles, medium-bellied muscles, and short-bellied muscles. Those rare individuals who possess a large percentage of long-bellied muscles are most likely to be successful in weightlifting and bodybuilding competition.

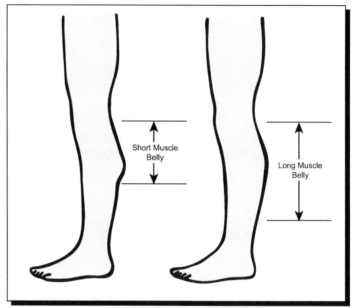

Figure 2-7

Gender Factors

Women who engage in strength training programs develop muscular strength at about the same rate as men. Research by Westcott (1974; 1979) indicates that both males and females can increase the strength of their bench press muscles (pectoralis major, anterior deltoid, and triceps) by 3 to 6 percent per week, over a period of several weeks. It is also known that males and females do not differ in strength per square centimeter of muscle tissue.

With respect to muscle size and effective muscle strength, however, there are definite sex-related differences. Although males and females gain strength at similar rates, post-pubescent males typically have larger muscles, which provides a significant strength advantage. Furthermore, strength training increases muscle size to a greater degree in males than in females. The reason appears to be related to the male sex hormone testosterone, which plays a major role in muscle growth and hypertrophy.

By virtue of their genetic make-up, males generally have a greater potential for muscle size and strength than females. Nonetheless, most females can develop lower body strength that compares favorably to males on a pound-for-pound basis. Westcott (1986) assessed quadriceps muscle strength in 907 adults on a Nautilus leg extension machine. On average, males could perform 10 strict repetitions with 62 percent of their bodyweight, while females could perform 10 strict repetitions with 55 percent of their bodyweight (see Table 2-1).

Quadriceps Strength for Men and Women		
	Men	*Women*
Age (years)	43	42
Body weight (lb.)	191	143
10-rep maximum (lb.)	119	79
Strength quotient (body weight)	62%	55%
Strength quotient (lean body weight)	74%	73%

Table 2-1

When evaluated by lean body weight, there was essentially no difference in quadriceps strength between the male and female subjects. On average, both genders could complete 10 strict repetitions with approximately 75 percent of their lean body weight. Accordingly, it is logical to conclude that relative leg muscle strength is similar in men and women.

With respect to strength gain, men typically increase their exercise weight loads more than women over a given time period. For example, after 10 weeks of strength training, a 175-pound male may improve his maximum bench press by 50 pounds (150 pounds to 200 pounds), whereas a 125-pound female may improve her maximum bench press by 25 pounds (75 pounds to 100 pounds). Notably, both the heavier male and the lighter female, however, experienced a 33-percent increase in their maximum bench press performance.

Research with hundreds of male and female resistance training participants has shown similar gains in muscle strength over the same time period (Westcott and Guy 1996). It may therefore be assumed, however, that men and women have similar responses to and attain comparable benefits from similar strength training programs.

Age Factors

Many people believe that boys and girls under 15 years are too young, while men and women over 55 years are too old, to benefit from strength training. In fact, people of all ages can increase their muscle size and strength through a basic program of resistance exercise.

As a case in point, the muscle development was assessed in more than 400 previously untrained people of all ages who performed eight weeks of standard Nautilus exercise (Westcott 1995). All of the program participants significantly increased their lean (muscle) weight. The youths (average age of 12 years) added approximately four pounds of lean weight, the middle-aged adults (average age of 45 years) added approximately three pounds of lean weight, and the older adults (average age of 65 years) added approximately three pounds of lean weight.

Of course, part of the youths' gain in lean weight was due to normal growth maturation processes. The older adults, however, increased their muscle mass as much as the middle-aged adults. In a follow-up study with more than 1600 men and women, there were no significant differences in muscle development among any of the age groups involved (20s, 30s, 40s, 50s, 60s, 70s). Similar to prior research, the average muscle gain was approximately three pounds in all of the age categories (Westcott et al. 2009). These results are consistent with other studies on senior strength training and indicate that older adults can build muscle tissue at the same rate as younger adults (Frontera et al. 1988; Fiatarone et al. 1994).

Likewise, both the younger and older adult participants increased their strength performance by 50 to 60 percent over the training period. The youth participants showed a higher rate of strength performance (60 to 75 percent over the same training duration), which, like their greater lean weight gain, was probably due to normal growth and maturation processes (Faigenbaum et al. 1993; Westcott 1994).

Arguably, some individuals may question the advisability of regular resistance exercise for preadolescents and seniors. This activity, however, is the most effective means for building strong muscles and bones, both of which are very important for these age groups. Properly performed strength training is a safe and productive form of exercise for people of all ages. The youth, adult, and senior participants in these studies did not experience any exercise-related injuries.

Physique Factors

To a large degree, a person's basic body build is determined by inherited characteristics, including an individual's skeletal frame, muscle cells, and fat cells. Generally speaking, there are four standard physique categories—ectomorphic, mesomorphic, endomorphic, and endomesomorphic (see Figure 2-8). These body types are largely determined by the number of muscle cells and fat cells with which a person is born. While it is possible to add fat cells throughout an individual's life, research indicates that humans do not increase the number of muscle cells (muscle fibers), even with strength training (Atherton et al. 1981; MacDougall 1985b).

❑ Ectomorphs: This body type is characterized by a relatively low number of muscle cells and a relatively low number of fat cells. Ectomorphs typically have a slight, linear appearance, and are best-suited for endurance activities, such as distance running.

❑ Mesomorphs: Mesomorphic physiques are characterized by a relatively high number of muscle cells and a relatively low number of fat cells. These individuals have a more rectangular appearance and a medium body weight. Bodybuilders, sprinters, wrestlers, and gymnasts typically have mesomorphic physiques.

❑ Endomorphs: This body type is characterized by a relatively low number of muscle cells and a relatively high number of fat cells. Endomorphs generally have a heavy, round appearance, and are less likely to excel in athletic activities.

❑ Endomesomorphs: People in this category have features of both mesomorphs and endomorphs, i.e., a relatively high number of muscle cells and a relatively high number of fat cells. Football linemen, shot putters, and discus throwers tend to have endomesomorphic physiques.

Top left photo: esolla/iStock/Thinkstock; top right photo: 63alfred/iStock/Thinkstock; bottom left photo: ferlistockphoto/iStock/Thinkstock; bottom right photo: shironosov/iStock/Thinkstock

Figure 2-8

Because mesomorphs have the largest number of muscle cells, these individuals have the greatest potential for developing muscular physiques. Ectomorphs and endomorphs, however, may add significant amounts of muscle through standard strength training and higher protein diets (Westcott et al. 2013). As noted previously, muscle hypertrophy is achieved by increasing the size of existing muscle fibers, rather than by increasing the number of muscle fibers. Regarding fat accumulation, appropriate exercise and proper nutrition are also the most effective means for avoiding enlarged fat cells.

Muscle Fiber Factors

There are two basic categories of muscle fibers—type-1 fibers and type-2 fibers. Type-1 muscle fibers, also known as slow-twitch fibers, are characterized by smaller motor units, more mitochondria, slower contraction speeds, and longer performance durations. Elite endurance athletes typically possess a very high percentage of type-1 muscle fibers.

Type-2 muscle fibers, also known as fast-twitch fibers, are characterized by larger motor units, fewer mitochondria, faster contraction speeds, and shorter performance durations. Elite power athletes typically possess a very high percentage of type-2 muscle fibers and elite endurance athletes generally have a high percentage of type-1 muscle fibers. For example, champion sprinters may have more than 80-percent fast-twitch muscle fibers in their quadriceps muscles, whereas champion marathon runners generally have more than 80-percent slow-twitch muscle fibers in their quadriceps muscles.

During the performance of resistance exercise, the slow-twitch muscle fibers are activated first, followed by the fast-twitch muscle fibers. Due to their physiological characteristics, however, the less enduring fast-twitch muscle fibers fatigue first, followed by the more enduring slow-twitch muscle fibers. A hypothetical example of biceps muscle fiber activation is presented in Figure 2-9.

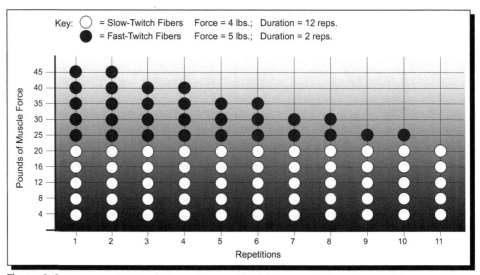

Figure 2-9

Assume that an individual has 10 biceps fibers, five of which are slow-twitch and five of which are fast-twitch. Assume that each slow-twitch fiber can produce four pounds of force and that each fast-twitch fiber can produce five pounds of force. Assume that each slow-twitch fiber can endure 12 repetitions and that each fast-twitch fiber can endure two repetitions.

At this point, the exerciser starts to perform a set of 25-pound dumbbell curls. To produce 25 pounds of muscle force, the individual activates five slow-twitch fibers (20 pounds of force) first, followed by one fast-twitch fiber (five pounds of force). After two repetitions, the first fast-twitch fiber fatigues and a fresh fast-twitch fiber replaces it. After two more repetitions, the second fast-twitch fiber fatigues, and a fresh fast-twitch fiber replaces it. After two more repetitions, the fourth fast-twitch fiber fatigues, and a fresh fast-twitch fiber replaces it. After two more repetitions, the last fast-twitch fiber fatigues, leaving only 20 pounds of force from the more-enduring slow-twitch fibers.

Obviously, an insufficient level of force exists to lift 25 pounds of resistance, so the exercise set must end after 10 repetitions. If, after resting, the individual performs a second set of dumbbell curls, the same muscle fibers will be activated, in the same order as the first set. One means for providing greater stimulus to the more enduring slow-twitch fibers is to immediately switch to a 25-pound dumbbell and perform as many additional repetitions as possible with proper form. This type of training is discussed in Chapter 6.

Experience Factors

Training experience implies the length of time a person has been involved in a strength training program. Generally speaking, the person who has trained regularly for two years will make smaller strength gains than an individual who has trained for only two weeks. During the early stages of a strength training program, improvement usually occurs quickly due to motor learning factors.

Motor learning is the neurological response to performing a new exercise. As the new exercise is practiced, the more effective motor units (muscle fibers) are automatically activated to facilitate the specific movement pattern and force production. As a person's strength approaches their genetic potential, the increases are much smaller and less frequent. In fact, progress appears to slow considerably during the first three months of training (Westcott 1985a; 1985b).

Figure 2-10 illustrates a typical strength improvement curve over a three-month training period. Although the participant achieves a 40-percent strength gain during the first month of training, the strength increase is only 10 percent during the second month, and about 2.5 percent during the third month.

The process of expending more and more effort and experiencing less and less improvement can be discouraging. Accordingly, it is essential to use training experience in the most productive manner possible. First, it must be understood that if a person continues to perform the same exercise routine, progress will normally plateau after several months of training. Second, due to the motor learning and skill specificity aspects of muscular activity, a change in exercise is usually accompanied by a higher rate of performance improvement.

Consequently, individuals who engage in strength training on a regular basis should routinely alter their training program in order to experience progress and maintain motivation. For example, Bill has been unable to complete more than 10 repetitions with 150 pounds in the leg extension exercise. Rather than remain on a plateau in this exercise, he replaces leg extensions with leg presses. By so doing, he continues to train the quadriceps muscles, but the movement pattern is different enough to require a new neuromuscular response.

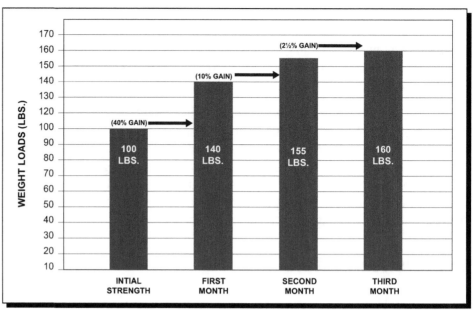

Figure 2-10

The result is noticeable performance improvement in the leg press exercise, due to both motor learning factors and muscle development. When progress in the leg press plateaus, Bill returns to the leg extension exercise. After a few training sessions, he surpasses his previous performance level in this exercise, and continues to make progress.

In summary, experienced strength training participants are less likely to see consistent progress, because they are closer to their strength potential. By frequently changing the exercises they do, they can continue to make performance improvements, which stimulates strength development and enhances training motivation.

Technique Factors

Training technique may have a profound influence on strength development and injury prevention. For example, John can curl 75 pounds in strict form, because his biceps are not assisted by larger muscle groups. John, however, can cheat curl 125 pounds by bending forward and initiating the movement with his large hip extensor muscles to give the barbell upward momentum.

In the first instance, John uses a controlled lifting movement that is characterized by consistent application of biceps force throughout the range of motion. This technique provides excellent stimulus for the biceps muscles and poses little risk of injury.

In the second scenario, John uses a fast lifting movement that is characterized by explosive involvement of assisting muscle groups and momentum. High levels of biceps force are required to overcome inertia at the beginning of the movement, but little biceps force is required throughout the remaining range of motion. Although this technique provides stimulus to the biceps muscles, it places significant stress on the connective tissue and carries a higher risk of injury (Finamore 1989).

In the author's opinion, John will achieve better biceps development by performing strict curls with 75 pounds than by performing cheat curls with 125 pounds. Generally speaking, the use of assisting muscle groups and momentum reduces the training stimulus to the target muscle group.

Another aspect of training technique is the resetting of neuromuscular inhibition levels as a result of regular practice (Ikai and Steinhaus 1961). In other words, the safety mechanisms responsible for prohibiting maximum force production may be adjusted through exercise familiarity, thereby enabling the exerciser to use a greater percentage of his potential strength.

It should also be noted that a muscle produces greater tension when it is stretched just prior to contraction. For example, a standing long jump is initiated by a quick downward movement to pre-stretch the thigh muscles so that they can contract more forcefully. Likewise, when a person quickly lowers the bar just before the upward phase of the bench press, additional force can be exerted as a result of the pre-stretch.

It would appear that the stretch reflex and the elastic properties of muscle tissue are largely responsible for the greater contractile strength associated with pre-stretching movements. Because quick movements with heavy weight loads may increase the risk of injury, however, pre-stretching as a standard strength training technique is not recommended.

Specificity Factors

People frequently equate hard work with success, but this factor is only true when there is a strong relationship between the work being done and the desired outcomes. Both a ten-mile run and three sets of heavy squats are hard work, but the physiological responses to each type of exercise are quite different. Both the serious distance runner and the serious weightlifter may train an hour or more each day, but their physical appearances are strikingly dissimilar.

Training that involves long periods of low-intensity exercise may develop cardiovascular endurance but does not improve muscle strength. Conversely, training that involves short periods of high-intensity exercise develops muscle strength but may not improve cardiovascular endurance. Experiments with laboratory animals (Gordon 1967) indicate that endurance training produces an increase in endurance enzymes, but a decrease in contractile proteins, while strength training produces an increase in contractile proteins, but a decrease in endurance enzymes.

An individual should train in a specific manner to obtain specific results: strength training for muscle development and endurance training for cardiovascular development. Figure 2-11 indicates the approximate positions of various activities along the strength-endurance continuum. Note that strength-related activities are of relatively high intensity and short duration, whereas endurance-related activities are of relatively low intensity and long duration.

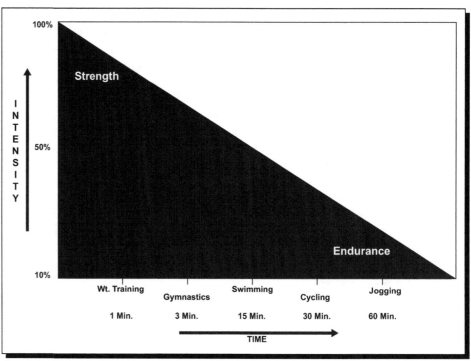

Figure 2-11

References

1. Atherton GW, James NT and Mahan M. (1981). Studies on muscle fibre splitting in skeletal muscle. *Experientia.* 37:308-310.
2. Faigenbaum AL, Zaichkowsky W, Westcott W, et al. (1993). The effects of twice-a-week strength training program on children. *Ped. Exerc. Sci.* 5:339-346.
3. Fiatarone M, O'Neill E, Ryan N, et al. (1994). Exercise training and nutritional supplementation for physical frailty in very elderly people. *New Eng. J. Med.* 330(25):1169-1175.
4. Finamore LV. (1989). Survey of Massachusetts high school football team strength and conditioning programs. Master's thesis. Vermont College of Norwich University.
5. Frontera W, Meredith C, O'Reilly K, et al. (1988). Strength conditioning in older men: Skeletal muscle hypertrophy and improved function. *J. Appl. Physiol.* 64(3):1038-1044.
6. Gordon HH. (1967). Anatomical and biomechanical adaptations of muscles to different exercises. *JAMA.* 201:755-758.
7. Hurley BF, Hagberg JM, Goldberg AP, et al. (1988). Resistive training can reduce coronary risk factors without altering VO2 max or percent body fat. *Med. Sci. Sports Exerc.* 20:150-154.
8. Ikai M and Steinhaus AH. (1961). Some factors modifying the expression of human strength. *J. Appl. Physiol.* 16:157-163.
9. Lamb DR. (1978). Physiology of exercise: Response and adaptations. New York: Macmillan.
10. MacDougall JD. (1978). Determining factors of strength: Part two. *Nat. Strength Cond. Assoc. J.* (1985b). 7:10-17.
11. Westcott WL. (1974). Effects of varied frequencies of weight training on the development of strength. Master's thesis. The Pennsylvania State University.
12. Westcott WL. (1979). Female response to weight training. *J. Phys. Ed.* 77:31-33.

13. Westcott WL. (1985a). The inevitable strength plateau. Schol. Coach. 55:30-31.

14. Westcott WL. (1985b). Combating disappointment when strength training progress slows. *J. Phys. Ed.* Prog. 81:D14-D15.

15. Westcott WL. (1986). Building strength at the YMCA. Champaign, Ill.: Human Kinetics.

16. Westcott WL. (1994). Studies show significant gains in young muscles. *Nautilus.* 3:2,6-7.

17. Westcott WL. (1995). *Strength fitness: Physiological principles and training techniques.* 4th ed. Dubuque, IA: Brown and Benchmark.

18. Westcott WL, Guy J. (1996). A physical evolution: Sedentary adults see marked improvements in as little as two days a week. IDEA Today. 14(9):58-65.

19. Westcott WL, Winett RA, Annesi JJ, et al. (2009). Prescribing physical activity: Applying the ACSM protocols for exercise type, intensity, and duration across three training frequencies. *Phys. Sportsmed.* 37(2):51-58.

20. Westcott WL, Apovian CM, Puhala K, et al. (2013). Nutrition programs enhance exercise effects on body composition and resting blood pressure. *Phys. Sportsmed.* 41(3):85-91.

CHAPTER 3:
Muscle Contraction and Movement Mechanics

A working knowledge of muscle structure and function is essential for understanding and applying the training principles and procedures for optimal strength development. In other words, to most effectively work the muscles, it is essential to know how the muscles work.

Muscle is very active tissue that makes up approximately half of the body's lean weight (the other half consists of bones, blood, organs, and skin). Muscle tissue is about 75-percent water and about 25-percent protein (specifically, the myosin and actin protein filaments that are responsible for all muscle actions). Each relatively large myosin protein filament is surrounded by six relatively small actin protein filaments. These two types of protein filaments are connected by cross-bridges (extensions of the myosin protein filaments). As illustrated in Figure 3-1, an arrangement of one myosin protein filament surrounded by six actin protein filaments on each end constitute a sarcomere, which is the smallest functional unit of muscle contraction.

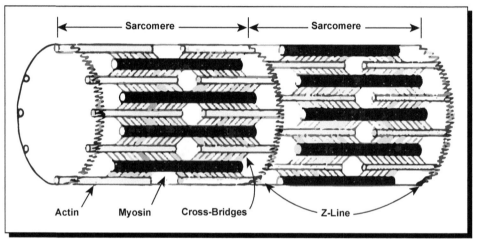

Figure 3-1

Long series of sarcomeres make up muscle fibers, which are actually muscle cells. Bundles of muscle fibers form independent components within the muscle known as fasiculi. Bundles of fasiculi comprise a particular muscle, such as the biceps brachii or the latissimus dorsi.

Muscle Contraction

Muscle contraction is dependent upon an electrical impulse sent from the central nervous system to specific motor units. As shown in Figure 3-2, a motor unit consists of a motor nerve and all of the individual muscle fibers that it innervates (activates). A slow-twitch motor unit may include up to 100 slow-twitch muscle fibers, while a fast-twitch motor unit may include more than 500 fast-twitch muscle fibers.

The electrical impulse initiates the energy production necessary for muscle contraction. This process involves the splitting of adenosine triphosphate (ATP) into adenosine diphosphate (ADP), inorganic phosphate (P), and energy. Every muscle fiber within an activated motor unit contracts completely and simultaneously, which produced maximum tension. Accordingly, relatively low muscle force can be attained by activating a small number of motor units, while relatively high muscle force can be attained by activating a large number of motor units.

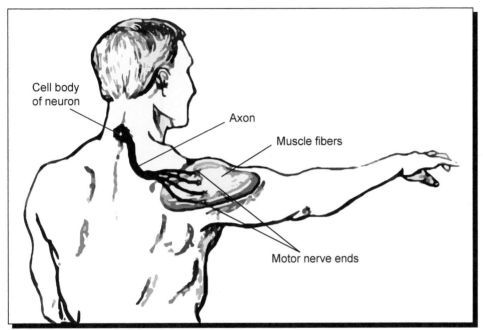

Figure 3-2

The actual contraction is accomplished by the myosin cross-bridges pulling the surrounding actin protein filaments at each end toward the center of the myosin protein filament. As this action simultaneously occurs in the adjacent sarcomeres of the activated muscle fibers, the muscle shortens with enough force to overcome the resistance and produce the desired joint movement.

Muscle contraction (shortening) in one muscle group must always be matched with muscle relaxation (lengthening) in the opposing muscle group. For example, when the biceps muscles in the front of the arms contract and shorten, the opposing triceps muscles in the rear of the arms must relax and lengthen in order to perform a barbell curl.

Muscle contractions, perhaps more accurately called muscle actions, are involved in holding a resistance, lifting a resistance, and lowering a resistance. These three aspects of muscle force production are known as isometric or static muscle contractions, concentric or positive muscle actions, and eccentric or negative muscle actions.

❏ Isometric muscle contraction: During an isometric muscle contraction, the muscle exerts enough force to match the resistance force and hold it in a stationary position. Although the muscle exerts force, there is no visible movement. As illustrated in Figure 3-3a, John can produce a maximum biceps force to hold a 100-pound barbell at 90 degrees of elbow flexion.

Figure 3-3a

❏ Concentric muscle action: During a concentric muscle action, the muscle exerts enough force to shorten and overcome the resistance force, (typically a lifting movement). As shown in Figure 3-3b, John can produce enough concentric biceps force to curl an 80-pound barbell from his hips to his shoulders. In other words, John's maximum concentric muscle force is about 80 percent of his maximum isometric muscle force. Although John is capable of producing 100 pounds of biceps muscle force, biomechanical factors (such as internal muscle friction) decrease his effective muscle force output by about 20 percent (depending on the speed of movement).

Figure 3-3b

❏ Eccentric muscle action: During an eccentric muscle action, the muscle exerts enough force to lengthen under control, while being overcome by the resistance (typically a lowering movement). As illustrated in Figure 3-3c, John can produce enough eccentric biceps force to slowly lower a 120-pound barbell from his shoulders to his hips. In other words, John's maximum eccentric muscle force is about 120 percent of his maximum isometric muscle force. Although John is still capable of producing 100 pounds of biceps muscle force, biomechanical factors (such as internal muscle friction) increase his effective muscle force output by about 20 percent (depending on the speed of movement).

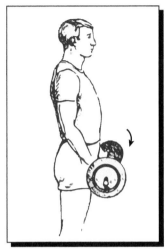

Figure 3-3c

Compared to isometric muscle strength, biomechanical factors decrease concentric muscle force output by approximately 20 percent and increase eccentric muscle force output by approximately 20 percent. This factor is why trainees can lower about 40 to 50 percent more resistance than they can lift at the same movement speed. Accordingly, it is recommended that resistance exercise be performed with both controlled lifting (concentric) and controlled lowering (eccentric) movements in order to maximize muscle activation throughout each repetition.

Muscle Function

Muscles that are primarily responsible for a specific joint action are called prime mover muscles. For example, the biceps muscles are prime movers for elbow flexion movements, such as barbell curls. The muscles that perform the opposite joint action are called antagonist muscles. In this case, the triceps muscle that perform elbow extension movements serve as antagonists to the biceps muscles. It should be kept in mind that the biceps muscles are responsible for both the lifting phase (concentric biceps action) and the lowering phase (eccentric biceps action) of the barbell curl exercise. The antagonist triceps muscles are essentially passive throughout the performance of barbell curls.

Other muscles, known as stabilizer muscles, contract isometrically during controlled curling actions. For example, the lower back (erector spinae) muscles perform static contractions to maintain an erect posture during barbell curls. Likewise, the chest (pectoralis major) and upper back (latissimus dorsi) muscles perform isometric contractions to keep the upper arms against the sides throughout each controlled barbell curl repetition.

Although the biceps brachii are the prime mover muscles for barbell curls, other muscle groups assist with elbow flexion. The assisting muscles include the radiobrachialis muscles of the forearms and the brachialis muscles of the upper arms.

While the barbell curl is clearly an exercise for the biceps muscles, this single-joint action actually involves several other muscle groups as joint stabilizers and movement assistants. Obviously, exercises that involve multi-joint actions (e.g., barbell squats, barbell bench presses, seated cable rows) engage a large number of prime mover, stabilizer, and assistant muscle groups throughout every repetition.

Muscle Fatigue and Muscle Soreness

During a standard set of resistance exercise, the muscles experience progressive strength reduction until they are unable to lift the weight. This situation is generally referred to as momentary muscle fatigue, and is typically accompanied by some degree of localized discomfort. Although the definitive causes of momentary muscle fatigue have not been quantified, it would appear that the temporary depletion of energy sources, the accumulation of lactate, the increase in tissue acidity, and the interference with neuromuscular transmission all contribute to this common experience. Fortunately, momentary muscle fatigue passes quickly, as energy sources are replenished, localized lactate is removed, tissue acidity decreases, and neuromuscular transmission returns to normal during relative brief (e.g., one to three minutes) recovery periods between successive exercise sets.

More is understood about the muscle discomfort that is typically experienced for one to three days after a challenging strength training session. Known as delayed onset muscle soreness (DOMS), this common resistance training response results from tissue microtrauma that actually occurs during the exercise performance. High-effort resistance training that involves significant eccentric muscle actions causes microscopic tears in the muscle fibers and connective tissue.

Depending on the severity of the microtrauma, the resulting inflammatory process many cause muscle discomfort from 24 to 72 hours after the exercise session. A moderate amount of delayed onset muscle soreness may be associated with effective strength training sessions. Intense or prolonged muscle soreness, however, suggests excessive tissue microtrauma occurs that seriously delays muscle recovery and diminishes muscle remodeling.

Types of Resistance Exercise

You can exercise your muscles differently, depending on the type of resistance you use in your training program. Effectiveness, safety, and personal preference are key factors when selecting your exercise mode.

❏ Isometric Exercise:
Isometric exercise involves static muscle contraction undertaken against a stationary resistance, such as pushing against the top of a doorway. While isometric exercise can effectively build muscle strength, its lack of movement is associated with certain training problems. First, isometric exercise increases muscle strength

primarily at the joint positions used. To develop full-range muscle strength with isometrics, it is typically necessary to train statically at several positions throughout the movement range.

Second, static muscle contractions tend to block blood flow, which may produce relatively high blood pressure responses. For this reason, older individuals and persons with cardiovascular problems should generally avoid isometric forms of exercise.

Third, most people have difficulty assessing their exercise effort and training progress with isometric strengthening programs. The lack of movement may make monotony and motivation serious obstacles to regular isometric training.

❑ Isokinetic Exercise:

Although there are a few exceptions, isokinetic exercise generally involves only positive muscle contractions against an accommodating hydraulic or electronic resistance. The training device maintains a constant movement speed, and the muscle force you apply determines the resistance force you receive. In other words, if you apply a low level of muscle force, you receive a low level of resistance force. Similarly, if you apply a high level of muscle force, you receive a high level of resistance force. For example, if you use a low-effort arm stroke when swimming, you encounter low isokinetic resistance from the water. On the other hand, if you use a high-effort arm stroke, you encounter high isokinetic resistance from the water.

Because isokinetic exercise never exceeds momentary muscle force production, it is frequently employed in muscle rehabilitation programs. Healthy exercisers, however, who inadvertently exert less muscle effort automatically encounter less resistance and may gain fewer strength benefits from this type of training.

❑ Isotonic Exercise:

Isotonic exercise has several differences in comparison with isokinetic exercise. First, isotonic exercise includes both positive and negative muscle contractions. Second, isotonic exercise does not require a constant movement speed. For example, the exerciser may perform successive repetitions at various (typically slower) movement speeds. Third, the exerciser controls the training effort level by selecting a certain resistance force, which requires the target muscles to respond accordingly. In other words, the more resistance a person selects, the more muscle force the individual must exert to perform each repetition.

Isotonic exercise, the most popular and effective type of strength training, may be performed with a constant level of resistance or with a variable resistance. Although the same principles apply, each type of resistance has a different pattern of muscle force production.

Dynamic Constant Resistance Exercise

Dynamic constant resistance exercise uses a fixed resistance, such as a barbell. Although the resistance does not change, leverage factors cause the muscle force exerted to be lower in some positions and higher in other positions. In

Figure 3-4, the barbell provides 100 pounds of resistance force throughout the pressing movement. Due to movement mechanics (leverage factors), however, the muscle force increases from 100 pounds in the bottom position to 140 pounds in the top position. Consequently, this form of isotonic exercise may provide a less-than-ideal matching of muscle force and resistance force throughout the movement range.

Figure 3-4

Dynamic Variable Resistance Exercise

As the term implies, dynamic variable resistance exercise uses a resistance that changes throughout the movement range. For example, well-designed resistance machines incorporate a counter-leverage cam mechanism to automatically vary the resistance force in accordance with muscle force, as the muscle force changes throughout the movement range. In other words, dynamic variable resistance provides proportionately less resistance in positions of lower muscle force and proportionately more resistance in positions of higher muscle force. The resistance machine shown in Figure 3-5 smoothly increases the resistance from 100 pounds in the bottom position to 140 pounds in the top position. This feature results in a relatively consistent matching of muscle force and resistance force throughout the movement range.

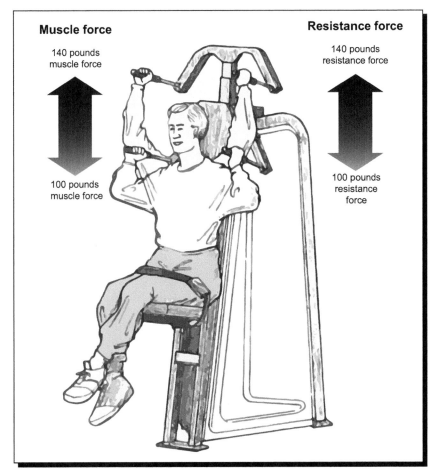

Figure 3-5

CHAPTER 4:
Research-Based Training Recommendations

During the past four decades the author has been privileged to conduct several research studies on strength training. This chapter will present the results of these and other investigations on the following topics: (1) research on strength training variables including, training frequency, training sets, exercise resistance, exercise repetitions, exercise progression, exercise speed, exercise range, training periodization, training time, activity order, activity integration, and circuit strength training; and (2) research on cardiovascular response to strength training, including exercise heart rate and exercise blood pressure.

Most of the studies presented in this chapter were conducted with average men, women, boys, and girls. The results are therefore most generalizable to average people who seek higher levels of strength fitness. The research findings may not be applicable to highly trained athletes such as competitive bodybuilders and weightlifters.

RESEARCH ON STRENGTH TRAINING VARIABLES

Training Frequency

Many people in our fast-paced society have difficulty maintaining a regular training schedule. While most strength training proponents advocate an every-other-day work-rest sequence, not everyone can follow this training pattern. Some enthusiasts find a few minutes every day for a short workout, while others prefer a longer training session once or twice a week.

The results of one study (Westcott 1974) that compared different frequencies of training on strength development in college age males can provide insight into the issue of training frequency. In an attempt to isolate the frequency variable, total training workloads were equated on a weekly basis. More specifically, all 55 subjects performed 60 repetitions per week with the bench press exercise. Group A trained one day per week and completed all 60 repetitions (12 sets of five reps) in a single session. Group B trained two days per week, and completed 30 repetitions (six sets of five reps) each session. Group C trained three days per week and performed 20 repetitions (four sets of five reps) each session. Group D trained five days per week and executed 12 repetitions (two sets of six reps) each session. Table 4-1 presents the training protocols followed by the four experimental groups.

Group (N)	Repetitions per training session per week	Training sessions per week	Repetitions percent increase	Mean
A 16	60	1	60	19%
B 20	30	2	60	17%
C 13	20	3	60	24%
D 6	12	5	60	21%

Table 4-1. Effects of different training frequencies on the development of muscle strength (N = 55)

All of the subjects were tested for maximum bench press strength (1-RM) at the beginning and every 2 ½ weeks during the 7 ½-week training period. As presented in Table 4-1, the subjects made excellent strength gains in the bench press exercise. Statistical analyses showed no significant differences among the four training groups, indicating that all of the training frequencies were equally effective for improving bench press strength. These results suggest that shorter, more frequent workouts and longer, less frequent workouts may both be productive for increasing muscle strength during the initial training period.

The researchers conducted two large-scale training frequency studies, the first with more than 1,100 subjects (Westcott and Guy, 1996), and the second with more than 1,700 participants (Westcott et al, 2009). Because both studies produced very similar results, only the latter and larger research study is addressed in this section.

All of the participants in this study performed the same full-body strength training protocol (one set, 8 to 12 repetitions, 12 standard weight-stack machine exercises) for a period of 10 weeks. Some of the subjects trained one day each week, some trained two non-consecutive days each week, and others trained three non-consecutive days each week.

The one-day-per-week trainees experienced a relatively small (0.75-pound) increase in lean (muscle) weight. Both the two-day-per-week trainees and the three-day-per-week trainees attained a statistically significant 3.1-pound increase in lean (muscle) weight. These results indicate that performing a full-body strength workout once a week is less productive than performing the same workout two or three days a week. It should also be noted that both the two and the three weekly strength training sessions elicited essentially the same level of muscle development.

On the other hand, research with advanced exercisers reveals that at least three recovery days are needed following a challenging resistance training session for muscles to remodel to a higher level of strength (McLester et al. 2003). One day after a hard workout (eight exercises, eight sets, eight repetitions), the subjects' strength levels were well below their pre-training abilities. Two days after the workout, their strength levels were still slightly below baseline. Three days after the workout, the subjects' strength levels were significantly higher than baseline, where they remained at this elevated level throughout the fourth post-training day.

Based on these findings, it would appear that advanced exercisers should take three to four recovery days between resistance training sessions for the same muscle groups. For example, a person who performs a total-body strength workout might train on Wednesdays and Saturdays to ensure sufficient time for muscle remodeling to occur to higher strength levels. A person who prefers to train more frequently may perform a split workout routine, such as doing chest and triceps exercises on Mondays and Thursdays, doing back and biceps exercises on Tuesdays and Fridays, and doing leg, shoulder, and core exercises on Wednesdays and Saturdays.

❏ Summary:
Based on the results of large-scale research studies, it would appear that beginning exercisers can attain similar and significant gains in muscle mass and muscle

strength by performing two or three non-consecutive resistance training sessions each week. These findings are in complete agreement with the American College of Sports Medicine (ACSM) strength training guidelines (ACSM 2014). However, studies with advanced exercisers indicate that optimal muscle remodeling occurs between 72 and 96 hours after a challenging strength training session. Accordingly, it is recommended that advanced exercisers take three to four recovery days between successive workouts for the same muscle groups.

Training Sets

Little agreement exists in the literature concerning how many sets of exercise a person should perform to achieve the optimal strength results. Bodybuilders typically execute multiple sets with each exercise, whereas many fitness centers advocate a single-set training policy.

❑   DeLorme-Watkins Program:
Following World War II, Thomas DeLorme and Arthur Watkins (1948) experimented with strength training for purposes of muscle rehabilitation. Their work produced one of the first systematic and progressive weight training regimens to receive approval form both medical and physical education professionals. Although performed under clinical conditions, they obtained excellent results by using three sets of 10 repetitions each.

The first set of 10 repetitions is performed with 50 percent of the heaviest weight load that can be lifted 10 times, and serves as a first-level warm-up. The second set of 10 repetitions, which is conducted with 75 percent of the heaviest weight load that can be lifted 10 times, serves as a second-level warm-up. The final set of 10 repetitions, executed with the heaviest weight ad that can be lifted 10 times, is the actual stimulus for strength development. The heaviest weight load that can be lifted 10 times is called the 10 repetition maximum (10-RM) weight load.

The heaviest weight load that John can press 10 times in succession (10-RM weight load) is 100 pounds. According to the DeLorme-Watkins training formula, John should do the following workout:

First set: 10 repetitions with 50 pounds

Second set: 10 repetitions with 75 pounds

Third set: 10 repetitions with 100 pounds

As John's muscles respond to the training stimulus, he will be able to complete more than 10 repetitions with 100 pounds. DeLorme and Watkins recommended that a new 10-RM weight load should be established, when the exerciser can perform 15 repetitions with the previous 10-RM weight load. This technique ensures the gradual and progressive loading of the muscles in accordance with the stress adaptation principle. This regimen represents what is generally known as a double-progressive training approach, because the exerciser alternately increases the exercise repetitions and the exercise resistance.

❏   Berger Program:

Beginning in 1962, Richard Berger conducted several studies involving different combinations of sets and repetitions. One of Berger's first experiments (1962b) dealt with the optimum number of repetitions that a person should perform when training with a single set. His findings indicated that one set of the 4-RM, 6-RM, or 8-RM weight load produced greater strength gains than one set of the 2-RM, 10-RM, or 12-RM weight load. Accordingly, he concluded that training with three to nine repetitions encompassed the optimum number of repetitions for increasing strength when training with one set, three times weekly.

Berger's best-know study (1962a) compared all combinations of one, two, and three sets with two, six, and 10 repetitions per set. The results of this study suggested that three sets of six repetitions each with the 6-RM weight load was the most effective training stimulus for gaining muscular strength. Although subsequent investigations by Berger (1963) and other researchers (O'Shea 1966) did not confirm the superiority of this training program, three sets of six repetitions became a very popular training format, especially for multi-muscle exercises, such as squats and bench presses.

Example

The heaviest weight load that Mary can curl six times in succession (6-RM weight load) is 50 pounds. According to the Berger training format, Mary should perform the following workout:

First set: six repetitions with 50 pounds

Second set: six repetitions with 50 pounds

Third set: six repetitions with 50 pounds

When Mary begins training with the 6-RM weight load, she will probably execute fewer than six repetitions in the second and third sets due to the cumulative effects of fatigue. As her level of strength increases, however, she will be able to complete six repetitions in all three sets. At that time, her weight load should be increased by 5 percent and the strength building process will begin anew. Like the DeLorme-Watkins program, the Berger system utilizes a double-progressive training protocol.

❏   Pyramid Program:

Westcott (1979) compared the training effects of the DeLorme-Watkins system and the Berger system, along with a third program that involved three sets with increasing weight loads and decreasing repetitions. The latter is a type of pyramid program frequently used with multi-muscle exercises, such as squats and bench presses, in which successive sets are done with heavier resistance and fewer repetitions. The pyramid program was based on the exerciser's 1-RM weight load, i.e., the heaviest weight load that can be lifted one time. In this regimen, the first set consisted of 10 repetitions with 55 percent of the 1-RM weight load, the second set required five repetitions with 75 percent of the 1-RM weight load, and the third set was a single lift with 95 percent of the 1-RM weight load.

Example

The heaviest weight load that Susan can bench press once (1-RM weight load) is 100 pounds. According to Westcott's pyramid training protocol, Susan should perform the following workout:

First set: 10 repetitions with 55 pounds

Second set: five repetitions with 75 pounds

Third set: one repetition with 95 pounds

The pyramid program is similar to the DeLorme-Watkins program in that both regimens involve two progressively heavier warm-up sets and one set designed to produce the training effect. They differ with respect to the relative amount of resistance used for the training stimulus in the final set.

Program Comparison

All of the participants in Westcott's study improved their bench press performance, and the rates of strength development for the three training groups were similar. Comparative results of the DeLorme-Watkins system, the Berger system, and the pyramid program are summarized in Table 4-2. Because there were no statistically significant differences in strength gains among the three training groups, these exercise protocols may be equally effective for developing muscle strength. Due to the near-maximum resistance used in the final set, however, the pyramid program may pose a higher risk of injury over an extended training period.

Group	Berger	DeLorme-Watkins	Pyramid
Subjects	5	4	5
Mean improvement per week	3.7%	4.3%	4.3%

Table 4-2. Improvement in bench press performance by groups training with Berger, DeLorme-Watkins, and pyramid programs (N = 14)

❏ Single Sets vs. Multiple Sets:

The author conducted two studies examining the effects of single sets and multiple sets on strength development. The first study (Westcott 1986c) compared training with one, two, and three sets of exercises performed on weight stack machines. Due to injuries, illnesses, and drop-outs, the number of subjects who completed the three-set program was too small to include in the data analyses. Consequently, this study actually compared 22 subjects who performed one set with 22 other subjects who performed two sets of five exercises: leg extension, leg curl, torso pullover, arm extension, and arm curl. As illustrated in Table 4-3, the results showed no statistically significant differences in strength development between the subjects who performed one set of each exercise and the subjects who performed two sets of each exercise.

Group	One set	Two sets
Subjects	22	22
Mean improvement per week (5 exercises)	15.8%	15.0%

Table 4-3. Improvement in strength performance by groups training with one or two sets per exercise (N = 44)

The second study (Westcott et al. 1989) was similar to Berger's research in that it compared all combinations of one, two, and three sets of five, 10 and 15 repetitions for improvements in bar-dip and chin-up performance.

To enable the subjects to complete the prescribed number of dips and chins in their exercise protocol, all training was performed on a computerized air-pressure apparatus that lifted a given percentage of the exerciser's bodyweight during each bar-dip and chin-up. The resistance-assistance machine was individually programmed so that each participant experienced muscle failure at the end of their training session.

Each subject performed one of the three prescribed exercise protocols three days each week throughout the 10-week study. Whenever a subject could complete their specific training program with a given resistance, the level of machine assistance was reduced slightly to make the workout more demanding.

Training Protocols*

1 set X 5 reps	2 sets X 5 reps	3 sets X 5 reps
1 set X 10 reps	2 sets X 10 reps	3 sets X 10 reps
1 set X 15 reps	2 sets X 15 reps	3 sets X 15 reps

*For example, a subject in the two sets of 10 reps group would perform two sets of 10 bar-dips and two sets of 10 chin-ups.

All subjects were tested for the maximum number of dips and chins they could perform in strict technique with their full bodyweight, the total number of which determined the subject's pre-training and post-training scores. As illustrated in Table 4-4, all of the training groups made excellent improvements in their bar-dip and chin-up performance. There were no statistically significant differences among the subjects who did one set of each exercise, the subjects who did two sets of each exercise, or the subjects who did three sets of each exercise, regardless of the number of repetitions performed.

Group	One set	Two sets	Three sets
Subjects	10	35	32
Mean improvement	4.8 reps	4.1 reps	5.2 reps

Table 4-4. Improvement in bar-dip and chin-up performance by groups training with one, two, and three sets per exercise (N = 77)

There have been three major meta-analyses of training sets, each of which has produced different results. The first review of research studies on different training sets (Carpinelli and Otto 1998) concluded that single-set training was just as effective as multiple-set training for increasing muscle strength. The second meta-analysis (Rhea et al. 2003) determined that one-set training was less productive than two-set training, that two-set training was less productive than three-set training, and that three-set training was less productive than four-set training. The third meta-analysis (Krieger 2009) found that one-set training and four-set training achieved similar strength gains, and that two-set training and three-set training elicited similar strength gains. Unlike the two previous studies, however, this investigative effort indicated that two to three exercise sets provided the most effective training protocol for increasing muscle strength.

Due to the lack of consensus regarding the optimum number of training sets, a common-sense approach would be to have new participants perform one good set of each resistance exercise. More than 2,800 participants in the strength training research studies conducted by the author and his colleagues have averaged approximately one pound per month muscle gain (through six months) by performing one set of 12 basic resistance exercises, two or three days per week.

❑ Summary:

Three major reviews on the optimum number of training sets for strength development have produced different results, ranging from recommendations of one-set per exercise, two or three-sets per exercise, and four-sets per exercise. Based on exercise selection, each of these recommendations for training sets could be obtained within the parameters presented in ACSM's Guidelines for Exercise Testing and Prescription (2014). These guidelines call for two to four exercise sets for each major muscle group, which may be achieved in a variety of ways, such as performing one set of two different exercises for a given muscle group or by completing four-sets of the same exercise.

ACSM's Guidelines for Exercise Testing and Prescription (2014) also state that single-set strength training can be effective for beginning exercisers and older adults. All factors considered, one set of each resistance exercise appears to be a productive training protocol for new exercisers. On the other hand, on an individual basis, more experienced participants who desire greater training volume may arbitrarily decide to progress to doing two, three, or four sets of each resistance exercise.

Exercise Resistance

For decades, the overload principle has been the key concept in strength training. Overloading involves using progressively heavier resistance to work the muscles more intensely, thereby stimulating further strength development. For example, if Mark can curl 100 pounds one time, then doing one repetition with 105 pounds will overload his biceps. Similarly, if Mark can curl 50 pounds 20 times, then 20 repetitions with 55 pounds would also overload his biceps.

Using a high level of resistance (i.e., one-repetition maximum) may increase the risk of injury, while performing a high number of repetitions (e.g., 20 or more) may decrease the strength-building stimulus. So, what is the most appropriate guideline for applying the overload principle? Muscle strength can be developed most effectively by working the target muscle to fatigue within the body's anaerobic energy system.

This system supplies energy for high-effort exercise lasting less than 90 seconds. For practical purposes, about 50 to 70 seconds of continuous muscle work to the point of muscle fatigue is preferred. Most people can perform about 50 to 70 seconds of resistance exercise with 75 percent of their maximum weight load (i.e., 75 percent of the heaviest weight that they can lift one time). At a moderate speed (about six seconds per repetition), this factor corresponds to about 8 to 12 controlled repetitions.

Fortunately, it is possible to estimate 75 percent of maximum resistance without doing an all-out lift. In general, the weight that can be lifted 10 times to fatigue is approximately 75 percent of maximum resistance. Training with this weight load creates a high stimulus for strength development and poses a low risk of tissue injury. Although 75 percent of maximum resistance is standard strength training procedure, periodically using lower and higher training loads (between 60 and 90 percent of maximum resistance) not only offers a welcome change of pace, it also provides both physiological and psychological benefits.

Exercise Repetitions

An inverse relationship exists between the weight load utilized for a particular exercise and the number of repetitions that can be executed. When a person uses the heaviest weight load possible, only a single lift can be performed. As the weight load is reduced, more repetitions can be completed. It should be noted, however, that Berger (1965) found that resistance training with less than 65 percent of maximum weight load was not very effective for strength development.

Beginning in 1948, a considerable amount of research was conducted to determine the optimum number of repetitions for developing muscle strength through resistance training. DeLorme (1948), the father of modern strength training, developed a highly productive exercise regimen, based on 10 repetitions per set. Berger (1962a) compared nine different strength training programs and determined that three sets of six repetitions produced the greatest strength gains.

In a 1963 investigation, however, Berger found no significant differences among training programs utilizing two, six, or 10 repetitions per set. O'Shea (1966) also determined that no significant differences existed among training programs using two and three repetitions, five and six repetitions, or nine and 10 repetitions. In a similar study, Withers (1970) discovered no significant differences among training programs incorporating three, five, or seven repetitions per set. Subsequently, during the 1970s, Nautilus machine-based exercise programs had a major impact on strength training protocols. As a result, one set of 8 to 12 repetitions became standard procedure for many strength training participants (Darden 1977).

Jones (1986) conducted a considerable amount of research in the area of muscle endurance. He found that subjects with low muscle endurance required only four or five repetitions to reduce their starting strength by 25 percent, while subjects with high muscle endurance required 15 to 16 repetitions to reduce their starting strength by 25 percent. Jones suggested that the differences in muscle endurance may be due to inherent physiological characteristics that are not altered by training. If Jones' hypothesis is correct, it might partly account for the inconsistent findings and recommendations with regards to the optimum number of resistance training repetitions.

Westcott (1995a) examined differences in muscle performance with a given sub-maximum resistance. This study involved 141 male and female study subjects who were tested on a Nautilus 10-degree chest machine to determine the heaviest weight load that they could perform one time. After a five-minute rest, the participants completed as many strict repetitions as possible with 75 percent of their maximum weight load. The findings of this study showed that most subjects performed 8 to 12 repetitions with 75 percent of their maximum weight load (see Figure 4-1).

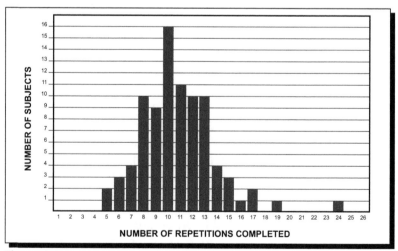

Figure 4-1

As shown in Table 4-5, the mean score for all subjects was 10.5 repetitions. It was apparent, however, that the subjects varied considerably in the number of repetitions they could complete with the same percentage of their maximum resistance. Two subjects completed only five repetitions, while one subject performed 24 repetitions with the same relative resistance (75 percent of maximum).

	Group A (4 secs/rep)	Group B (6 secs/rep)	Group C (8 secs/rep)	Group D (14 secs/rep)
Training protocol	(4 secs/rep)	(6 secs/rep)	(8 secs/rep)	(14 secs/rep)
Repetitions per set	10	10	10	5
Time per set	40 secs.	60 secs.	80 secs.	70 secs.
Average strength improvement	+22 lb.*	+22 lb.*	+23 lb.*	+27 lb.*
*Statistically significant improvement (p<.05)				

Table 4-5. Changes in overall strength using different movement speeds (N = 198)

Accordingly, it would appear that while most people have moderate levels of muscular endurance, some people have high levels of muscle endurance, while still others have low levels of muscle endurance. Because all of the subjects in this study exercised regularly with one set of 8 to 12 repetitions, their relative muscle endurance would seem to be independent of the training procedures. These results tend to support Jones' (1986) contention that performance differences with the same relative level of resistance are due to inherent physiological characteristics. It is possible, however, that differences in muscle fiber types may be a major factor in the number of repetitions that a person can complete with a given sub-maximum weight load.

Based on these findings, as well as subsequent research in which the exercise duration was matched to each individual's muscle endurance (Westcott 1987), the following repetition guidelines are recommended. People with low-endurance muscles generally attain better results by training with about five to eight repetitions (30 to 50 seconds) per set. People with moderate-endurance muscles typically achieve better results by training with about 8 to 12 repetitions (50 to 70 seconds) per set. People with high-endurance muscles generally gain better results by training with about 12 to 15 repetitions (70 to 90 seconds) per set. Because most people have moderate-endurance muscles, 8 to 12 repetitions per set are suggested as standard training procedure. On the other hand, it is advisable to periodically perform higher or lower repetitions per set for a change of pace, and to promote a fresh strength-building stimulus.

❏ Summary:

As a result of widely published strength training guidelines, many participants follow an 8 to 12 repetition protocol. Westcott's (1986L) research indicates that this is a safe and effective training recommendation, given that most individuals can perform 8 to 12 strict repetitions with 75 percent of their maximum resistance. With respect to training specificity, however, it may be advisable for individuals with low-endurance muscles to train with fewer repetitions and for persons with high-endurance muscles to train with more repetitions.

Exercise Progression

Continued strength development depends on progressive resistance exercise that gradually places more stress on the target muscles. A double-progressive training protocol alternately increases repetitions and resistance in a systematic manner. For example, if Mary can do eight lateral raises with 50 pounds, she should continue training with 50 pounds until she can do 12 repetitions, at which time she should increase the resistance by about 5 percent. In other words, she should add 2.5 pounds to the weight stack and train with 52.5 pounds, until which time she can again perform 12 repetitions of the exercise.

Alternately increasing the number of exercise repetitions up to 12 and then increasing the exercise resistance by 5 percent (or less) ensures gradual strength gains, with a relatively low risk of injury. Although there are other progression protocols, this system fatigues the target muscles within 50 to 70 seconds of continuous resistance exercise and virtually eliminates the possibility of doing too much too soon.

Exercise Speed

Perhaps the area of greatest controversy in the field of strength training is movement speed. Advocates of fast strength training believe that faster movement speeds enhance explosive muscle power (Counsilman 1976). Conversely, proponents of slow strength training contend that slower movement speeds increase strength development and reduce injury potential (Pipes 1979).

In 1970, Moffroid and Whipple compared the effects of two movement speeds on muscle strength. One group of subjects performed an isokinetic knee extension at a speed of 36 degrees per second. Another group of subjects performed an isokinetic knee extension at a speed of 108 degrees per second. The results showed that the slower-trained subjects made greater strength gains when tested at the slower speed, and that the faster trained subjects made greater strength gains when tested at the faster speed. A study by Coyle et al. (1981) produced similar results. The slower-trained subjects (60 degrees per second) showed more strength improvement at the slower speed, while the faster trained subjects (300 degrees per second) showed more strength improvement at the faster speed.

Both of these studies revealed a specificity of training effect. In other words, slower training appeared to be more effective for strength development at slower speeds, and faster training appeared to be more effective for strength development at faster speeds.

Palmieri (1987) trained 54 subjects with squats, leg extensions, and heel raises. One group trained with slow movement speeds, another group trained with fast movement speeds, and a third group combined both slow and fast movement speeds. All of the training groups improved in leg power, but there were no significant differences with respect to the training speed. Palmieri's findings indicated that slow strength training, fast strength training, and mixed strength training (i.e., slow and fast) may be equally effective for developing power.

Research by Rosentswieg, Hinson, and Ridgway (1975) found significantly greater strength stimulus with slower muscle contractions. Similarly, a study by Van Oteghen (1975) also reported significantly greater strength development with slower speed training. Gettman and Ayres (1978) examined the effects of training speed on body composition. Their findings showed that subjects who trained with slow-movement speeds improved body composition more than subjects who trained with fast-movement speeds.

In an attempt to reduce hard-to-control variables between training groups, Westcott (1986a) conducted a study in which all of the subjects received both experimental treatments. Each participant trained one leg at a relatively slow speed (60 degrees per second) and the other leg at a relatively fast speed (240 degrees per second) on an isokinetic resistance apparatus. All subjects followed the same strength training protocol. Upon securing the left leg to the training apparatus, they performed 20 seconds of knee extensions at 60 degrees per second for three sets of exercise, with a 40-second recovery period between sets. Upon securing the right leg to the training apparatus, they then performed 20 seconds of knee extensions at 240 degrees per second for three sets of exercise, with a 40-second recovery period between sets.

After training three times per week for three weeks, each leg was retested for maximum strength at 60 and 240 degrees per second. The slow-trained leg showed significant strength gains at both movement speeds, whereas the fast-trained leg did not improve strength at either movement speed. The results of this study indicated that resistance training at a relatively slow speed of 60 degrees per second may be more effective than resistance training at a relatively fast speed of 240 degrees per second for improving muscle strength at both speeds of movement.

As shown in Figure 4-2, when momentum is minimized with isokinetic resistance, both muscle tension (the area under each force curve) and muscle force (the height of each force curve) decrease as the movement speed increases. Accordingly, moderate-to-slow training speeds appear to provide a greater strength building stimulus than fast training speeds, when exercises are performed without momentum.

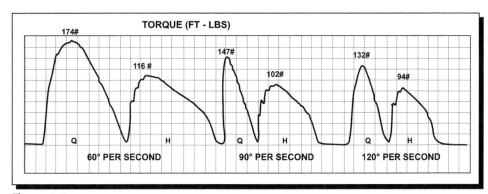

Figure 4-2

Exercise speed may be divided into three categories: fast, moderate, and slow. A fast exercise speed is one that cannot be stopped at a given point in the movement range. Fast exercise speeds emphasize momentum, which may reduce muscle activation and increase injury risk. Repetitions that take two seconds or less qualify as fast.

A moderate exercise speed is one that can be stopped upon request to do so. Moderate exercise speed deemphasizes momentum, increases muscle effort, and reduces injury risk. Repetitions that take between four and six seconds are of moderate speed.

A slow exercise speed is one that is performed with meticulous control. Slow exercise speed minimizes momentum and maximizes muscle tension. Lifting movements that take eight or more seconds are considered slow. Research indicates that moderate-to-slow exercise speeds are effective for increasing muscle strength. As such, training at these speeds is recommended for safe and successful strength training.

Moderate-to-slow exercise speeds have the following training advantages over fast exercise speeds:

- A longer period of muscle tension
- A higher level of continuous muscle force
- A lower level of momentum
- A lower risk of tissue injury

Six-second repetitions have a long, almost 50-year history of success, and may be considered standard training procedure (ACSM 2006) in some quarters. It should be noted, however, that other moderate-to-slow movement speeds may be equally effective, as indicated by one of the various research studies conducted by Westcott and his colleagues. In a study by Westcott (1995b), 198 study participants performed one set of 8 to 12 repetitions on 13 Nautilus machines for a period of eight weeks. Group A trained with four-second repetitions, Group B performed six-second repetitions, Group C used eight-second repetitions, and Group D completed 14 second repetitions.

As shown in Table 4-5, all four groups achieved significant improvements in muscle strength (average strength gains for all 13 resistance exercises). Based on these findings, moderate-to-slow movement speeds that fatigue the target muscles within the anaerobic energy system (40 to 80 seconds) appear to produce similar improvements in muscle strength.

❏ Summary:

Moderate-to-slow repetition speeds are effective for safely increasing muscle strength, because they provide more muscle tension, more muscle force, less momentum, and less tissue trauma than fast movement speeds. Repetition speeds between four and eight seconds are recommended for most practical purposes of muscle and strength development.

Exercise Range

Most people need to perform full-range resistance exercise to develop full-range muscle strength. Based on the work of Jones and colleagues (1988), muscle strength is specific to the movement range that is trained. For example, resistance-machine back extensions performed in one-half of the movement range have their greatest strengthening effect in that area (Jones et al. 1988).

Full-range muscle strength is especially important for patients with low back pain. Individuals who have minimal strength in the position of full trunk extension may be more likely to experience low back pain. Fortunately, training the lower back muscles through their full movement range can significantly increase strength and reduce pain in this part of the body (Jones et al. 1988).

Because full-range muscle strength enhances physical performance and reduces injury risk, full-range resistance exercise should be performed whenever possible. Although the range of joint movement varies among individuals, it is advisable to train from the position of full muscle stretch to the position of complete muscle contraction. Keep in mind that when the target muscle (e.g., biceps) is fully contracted, the opposing muscle (e.g., triceps) is fully stretched. For this reason, full-range resistance training may enhance joint flexibility, as well as increase muscle strength.

Training Periodization

When exercisers make successive training sessions a little more demanding, they will experience continuous strength development up to a point. Unfortunately, the muscles do not respond in this manner indefinitely. After several months of strength exercise, the muscles may require periodic variations in training stress to stimulate further adaptations.

Exercise periodization is simply a systematic means for changing the training stimuli. An example of such an approach might involve a three-month program of exercise periodization that progresses from higher repetitions with lower resistance to lower repetitions with higher resistance. As presented in Table 4-6, the first-month training protocol entails 12 to 16 repetitions with about 65 percent of maximum resistance. The lower resistance provides less stress to the muscles, tendons, ligaments, and bones, thereby reducing the risk of tissue injury during the initial conditioning phase.

Month	Exercise resistance	Exercise repetitions
First	About 65 percent maximum	12 to 16 reps per set
Second	About 75 percent maximum	8 to 12 reps per set
Third	About 85 percent maximum	4 to 8 reps per set

Table 4-6. Sample three-month periodization program

The second-month training protocol encompasses 8 to 12 repetitions with about 75 percent of maximum resistance. This phase is a basic strength-building period that provides a solid foundation for the final training phase.

The third-month training protocol comprises doing four to eight repetitions with about 85 percent of maximum resistance. The higher resistance may provide greater strength stimulus, and should be well-tolerated by the musculoskeletal system after two months of progressive conditioning.

Following three months of regular resistance exercise, it may be advisable to take a few days of active rest before repeating the training cycle. Active rest refers to non-strength-building activities, such as walking, jogging, cycling, swimming, tennis, and basketball.

Although there are numerous periodization variations, the three-month training model fits well with most sports seasons. Repeating the training cycle provides a systematic change in the exercise stimulus. Assuming positive muscle adaptations, an individual should begin each new training cycle at a higher strength level.

Training Time

Most people feel that training time is a matter of personal preference, with little bearing on a person's strength development. Some individuals seem to function best in the morning, while others tend to be more productive in the evening. Because most sports practice sessions are held after school, athletes grow accustomed to training in the afternoon. Without exploring the area of biorhythms, it would seem to make sense that once a training schedule has been established, a person will probably perform best at their regular workout time. It is also logical, however, to assume that the cumulative effect of general fatigue may influence physical performance later in the day.

Westcott (1986c) decided to test this hypothesis on an important muscle group that typically works sixteen hours a day, even while driving the car, sitting in the office, or studying in the library—the trapezius and posterior neck muscles. These muscles maintain the head in an erect position throughout a person's working hours. Needless to say, the neck extensors are key muscles with regard to safety and performance in sports, such as football and wrestling.

The subjects in this study by Westcott were 10 men and women who regularly participated in a strength training program. All of the participants had sedentary occupations that required a minimum amount of physical exertion. Each subject was evaluated for neck extension strength on a Nautilus neck machine, with a weight load that could be lifted at least 10 repetitions. The subjects were randomly tested with the same weight load before 10:00 a.m. and after 5:00 p.m. on nonconsecutive days.

The results showed that the subjects completed 44 percent more repetitions in the morning session than in the evening session. The morning performance exceeded the evening performance in every instance, even though many of the subjects normally trained later in the day.

These statistically significant findings suggest that daily fatigue may have a profound effect on the neck extensor muscles. It would appear that a person having to hold their head in an upright position for several hours a day may reduce neck strength substantially.

❑ Summary:
In accordance with training frequency recommendations, an individual should schedule workouts at the peak of muscle building processes to obtain maximum strength benefits. Similarly, a person should train when both their energy levels

and their strength levels are the highest to achieve the best results. The findings from one study indicate that the neck extensor muscles perform significantly better at the beginning of the day than at the end of the day. It may, therefore, be advisable to perform neck strengthening exercises earlier in the day, when the fatigue level of these muscles is lower. While it is possible that morning strength workouts may produce excellent overall results for the same reason, individual training preferences should certainly be taken into consideration when deciding when to work out.

Activity Order

Some individuals want to combine their strength training and endurance training. In that regard, it is generally recommended that people who perform challenging strength workouts and challenging endurance workouts do so on the same day, followed by at least one recovery day.

Westcott (2005) researched the effects of activity order on exercise performance. The 205 subjects in this study were randomly assigned to perform 25 minutes of strength training (12 weight stack machine exercises), followed by 25 minutes of aerobic activity (treadmill walking and stationary cycling), or to perform 25 minutes of aerobic activity, followed by 25 minutes of strength training.

After 10 weeks of training, the subjects who always performed strength training, followed by endurance exercise, experienced a mean strength gain of 16 pounds. Similarly, the subjects who always performed endurance exercise, followed by strength training, experienced a similar mean strength gain of 15 pounds. In other words, there were no significant differences in strength development, whether the strength training was performed before or after the endurance exercise.

❏ Summary:
The participants in this study performed a basic strength-training protocol (one set of 8 to 12 repetitions at about 75 percent of maximum resistance), and a standard endurance exercise protocol (25 minutes of walking and cycling at about 75 percent of maximum heart rate). When performed in this manner, activity order appears to have no effect on strength development. As such, this training factor may therefore be a matter of personal preference.

Activity Integration

Strength training and flexibility exercise are complementary activities that should be performed together for best results in both areas. Basically, the capacity of a muscle to contract and shorten and the ability of a muscle to relax and lengthen represent two sides of the same coin. Strength exercise performed through the full range of movement enhances joint flexibility. Similarly, training programs that combine resistance exercise and static stretching have been shown to elicit greater strength gains than resistance exercise alone.

A series of studies compared the effects of resistance exercise alone and resistance exercise plus static stretching on strength development in previously untrained participants (Westcott and LaRosa Loud 2000). Altogether, more than 150 men and women performed identical programs of resistance exercise (12 weight stack machines, one set of 8 to 12 repetitions, two or three days a week) for a period of 10 weeks. One group of subjects performed the strength training program without stretching. A second group of subjects performed the same strength training program with distributed stretching (a 20-second static stretch executed after each resistance exercise for the muscles just worked). A third group of subjects performed the same strength training program with consolidated stretching (six 20-second static stretches after the workout that cumulatively addressed all of the major muscle groups).

The results of these studies showed two things. First, the subjects who performed both resistance training and stretching exercise experienced approximately 20 percent greater strength gains than subjects who performed resistance training only (19.6 pounds vs. 16.4 pounds). Second, subjects who performed distributed stretching and subjects who performed consolidated stretching attained essentially equal increases in muscle strength.

❑ Summary:
Combined resistance training and stretching exercises produced a 20-percent greater strength gain than resistance training alone over a 10-week training period. It is recommended that trainees perform a 20-second static stretch after each resistance exercise or a series of static stretches following the workout to enhance both muscle strength and joint flexibility.

Combining strength and flexibility exercises is an excellent example of effective activity integration. Another example of activity integration that has proven productive for concurrently adding muscle and losing fat is combining strength and endurance exercise. This type of training program will be presenting in the following section on circuit strength training.

Circuit Strength Training

Circuit strength training has been defined as "a conditioning program in which an individual performs one set of exercise for a given muscle group (e.g., quadriceps), followed closely by one set of exercise for a different muscle group (e.g., hamstrings), and so on for all of the major muscle groups. Typically, 10 to 15 resistance exercises are done in close succession" (Westcott, in Burke 1998). Circuit strength training provides a time-efficient exercise program by eliminating rest periods that are necessary when performing successive sets for the same muscle groups. Because each circuit exercise is followed by an exercise for a different muscle group, it is possible to move quickly from station to station.

Training in this manner provides a dual conditioning benefit. At each strength training station, participants perform a set of resistance exercise utilizing the anaerobic energy system (typically 10 to 15 repetitions in about 60 seconds). Completing 10 to 15 different resistance exercises enables a comprehensive strength training session that addresses all of the major muscle groups. Moving quickly between exercise stations (e.g., approximately 30 seconds) results in a total workout time between 15 to 23 minutes.

Due to the relatively high and continuous exercise effort, the participant's heart rate generally reaches and remains within the target heart rate range throughout the entire training session. This situation provides an effective aerobic conditioning stimulus. Unlike most physical activities that specifically enhance either muscular strength (anaerobic exercise) or cardiovascular endurance (aerobic exercise), circuit strength training concurrently improves both of these fitness parameters.

Although numerous research studies have shown significant improvements in muscle strength, lean weight, and aerobic capacity as a result of circuit strength training (Gettman et al. 1981, Gettman et al. 1982, Harris and Holly 1987), a more comprehensive study was conducted by Messier and Dill in 1985. These researchers compared the effects of a standard weight training program (three days a week, 50 minutes per session), a typical running program (three days a week, 30 minutes per session), and a circuit strength training program (threee days a week, 20 minutes per session) on muscle strength and aerobic capacity. After 10 weeks of training, the average strength gain for the standard weight training participants was 23 percent, compared to 38 percent for the circuit training participants. In other words, the circuit training program was at least as productive as the standard weight training program for increasing muscle strength.

Similarly, the average improvement in aerobic capacity ($\dot{V}O_2max$) for the running group was 12 percent, compared to 11 percent for the circuit training group. No significant difference in cardiovascular enhancement was found between the running group and the circuit training group. Not only did the circuit strength training program concurrently increase muscular strength and cardiovascular endurance, it was as effective as standard weight training for eliciting strength gains, and as well as effective as running for eliciting aerobic gains. Furthermore, the circuit strength training program achieved similar physiological responses in much shorter exercise sessions (20 minutes) than the standard weight training program (50 minutes) and the running program (30 minutes).

In 2007, Westcott and colleagues researched the conditioning effects of a more comprehensive circuit training program on U.S. Air Force personnel. Their circuit training program alternated 10 resistance machine stations with 10 stationary cycling stations. Participants performed 60 seconds of continuous exercise at each station, for a total training time of 20 minutes. The relatively brief circuit training program was compared with the standard Air Force aerobic conditioning program that called for 60-minute sessions of aerobic activity.

After 12 weeks of training, only the circuit training program participants attained significant improvements in muscular strength/endurance (push-up and sit-up assessments) and aerobic performance (1.5 mile run time). Furthermore, significantly more circuit strength training program participants attained a passing score on the Air Force physical fitness test than did the standard aerobic training program participants.

More recently, Westcott and associates (2013) examined the effects of a combined circuit strength training on lean weight, fat weight, and resting blood pressure in men and women who were enrolled in a weight loss program. This program consisted of nine weight-stack machine exercises performed for one set of 8 to 12 repetitions each, interspersed with three five-minute bouts of stationary cycling, as detailed in Table 4-7. After 10 weeks of training, the three groups of 121 program participants averaged a five-pound fat loss (0.5 pounds per week), a two-pound muscle gain (0.2 pounds per week), and a blood pressure reduction of 2mmHg systolic and 2.5 mmHg diastolic. Basically, the relatively brief circuit training sessions resulted in concurrent decreases in fat weight and increases in lean weight, while also eliciting reductions in resting blood pressure.

1.	Leg extension	5.	Chest press	9.	Abdominal flexion
2.	Leg curl	6.	Lat pulldown	10.	Low back extension
3.	Leg press	7.	Shoulder press	11.	Torso rotation
4.	Cycle	8.	Cycle	12.	Cycle

- Weight stack machines – one set of 8 to 12 repetitions (six secs/rep)
- Cycle – Five minutes of interval training (20 secs higher effort, 20 secs lower effort

Table 4-7. Circuit strength training protocol implemented in the weight loss study.

❑ Summary:

Circuit strength training provides a time-efficient alternative to standard resistance training, because it reduces recovery periods between successive bouts of exercise. Circuit training may be performed either exclusively with resistance exercise or with various combinations of strength and endurance stations. Both types of circuit strength training have demonstrated concurrent improvements in muscle strength and cardiovascular endurance, as well as muscle gain and fat loss. Basically, longer rests between circuit stations enables heavier weight loads and facilitates strength development, whereas shorter rests between circuit stations necessitates lighter weight loads and favors cardiovascular conditioning.

Cardiovascular Response

As indicated in the previous section, resistance exercise can significantly increase cardiovascular fitness when performed in a circuit training format. Similar to aerobic activity, strength training has an acute impact on both heart rate and blood pressure, eliciting responses that are surprisingly similar.

❑ Heart Rate:

Whenever the demand for energy increases, the heart rate increases. The heart is similar to the fuel pump in an automobile, and the muscles are analogous to the engine. As the muscles perform work, the heart must pump blood to the worksites to replenish energy supplies and remove metabolic waste products. Because the heart pumps blood throughout the entire body, activity in any of the major muscle groups produces a faster heart rate. Although more oxygen is consumed by larger muscle groups, the heart-rate response is essentially the same for a leg extension and an arm extension (Hempel and Wells 1985).

Westcott (1985b, 2000) found that heart rate increases progressively during a 10-repetition set of resistance exercise. To maintain a heart rate within the target training zone, it is necessary to take relatively brief rests between the exercises. As illustrated in Figure 4-3, when 90-second rests were taken between a 10-exercise workout (one set of each exercise), the mean peak heart rates averaged 128 beats per minute. When the recovery periods were reduced to 60 seconds, the mean peak heart rates averaged 139 beats per minute. In contrast, when only 30 seconds were taken between exercises, the mean peak heart rates averaged 148 beats per minute.

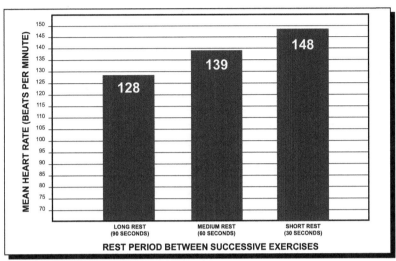

Figure 4-3

Because circuit strength training programs typically have short rest intervals, relatively high exercise heart rates (i.e., greater than 70 percent of maximum heart rate) can be maintained over a 15 to 25 minute training duration. Accordingly, it is understandable why circuit strength training has demonstrated significant improvements in aerobic capacity (Gettman et al. 1981; Gettman et al. 1982; Harris and Holly 1987).

❑ Blood Pressure:

A common misconception exists that strength training has an adverse effect on blood pressure. Although exercise physiologists are well aware that isometric strength training can cause unusually large increases in systolic and diastolic blood pressures, studies of blood pressure changes during non-isometric strength training have produced varied results. MacDougall et al. (1983) found extremely high systolic and diastolic blood pressures in bodybuilders during heavy leg exercises. In one subject, the intra-arterial blood pressure measured 400/300 mm Hg. It is possible that other factors, such as essential hypertension, use of anabolic steroids, and excessive body mass, may have been at least partly responsible for the unusually high blood pressure response (Wright 1978; Hunter and McCarthy 1982).

Freedson, Chang, and Katch (1984) reported blood pressure readings of 240/155 mm Hg during free weight and hydraulic bench press exercises. These readings were lower than the readings found by MacDougall et al. (1983), but higher than those obtained by Westcott and Howes (1983) and Westcott (1986b).

Westcott and Howes (1983) studied blood pressure responses in 24 adults during one-arm biceps curls with light, medium, and heavy weight loads. The mean systolic blood pressure increased gradually from 123 mm Hg at rest to

165 mm Hg during the final repetition with the 10-RM weight load. The mean diastolic pressure measured 75 mm Hg both before and immediately after the exercise set. Figure 4-4 shows that the systolic blood pressure response was directly related to the training intensity. The peak systolic readings were 143 mm Hg with the light weight load, 151 mm Hg with the medium weight load, and 165 mm Hg with the heavy weight load.

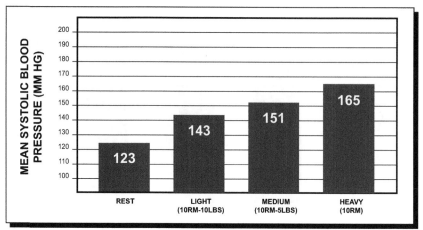

Figure 4-4

Based on the findings of this study, it would appear that biceps curls performed with the 10-RM weight load do not produce abrupt, excessive, or unusual blood pressure responses. In fact, the 34-percent increase in systolic pressure was similar to 35-percent increase in systolic pressure measured on 23 subjects during a standard bout of stationary cycling (20 minutes at approximately 75 percent of maximum heartrate).

Because lower-body exercises involve more muscle mass and more muscle force than upper-body exercises, Westcott (1986b) examined blood pressure responses in 25 men and women during Nautilus machine duo-squats with heavy weight loads. The mean systolic blood pressure increased gradually from 127 mm Hg at rest to 190 mm Hg during the final repetition with the 10-RM weight load (see Figure 4-5). The mean diastolic pressure measured 73 mm Hg before and 61 mm Hg immediately after the exercise set.

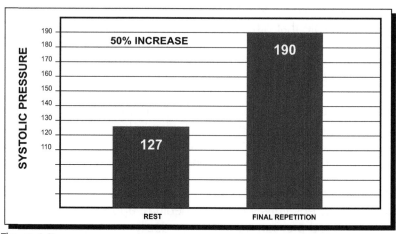

Figure 4-5

Although the Nautilus duo-squats produced a 50-percent increase in systolic blood pressure, the response pattern was similar to one-arm biceps curls. All of the subjects demonstrated a gradual, progressive, and predictable systolic blood pressure increase during the 10-repetition exercise sets. It should be noted that a systolic blood pressure of 190 mm Hg is well below the peak exercise level of 250 mm Hg recommended by the American College of Sports Medicine (ACSM 2010).

Westcott and Pappas (1987) examined the immediate effects of circuit strength training on blood pressure. The standing blood pressures of the 100 subjects were recorded 30 to 60 seconds before and 30 to 60 seconds after performing an 11-station strength training circuit. As presented in Figure 4-6, the mean pre-exercise blood pressure reading was 115/67 mm Hg, while the mean post-exercise blood pressure reading was 117/65 mm Hg.

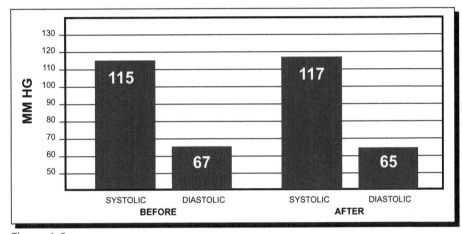

Figure 4-6

These results indicated that both systolic and diastolic blood pressure readings were essentially the same before and after more than 20 minutes of circuit strength training with relatively heavy resistance. Note that the participants in this study, most of whom had performed regular circuit strength training for over a year, recorded relatively low blood pressures both before (115/67 mm Hg) and after (117/65 mm Hg) the exercise session.

❏ Summary:

Based on the majority of blood pressure studies reviewed, it would appear that sensible strength training does not have an adverse acute effect on blood pressure in healthy adults. As presented in Chapter 1, research clearly demonstrates that regular resistance exercise results in reduced systolic and diastolic blood pressure readings.

Sensible strength training is characterized by continuous movement and continuous breathing throughout the exercise set. It should be emphasized that because prolonged isometric contractions or breath-holding can produce excessive blood pressure responses, both techniques should be avoided. It is highly recommended that persons with elevated resting blood pressures or other cardiovascular abnormalities consult their physician before beginning a strength training program.

SUMMARY OF RESEARCH-BASED TRAINING RECOMMENDATIONS

❏ Training Frequency:

Beginning exercisers may attain excellent results by training each major muscle group two or three non-consecutive days per week. Advanced exercisers require more recovery time for muscle remodeling, and are advised to train each major muscle group twice a week, with 72 to 96 hours rest between sessions.

❏ Training Sets:

Beginning participants may achieve significant gains in muscle strength and muscle mass by performing one set of each resistance exercise. Advanced participants may perform multiple sets of each exercise so that each major muscle group experiences two to four training bouts per session.

❏ Exercise Resistance:

Most exercisers will experience excellent results by training with approximately 75 percent of their maximum resistance. Periodically employing lower and higher training loads (between 60 and 90 percent of maximum resistance) is recommended.

❏ Exercise Repetitions:

Most exercisers will experience excellent results by training with 8 to 12 repetitions per set. People with low-endurance muscles typically respond better with lower repetition training (five to eight reps), and individuals with high-endurance muscles generally respond better with higher repetition training (12 to 15 reps).

❏ Exercise Progression:

To gradually increase muscle stress in a safe and productive manner, a double-progressive training protocol is recommended. Typically, this technique involves training with the same resistance until 12 repetitions can be completed and then increasing the resistance by approximately 5 percent.

❏ Exercise Speed:

Moderate-to-slow movement speeds are most effective for providing consistent muscle tension and enabling higher force production. Repetition speeds between four and eight seconds are recommended for most training purposes.

❏ Exercise Range:

Full-range exercise movements are recommended to develop full-range muscle strength, which enhances physical performance and reduces injury risk.

❏ Training Periodization:

Periodically changing the training protocol provides different muscular stimulation that may facilitate more consistent strength gains. A basic periodization approach is to systematically increase the exercise resistance and decrease the exercise repetitions over a three-month training period.

❏ Training Time:

Resistance exercise should be performed when both strength levels and energy levels are high, which is largely a matter of personal preference.

❏ Activity Order:

When combining a basic strength training protocol and a standard endurance exercise protocol in the same workout session, the order in which these activities are performed is essentially a matter of personal preference.

❏ Activity Integration:

It is advisable to perform static stretching after resistance exercise to enhance both muscle strength and joint flexibility.

❏ Circuit Strength Training:

Circuit strength training reduces workout duration by eliminating the rest periods necessary in multiple-set protocols. Moving quickly between successive exercises has proven effective for improving muscle strength, cardiovascular endurance, and body composition.

❏ Heart Rate:

The shorter the rest period between successive exercises in a circuit strength training program, the higher the heart rate response throughout the training session, which may elicit cardiovascular conditioning effects.

❏ Blood Pressure:

The acute systolic blood pressure response to sensible strength training is a progressive increase within recommended parameters, as well as a rapid return to resting levels after the exercise session. The long-term effect is a significant reduction in resting systolic and diastolic blood pressure.

References

1. American College of Sports Medicine. (2013). *Guidelines for exercise testing and prescription,* 9th ed. Philadelphia: Lippincott, Williams and Wilkins.
2. American College of Sports Medicine. (2010). *Guidelines for exercise testing and prescription,* 8th ed. Philadelphia: Lippincott, Williams and Wilkins.
3. American College of Sports Medicine. (2014). *Guidelines for exercise testing and prescription,* 9th ed. Philadelphia: Lippincott, Williams and Wilkins.
4. Berger RA. (1962a). Effects of varied weight training programs on strength. *Res. Quart.* 33:168-181.
5. Berger RA. (1962b). Optimum repetitions for the development of strength. *Res. Quart.* 33:334-338.
6. Berger RA. (1963). Comparative effects of three weight training programs. *Res. Quart.* 34:396-397.
7. Berger RA. (1965). Comparison of the effects of various weight training loads on strength. *Res. Quart.* 36:141-146.
8. Carpinelli RN and Otto RM. (1998). Strength training: Single versus multiple sets. *Sportsmed.* 26(2):73-84.
9. Counsilman J. (1976). The importance of speed in exercise. *Schol. Coach.* 46:94-99.
10. Coyle EF, Feiring DC, Rotkis TC, et al. (1981). Specificity of power improvements through slow and fast isokinetic training. *J. Appl. Physiol.* 51:1437-1442.
11. Darden E. (1977). *Strength training principles: How to get the most out of your workouts.* Winter Park, Fla.: Anna Publishing Company, Inc.
12. DeLorme TL, and Watkins AL. (1948). Techniqeus of progressive resistance exercise. *Arch. Phys. Med.* 29:263.

13. Freedson P, Chang B, and Katch F. (1984). Intra-arterial blood pressure during free-weight and hydraulic resistive exercise. *Med. Sci. Sports. Exerc.* 16:131.

14. Gettman LR, and Ayres J. (1978). Aerobic changes through 10 weeks of slow and fast isokinetic training (abstract). *Med. Sci. Sports.* 10:47.

15. Gettman LR, Ward P, and Hagan RD. (1981). Strength and endurance changes through circuit weight training. *Nat. Strength Cond. Assoc. J.* 3:12-14.

16. Gettman L, Ward P, and Hagan RD. (1982). A comparison of combined running and weight training with circuit weight training. *Med. Sci. Sports Exerc.* 14:229-234.

17. Harris LA, and Holly RG. (1987). Physiological response to circuit weight training in borderline hypertensive subjects. *Med. Sci. Sports. Exerc.* 19:246-252.

18. Hempel LS, and Wells CL. (1985). Cardiorespiratory cost of the Nautilus express circuit. Phys. *Sportsmed.* 13:82-97.

19. Hunter, GR, and McCarthy JP. (1982). Pressure response associated with high-intensity anaerobic training. *Phys. Sports. Med.* 11:151-162.

20. Jones A. (1986). Exercise 1986: The present state of the art; now a science. Club Industry. 2:36A-64A.

21. Jones A, Pollock M, Graves J, et al. (1988). Safe, specific testing and rehabilitative exercise for the muscles of the lumbar spine. Santa Barbara, Calif.: Sequoia Communications.

22. Krieger JW. (2009). Single versus multiple sets of resistance exercise: A meta-regression. *J. Str. Cond. Res.* 23(6):1890-1901.

23. MacDougall JD, Tuxen D, Sale D, et al. (1983). Direct measurement of arterial blood pressure during heavy resistance training. *Med. Sci. Sports. Exerc.* 15:158.

24. McLester J, Bishop P, Smith J, et al. (2003). A series of studies –a practical protocol for testing muscular endurance recovery. *J. Str. Cond. Res.* 17(2):259-273.

25. Messier SP, and Dill M. (1985). Alternations in strength and maximal oxygen uptake consequent to Nautilus circuit weight training. *Res. Quart.* Exerc. Sport. 56:345-351.

26. Moffroid MT, and Whipple RH. (1970). Specificity of speed and exercise. *J. Am. Physical Ther. Assoc.* 50:1692-1699.

27. O'Shea P. (1966). Effects of selected weight training programs on the development of muscle hypertrophy. *Res. Quart.* 37:95.

28. Palmieri GA. (1987). Weight training and repetition speed. *J. Appl. Sport Sci. Res.* 1:36-38.

29. Pipes TV. (1979). High intensity, not high speed. *Athl. J.* 59:60-62.

30. Rhea MR, Alvar BA, Burkett IN, and Ball SD. (2003). A meta-analysis to determine the dose response for strength development. *Med. Sci. Sports Exerc.* 35(3):456-464.

31. Rosentswieg J, Hinson M, and Rigway M. (1975). An electromyographic comparison of an isokinetic bench press performed at three speeds. *Res. Quart.* 46:471-475.

32. Van Oteghan SL. (1975). Two speeds of isokinetic exercise as related to the vertical jump performance of women. *Res. Quart.* 46:78-84.

33. Westcott WL. (1974). Effects of varied frequencies of weight training on the development of strength. Master's thesis. The Pennsylvania State University.

34. Westcott WL. (1979). Female response to weight training. J. Phys. Edu. 77:31-33.

35. Westcott WL. (1985). Cardiovascular fitness and strength training. Paper presented at Nautilus National Fitness Seminar, Las Vegas.

36. Westcott WL. (1986a). Muscle development, safety make case for slow strength training. J. Phys. Edu. Prog. 82:E14-E16 (April).

37. Westcott WL. (1986b). Strength training and blood pressure. *Am. Fit. Quart.* 5:38-39.

38. Westcott WL. (1986c). Four key factors in building a strength program. *Schol. Coach.* 55:104-105.

39. Westcott WL. (1986d). How many reps per set? *Schol. Coach.* 56:72-73.

40. Westcott WL. (1995a). *Strength Fitness: Physiological Principles and Training Techniques*, 4th ed. Dubrigue IA: Brown and Benchmark.

41. Westcott WL. (1995b). The up and the down. *Nautilus*. 4(4):3-5.

42. Westcott WL. (1998). In Burke E, Ed. Precision heart rate training. Champaign IL: *Human Kinetics* (page 154).

43. Westcott WL. (2005). Combining strength and endurance exercise. *Fit Manage*. 21(1):24-27.

44. Westcott WL, and Howes B. (1983). Blood pressure response during weight training exercise. *Nat. Str. Cond. Assoc. J*. 5:67-71.

45. Westcott WL, and Pappas, M. 1987. Immediate effects of circuit strength training on blood pressure. *Am. Fit. Quart*. 6:43-44.

46. Westcott WL, Greenberger K, and Milius D. (1989). Strength training research: Sets and repetitions. *Schol. Coach*. 58:98-100.

47. Westcott WL, and Guy J. (1996). A physical evolution: Sedentary adults see marked improvements in as little as two days a week. *IDEA Today*. 14(9):58-65.

48. Westcott WL, O'Grady S. (2000). Heart rate and blood pressure response to strength exercise. *Fit. Manage*. 16(9):40-44.

49. Westcott, WL, and LaRosa Loud, R. (2000). Stretching for strength. *Fit. Manage*. 16(7):44-46.

50. Westcott WL, Annesi JJ, Skaggs JM, et al. (2007). Comparison of two exercise protocols on fitness improvement in poorly conditioned Air Force personnel. *Perceptual Motor Skills*. 104:629-636.

51. Westcott WL, Winett RA, Annesi JJ, et al. (2009). Prescribing physical activity: Applying the ACSM protocols for exercise type, intensity, and duration across 3 training frequencies. *Physician Sportsmed*. 37(2):51-58.

52. Westcott WL, Apovian C, Puhala K, et al. (2013). Nutrition programs enhance exercise effects on body composition and resting blood pressure. *Physician Sportsmed*. 41(3): 85-91.

53. Withers RT. (1970). Effects of varied weight training loads on the strength of university freshman. *Res. Quart*. 41:110-114

54. Wright JE. (1978). *Anabolic steroids and sports*. Natick, Mass.: Sports-Science Consultants.

CHAPTER 5:
Strength Training Exercises: Machines and Free Weights

This chapter presents an overview of recommended strength training exercises using machines and free weights. The first section provides detailed descriptions and precise photographs (beginning and ending positions) for standard resistance machine exercises. These exercises are categorized under seven headings: leg exercises; chest exercises; upper back exercises; shoulder exercises; arm exercises; midsection exercises; and neck exercises. The second section provides detailed descriptions and precise photographs (beginning and ending positions) for standard free weight exercises. These are categorized under the same seven headings.

Before a person selects their training exercises, they should be sure to read Chapter 6 on developing a specific strength training program. As such, those exercises should be selected that are most appropriate for attaining that individual's training objectives within the timeframe that the person has available. It should be noted that it is essential that the individual is comfortable with both the exercise equipment utilized and the training technique employed.

Pre-Performance Checkpoints

When strength exercises are performed, the following points to maximize muscle development and minimize injury risk should be observed:

- Perform each exercise slowly, about two to three seconds for lifting the resistance and about two to three seconds for lowering the resistance. This standard four- to six-second training procedure has consistently produced excellent results. The lowering phase is just as important as the lifting phase and should be performed in an equally slow and controlled manner.

- Perform each exercise through a full-movement range. This step is necessary for comprehensive muscle conditioning, from the fully stretched to the fully contracted positions.

- Begin with one set of each exercise. Although single-set training is an effective and efficient means of increasing muscle strength and size, additional exercise sets can be added if so desired.

- Begin with a weight load that fatigues the target muscles within 8 to 12 repetitions to emphasize the anaerobic energy system (about 50 to 70 seconds) and to optimize strength development. The standard repetition protocol can be employed, while alternating between lower (four to eight reps) and higher (12 to 16 reps) protocols to achieve variety and accommodate personal preference.

- Increase the weight load by 5 percent when the end number of repetitions in good form (e.g., 12 reps) can be completed. Gradual training progression is the key to continued strength improvement with a minimum risk of injuries.

- Breathe continuously throughout every repetition, exhaling while lifting the resistance and inhaling while lowering the resistance. This breathing pattern should reduce the chance of a high blood pressure response, while also enhancing exercise performance.

- Never compromise proper form for additional repetitions. Use correct technique to make sure that the target muscles are being trained productively and safely.

The machine and free-weight exercises are presented in the recommended training order. Exercises for the larger muscle groups are initially described, followed by exercises for the smaller muscle groups. Performing the exercises in this order enables individuals to work with heavier weight loads when they're fresh and with lighter weight loads when they're fatigued. This sequence does not mean that the smaller muscles are less important than the larger muscles. Rather, it is a reflection of the fact that it is physiologically and psychologically better to perform higher-energy exercises (e.g., leg presses) before lower-energy exercises (e.g., triceps extensions).

STANDARD RESISTANCE-MACHINE EXERCISES

Leg Exercises

❏ Leg Extension:

- Joint action—knee extension

- Prime-mover muscles—quadriceps

- Movement plane—sagittal

- Movement path—rotary

- Exercise technique—Sit on the seat and place the ankles behind the movement pad. Align the knees with the machine's axis of rotation. Push the seat-adjust lever to bring the seat back against the hips. Grip the handles lightly. Push the movement pad upward until the quadriceps are fully contracted. Return slowly to the starting position, and repeat.

- Technique tips:

  ✓ Keep the back against the seat.

  ✓ Maintain a neutral head position.

  ✓ Keep the ankles at 90 degrees of flexion.

  ✓ Exhale throughout the upward movement.

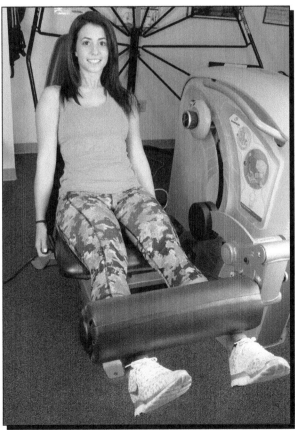

❏ Seated Leg Curl:

- Joint action—knee flexion

- Prime-mover muscles—hamstrings

- Movement plane—sagittal

- Movement path—rotary

- Exercise technique—Sit on the seat and push the leg-entry handle forward, slide the legs between the adjustable movement pads, and return the handle to its resting position. Align the knees with the machine's axis of rotation. Push the seat-adjust lever to bring the seat back against the hips. Grip the handles lightly. Pull the movement pad downward toward the hips until the hamstrings are fully contracted. Return slowly to the starting position, and repeat.

- Technique tips:

  ✓ Keep the back against the seat.

  ✓ Maintain a neutral head position.

  ✓ Keep the ankles at 90 degrees of flexion.

  ✓ Exhale throughout the downward movement.

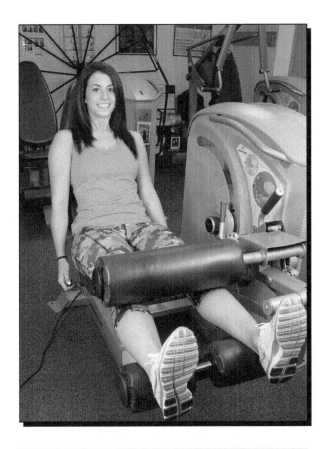

❏ Hip Adduction:

- Joint action—hip adduction

- Prime-mover muscles—hip adductors

- Movement plane—transverse

- Movement path—rotary

- Exercise technique—Sit with the hip joints aligned with the machine's axis of rotation. Place the thighs outside the appropriately positioned movement pads. Grip the handles lightly. Pull the movement pads together until they make contact. Return slowly to the starting position, and repeat.

- Technique tips:

  ✓ Keep the back against the seat.

  ✓ Maintain a neutral head position.

  ✓ Keep the ankles in a neutral position.

  ✓ Exhale throughout the inward movement.

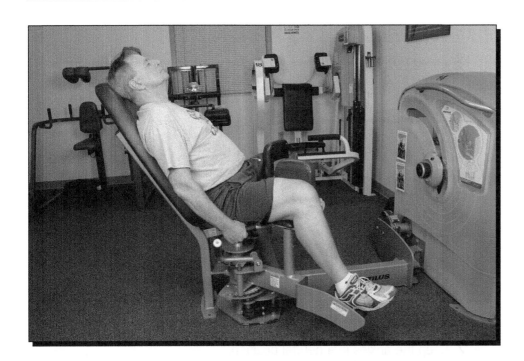

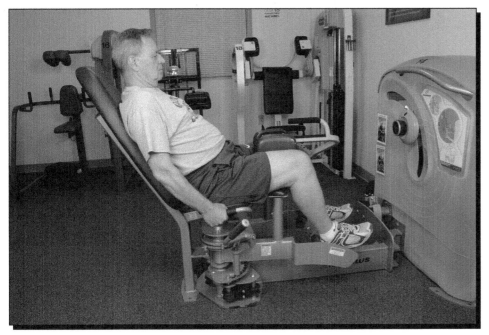

❏   Hip Abduction:

- Joint action—hip abduction

- Prime-mover muscles—hip abductors

- Movement plane—transverse

- Movement path—rotary

- Exercise technique—Sit with the hip joints aligned with the machine's axis of rotation. Place the thighs inside the movement pads. Grip the handles lightly. Pull the movement pads apart as far as possible. Return slowly to the starting position, and repeat.

- Technique tips:

  ✓ Keep the back against the seat.

  ✓ Maintain a neutral head position.

  ✓ Keep the ankles in a neutral position.

  ✓ Exhale throughout the outward movement.

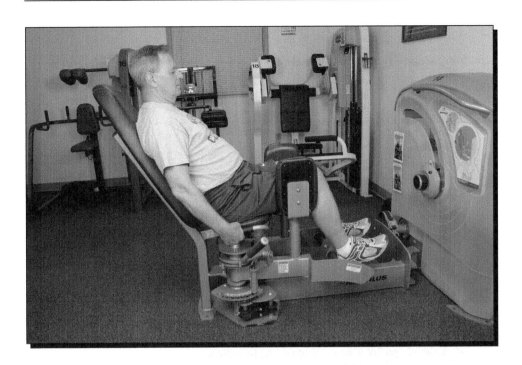

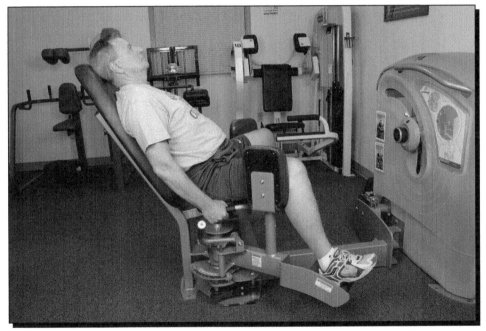

❏ Leg Press:

- Joint action—hip and knee extension

- Prime-mover muscles—hamstrings, gluteals, and quadriceps

- Movement plane—sagittal

- Movement path—linear

- Exercise technique—Sit with the feet evenly placed on the footpad, and the lower legs parallel to the floor. Crank the seat forward until the knees are flexed at 90 degrees. Grip the handles lightly. Push the footpad forward until the knees are fully extended. Return slowly to the starting position, and repeat.

- Technique tips:

  ✓ Keep the back against the seat.

  ✓ Maintain a neutral head position.

  ✓ Extend gently into a straight-leg position.

  ✓ Keep the feet, knees and hips in alignment throughout the exercise.

  ✓ Exhale throughout the forward movement.

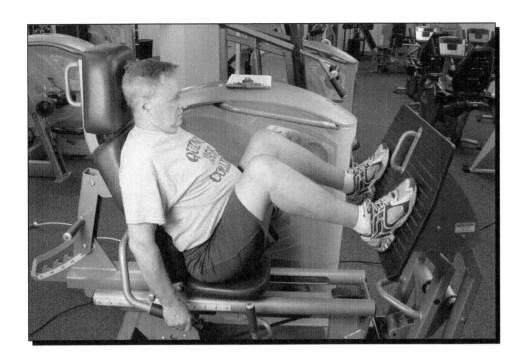

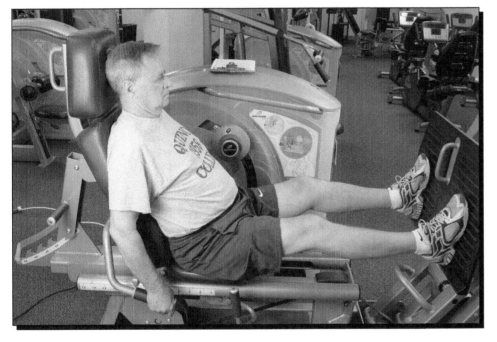

❏ Calf Press:

- Joint action—ankle extension (plantar flexion)

- Prime-mover muscles—gastrocnemius and soleus

- Movement plane—sagittal

- Movement path—rotary

- Exercise technique—Sit with the knees slightly bent, with the heels in the crease and the balls of the feet on the foot bar. Press the foot bar downward as far as possible. Return slowly to the starting position, and repeat.

- Technique tips:

    ✓ Keep the back straight.

    ✓ Maintain a neutral head position.

    ✓ Exhale throughout the pressing movement.

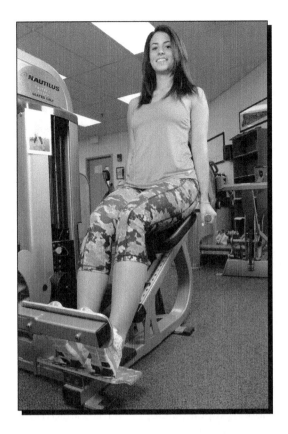

Chest Exercises

❏ Chest Cross:

- Joint action—shoulder horizontal flexion

- Prime-mover muscles—pectoralis major and anterior deltoid

- Movement plane—transverse

- Movement path—rotary

- Exercise technique—Sit with the shoulder joints aligned with the machine's axis of rotation. Place the front of the upper arms against the roller pads. Exert force against the roller pads to move them forward as far as possible. Return slowly to the starting position, and repeat.

- Technique tips:

  ✓ Keep the back against the seat.

  ✓ Maintain a neutral head position.

  ✓ Lead movements with the upper arms.

  ✓ When positioned properly, the upper arms should move parallel to the floor.

  ✓ Exhale throughout the forward movement.

❑ Chest Press:

- Joint action—shoulder horizontal flexion and elbow extension

- Prime-mover muscles—pectoralis major, anterior deltoid, and triceps

- Movement plane—transverse

- Movement path—linear

- Exercise technique—Sit with the chest directly behind the handles. Press the handles forward until the elbows are fully extended. Return slowly to the starting position, and repeat.

- Technique tips:

  ✓ Maintain a neutral head position.

  ✓ When positioned properly, the arms should move approximately parallel to the floor.

  ✓ Wide handles place greater emphasis on the pectoralis major muscles.

  ✓ Narrow handles place greater emphasis on the triceps muscles.

  ✓ Exhale throughout the forward movement.

❏ Incline Press:

- Joint action—shoulder horizontal flexion and elbow extension

- Prime-mover muscles—pectoralis major, anterior deltoid, and triceps

- Movement plane—transverse

- Movement path—linear

- Exercise technique—Sit with the shoulders approximately even with the handles. Press the handles upward until the elbows are fully extended. Return slowly to the starting position, and repeat.

- Technique tips:

  ✓ Maintain a neutral head position.

  ✓ When positioned properly, the arms should move perpendicular to the floor.

  ✓ Exhale throughout the upward movement.

❏ Weight-Assisted Bar Dip:

- Joint action—shoulder flexion and elbow extension

- Prime-mover muscles—pectoralis major, anterior deltoid, and triceps

- Movement plane—sagittal

- Movement path—linear

- Exercise technique—Grip the dip bars, place the knees on the platform and hold the bars in a straight-arm support position. Lower the body until the elbows are bent 90 degrees. Press up slowly to a straight-arm position, and repeat. Remove the knees from the platform in the top position.

- Technique tips:

  ✓ Maintain an erect posture.

  ✓ Maintain a neutral head position.

  ✓ Always enter and exit the knee platform in the top position.

  ✓ Exhale throughout the upward movement.

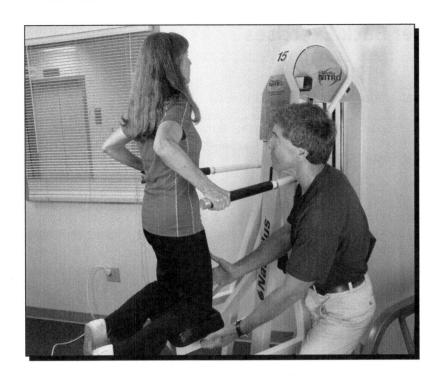

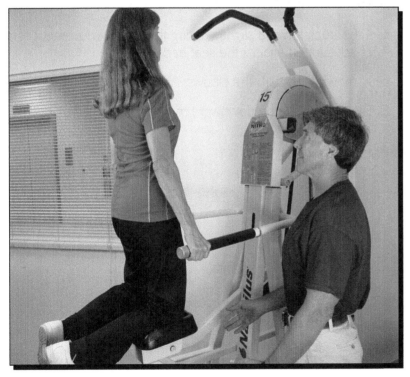

Upper Back Exercises

❏ Super Pullover:

• Joint action—shoulder extension

• Prime-mover muscles—latissimus dorsi, teres major, and triceps

• Movement plane—sagittal

• Movement path—rotary

• Exercise technique—Squeeze the seat-adjust lever to sit with the shoulders in line with the machine's axis of rotation (the red dot). Secure the seat belt and press the foot lever to position the movement pads. Place the arms on the movement pads, grip the crossbar lightly, and stretch the arms upward as far as comfortable. Pull the arms downward, until the crossbar contacts the midsection. Return slowly to the starting position, and repeat. After the final repetition, press the foot lever to remove the arms from the movement pads.

• Technique tips:

✓ Maintain a neutral head position.

✓ Curl the trunk forward slightly during the pulling movement to provide low back support against the seat back.

✓ Lead movements with the elbows.

✓ Exhale throughout the downward movement.

❑ Compound Row:

- Joint action—shoulder extension and elbow flexion

- Prime-mover muscles—latissimus dorsi, teres major, posterior deltoid, rhomboids, trapezius, and biceps

- Movement plane—sagittal

- Movement path—linear

- Exercise technique—Adjust the seat so that the arms are approximately parallel to the floor and adjust the chest pad so that the hands can just reach the handles. Pull the handles backward to the chest. Return slowly to the starting position, and repeat.

- Technique tips:

  ✓ Maintain an erect posture.

  ✓ Maintain a neutral head position.

  ✓ Keep the chest against the support pad throughout the exercise.

  ✓ Exhale throughout the backward movement.

❏ Pulldown:

- Joint action—shoulder extension and elbow flexion

- Prime-mover muscles—latissimus dorsi, teres major, and biceps

- Movement plane—sagittal

- Movement path—linear

- Exercise technique—Adjust the seat to just reach the handles and secure the thighs under the roller pads. Pull the handles downward below the level of the chin. Return slowly to the starting position, and repeat.

- Technique tips:

  ✓ Maintain an erect posture.

  ✓ Maintain a neutral head position.

  ✓ The palms should generally face each other throughout the exercise movement.

  ✓ Exhale throughout the downward movement.

❏ Weight-Assisted Chin-Up:

- Joint action—shoulder extension and elbow flexion

- Prime-mover muscles—latissimus dorsi, teres major, and biceps

- Movement plane—sagittal

- Movement path—linear

- Exercise technique—Grasp the chin bar, place the knees on the platform, and lower the body to a full-hanging position. Pull the body upward until the chin is above the chin bar. Return slowly to the full-hanging position, and repeat. Remove the knees from the platform in the top position.

- Technique tips:

  ✓ Maintain an erect posture.

  ✓ Maintain a neutral head position.

  ✓ Always enter and exit the knee platform in the top position.

  ✓ A shoulder-width grip with the palms toward the face is recommended for best results.

  ✓ Exhale throughout the upward movement.

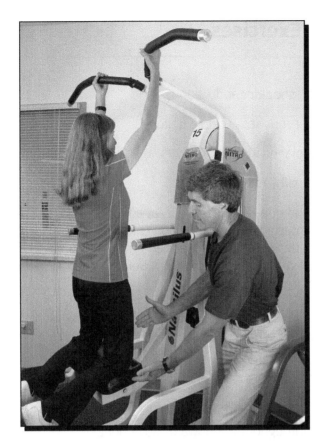

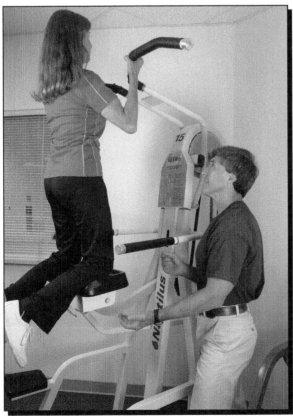

Shoulder Exercises

❏ Lateral Raise:

- Joint action—shoulder abduction

- Prime-mover muscles—middle deltoids

- Movement plane—frontal

- Movement path—rotary

- Exercise technique—Squeeze the seat-adjust lever to sit with the shoulders in line with machine's axis of rotation (the red dots). Place the arms against the sides inside the movement pads and grasp the handles. Lift the movement pads to a point just above horizontal. Return slowly to the starting position, and repeat.

- Technique tips:

  ✓ Keep the back against the seat.

  ✓ Maintain a neutral head position.

  ✓ Lead movements with the elbows.

  ✓ Exhale throughout the upward movement.

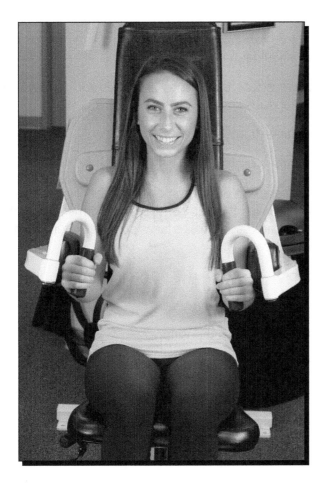

❏ Rear Delt:

- Joint action—shoulder horizontal extension

- Prime-mover muscles—rear deltoids, latissimus dorsi, teres major, rhomboids, and middle trapezius

- Movement plane—transverse

- Movement path—rotary

- Exercise technique—Sit with the shoulder joints aligned with the machine's axis of rotation. Place the back of the upper arms against the roller pads. Move the roller pads backwards as far as possible. Return slowly to the starting position, and repeat.

- Technique tips:

   ✓ Keep the back against the seat.

   ✓ Maintain a neutral head position.

   ✓ Lead movements with the upper arms.

   ✓ When positioned properly, the upper arms should move parallel to the floor.

   ✓ Exhale throughout the backward movement.

❏ Overhead Press:

- Joint action—shoulder abduction and elbow extension

- Prime-mover muscles—deltoids, triceps, and upper trapezius

- Movement plane—frontal

- Movement path—linear

- Exercise technique—Adjust the seat so that the shoulders are slightly lower than the handles. Press the handles upward until the elbows are fully extended. Return slowly to the starting position, and repeat.

- Technique tips:

  ✓ Keep the back against the seat.

  ✓ Maintain a neutral head position.

  ✓ Wide handles place a greater emphasis on the middle deltoid muscles.

  ✓ Narrow handles place a greater emphasis on the anterior deltoid muscles.

  ✓ Exhale throughout the upward movement.

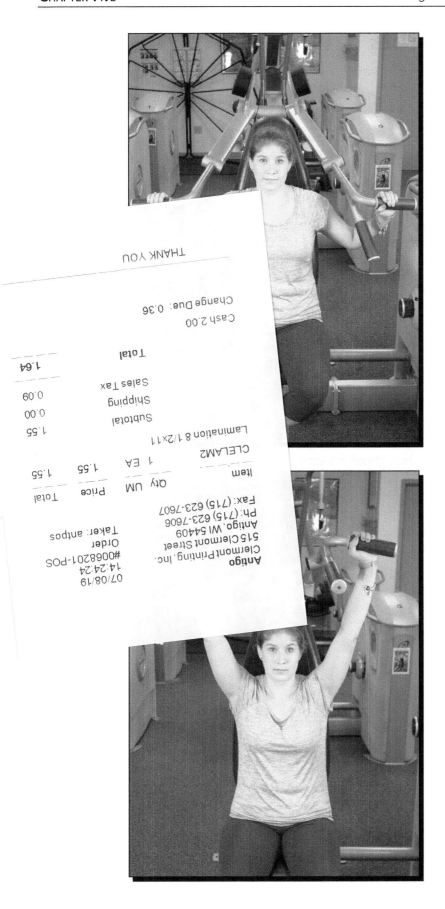

Arm Exercises

❏ Preacher Curl:

- Joint action—elbow flexion

- Prime-mover muscles—biceps

- Movement plane—sagittal

- Movement path—rotary

- Exercise technique—Adjust the seat to sit with the elbows in line with the machine's axis of rotation (the red dot). Partially stand, grip the movement bar loosely, and sit in a properly aligned position. Curl the movement bar upward as far as possible. Return slowly to the starting position and repeat. After the final repetition, partially stand and lower the movement bar to the resting position.

- Technique tips:

  ✓ Maintain an erect posture.

  ✓ Maintain a neutral head position.

  ✓ It is not necessary to fully extend the elbows between the repetitions.

  ✓ Exhale throughout the upward movement.

❑ Triceps Press:

- Joint action—shoulder flexion and elbow extension

- Prime-mover muscles—pectoralis major, anterior deltoid, and triceps

- Movement plane—sagittal

- Movement path—linear

- Exercise technique—Sit with the shoulders above the handles so that the elbows are bent 90 degrees. Secure the seat belt. Press the handles downward until the elbows are fully extended. Return slowly to the starting position, and repeat.

- Technique tips:

  ✓ Having the elbows away from the sides places a greater emphasis on the pectoralis major muscles.

  ✓ Having the elbows close to the sides places a greater emphasis on the triceps muscles.

  ✓ The body may lean slightly forward when performing the exercise.

  ✓ Exhale throughout the downward movement.

Midsection Exercises

❏ Abdominal Crunch:

- Joint action—trunk flexion

- Prime-mover muscles—rectus abdominis and hip flexors

- Movement plane—sagittal

- Movement path—rotary

- Exercise technique—Adjust the seat to sit with the navel in line with the red dot, with the feet under the roller pads. Place the elbows on the movement pads and grip the handles lightly. Pull the torso downward in a crunch movement, until the abdominal muscles are fully contracted. Return slowly to the starting position, and repeat.

- Technique tips:

  ✓ Keep the upper back against the seat.

  ✓ Keep the head neutral or slightly forward.

  ✓ Pause momentarily in a fully contracted position for best results.

  ✓ Exhale throughout the downward movement.

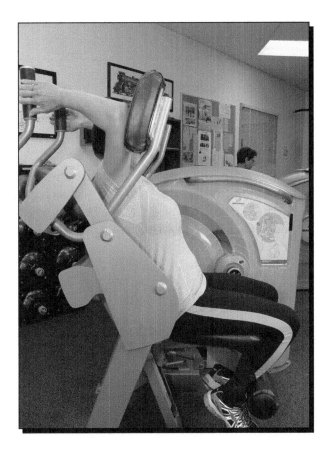

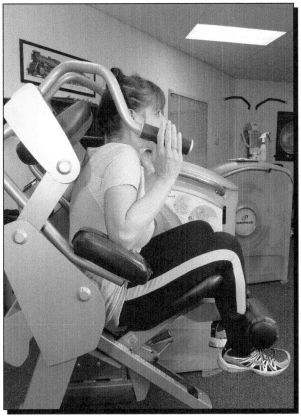

❏ Low Back Extension:

- Joint action—trunk extension

- Prime-mover muscles—erector spinae

- Movement plane—sagittal

- Movement path—rotary

- Exercise technique—Adjust the seat to sit with the navel in line with the red dot. Position the foot pad so that the knees are slightly higher than the hips. Secure both seat belts across the thighs. Push the movement pad backward until the low back muscles are fully contracted. Return slowly to the starting position, and repeat.

- Technique tips:

  ✓ Keep the hips against the seat.

  ✓ Maintain a neutral head position.

  ✓ Fold the arms across the chest.

  ✓ Exhale throughout the backward movement.

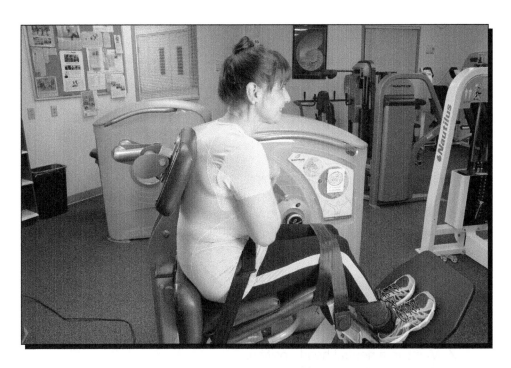

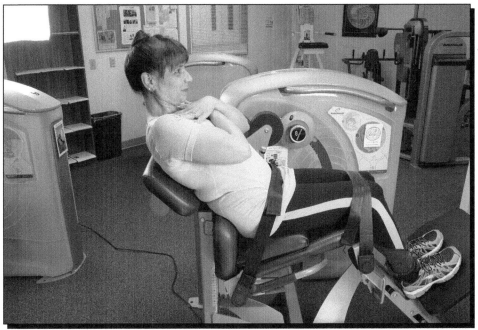

❏ Rotary Torso:

- Joint action—trunk rotation

- Prime-mover muscles—external obliques and internal obliques

- Movement plane—transverse

- Movement path—rotary

- Exercise technique—Sit with the hips against the seat ridge. Place the arms behind the movement pad to concurrently pull and push the pads in the desired direction. Turn the torso clockwise until the oblique muscles are fully contracted; return slowly, and repeat. Adjust the seat position. Turn the torso counterclockwise until the oblique muscles are fully contracted, return slowly, and repeat.

- Technique tips:

  ✓ Maintain an erect posture.

  ✓ Maintain a neutral head position.

  ✓ When the hips are stabilized, the trunk has a relatively short rotation range (about 70 degrees).

  ✓ Concurrently pulling one movement pad and pushing the other movement pad places equal resistance on each side of the torso.

  ✓ Exhale throughout the turning movements that lift the weight stack.

❑ Hanging Knee Lift (Legs Bent):

- Joint action—hip flexion

- Prime-mover muscles—rectus femoris, iliacus, psoas, and rectus abdominis

- Movement plane—sagittal

- Movement path—rotary

- Exercise technique—Grip the dip bars with the arms straight and the body supported in a vertical position. Lift both legs upward, with the knees bent, until the thighs are parallel to the floor. Return slowly to the starting position, and repeat.

- Technique tips:

  ✓ Maintain an erect posture.

  ✓ Maintain a neutral head position.

  ✓ Exhale throughout the lifting movement.

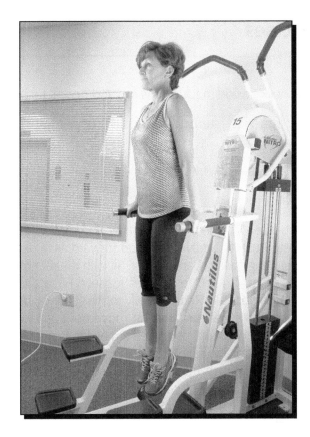

Neck Exercises

❏ 4-Way Neck:

- Joint action—neck flexion, neck extension, and neck lateral flexion

- Prime-mover muscles—sterncleidomastoid, upper trapezius, and levator scapulae

- Movement plane—sagittal/frontal

- Movement path—rotary

- Exercise technique—Sit with the face against the movement pad. Grasp the handles loosely. Push the movement pad forward as far as possible. Return slowly to the starting position, and repeat. Sit with the rear of the head against the movement pad. Grasp the handles loosely. Push the movement pad backward as far as possible. Return slowly to the starting position, and repeat. Sit with the side of the head against the movement pad. Grasp the handles loosely. Push one movement pad sideward as far as possible. Return slowly to the starting position, and repeat. Sit with the other side of the head against the movement pad. Grasp the handles loosely. Push the movement pad sideward as far as possible. Return slowly to the starting position, and repeat.

- Technique tips:

  ✓ Maintain an erect posture.

  ✓ Keep the torso in contact with the restraining pad.

  ✓ Exhale throughout the neck movements that lift the weight stack.

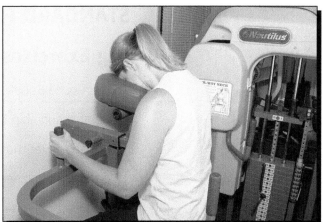
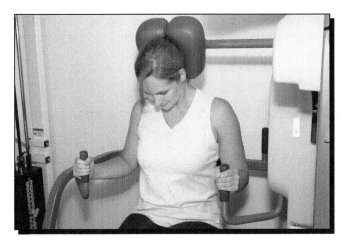
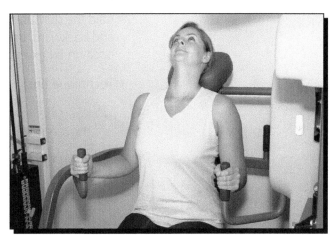

STANDARD FREE-WEIGHT EXERCISES

Leg Exercises

❏ Dumbbell Squat:

- Joint action—hip extension and knee extension

- Prime-mover muscles—hamstrings, gluteals, and quadriceps

- Movement plane—sagittal

- Movement path—linear

- Exercise technique—Stand with the feet shoulder-width apart or wider and hold the dumbbells in each hand beside the hips. Lower the hips downward and backward, until the thighs are parallel to the floor. Return to the standing position by extending the hips and knees, and repeat.

- Technique tips:

  ✓ Keep the head up and the back straight during the downward and upward movements.

  ✓ Keep the feet fully on the floor throughout each repetition.

  ✓ Keep the knees directly above the feet throughout each repetition.

  ✓ Exhale throughout the upward movement.

❏ Barbell Squat:

- Joint action—hip extension and knee extension

- Prime-mover muscles—hamstrings, gluteals, and quadriceps

- Movement plane—sagittal

- Movement path—linear

- Exercise technique—Stand with the feet shoulder-width apart or wider and position the bar on the shoulders, while it is still on the rack. Stand erect to lift the bar from the rack and step backward. Lower the hips downward and backward until the thighs are parallel to the floor. Return to the standing position by extending the hips and knees, and repeat.

- Technique tips:

  ✓ Keep the head up and the back straight during the downward and upward movements.

  ✓ Keep the feet fully on the floor throughout each repetition.

  ✓ Keep the knees directly above the feet throughout each repetition.

  ✓ Exhale throughout the upward movement.

  Note: This exercise should be performed with a spotter to assist the lifter, if needed.

❏ Dumbbell Deadlift:

- Joint action—hip extension and knee extension

- Prime-mover muscles—hamstrings, gluteals, quadriceps, erector spinae, and upper trapezius

- Movement plane—sagittal

- Movement path—linear

- Exercise technique—Stand with the feet shoulder-width apart or wider and hold a dumbbell in each hand beside the hips. Flex the hips and knees enough to touch the dumbbells to the floor. Return to the standing position, and repeat.

- Technique tips:

  ✓ Keep the head up during the downward and upward movement phases.

  ✓ Keep the arms straight throughout each repetition.

  ✓ Keep the knees directly above the feet throughout each repetition.

  ✓ Exhale throughout the upward movement.

❏ Barbell Deadlift:

- Joint action—hip extension and knee extension

- Prime-mover muscles—hamstrings, gluteals, quadriceps, erector spinae, and upper trapezius

- Movement plane—sagittal

- Movement path—linear

- Exercise technique—Stand with the feet shoulder-width apart or wider in front of a barbell. Flex the hips and knees enough to grasp the barbell with a shoulder-width mixed grip (the palms facing each other) and the arms straight. Lift the barbell upward to the thighs by extending the hips and knees. Return the barbell to the floor, and repeat.

- Technique tips:

    ✓ Keep the head up during the downward and upward movements.

    ✓ Keep the arms straight throughout each repetition.

    ✓ Keep the knees directly above the feet throughout each repetition.

    ✓ Exhale throughout the upward movement.

❏ Dumbbell Heel Raise:

- Joint action—ankle extension (plantar flexion)

- Prime-mover muscles—gastrocnemius and soleus

- Movement plane—sagittal

- Movement path—rotary

- Exercise technique—Stand with the feet shoulder-width apart on a stable, elevated surface, and hold a dumbbell in each hand beside the hips. Lift the body upward by rising onto the toes. Return slowly to the starting position, and repeat.

- Technique tips:

  ✓ Keep the head up and the back straight during the downward and upward movements.

  ✓ Keep the arms and legs straight throughout each repetition.

  ✓ Achieve maximum movement range by lifting and lowering the heels as far as comfortable each repetition.

  ✓ Exhale throughout the upward movement.

❏ Barbell Heel Raise:

- Joint action—ankle extension (plantar flexion)

- Prime-mover muscles—gastrocnemius and soleus

- Movement plane—sagittal

- Movement path—rotary

- Exercise technique—Stand with the feet shoulder-width apart on a stable, elevated surface, and hold a barbell against the front thighs, with the arms straight. Lift the body upward by rising onto the toes. Return slowly to the starting position, and repeat.

- Technique tips:

  ✓ Keep the head up and the back straight during the downward and upward movements.

  ✓ Keep the arms and legs straight throughout each repetition.

  ✓ Achieve maximum movement range by lifting and lowering the heels as far as comfortable each repetition.

  ✓ Exhale throughout the upward movement.

❏ Dumbbell Lunge:

- Joint action—hip extension and knee extension

- Prime-mover muscles—hamstrings, gluteals, and quadriceps

- Movement plane—sagittal

- Movement path—linear

- Exercise technique—Stand with the feet less than shoulder-width apart, and hold a dumbbell in each hand beside the hips. Step forward with the left foot so that the left knee is flexed about 90 degrees and the right shin is parallel to the floor. Return to the standing position by extending the hips and knees. Repeat, stepping forward with the right foot.

- Technique tips:

  ✓ Keep the head up and the back straight during the downward and upward movements.

  ✓ Step forward far enough so that the knee is directly above the foot.

  ✓ Exhale throughout the upward movement.

❏ Dumbbell Step-Up:

- Joint action—hip extension and knee extension

- Prime-mover muscles—hamstrings, gluteals, and quadriceps

- Movement plane—sagittal

- Movement path—linear

- Exercise technique—Stand with the feet less than shoulder-width apart, in front of a sturdy step or box, and hold a dumbbell in each hand, beside the hips. Place the left foot on the step and lift the body to a standing position (both feet) on the step by extending the left hip and knee. Step down with the left foot, followed by the right foot to the starting position on the floor. Repeat, stepping upward with the right foot.

- Technique tips:

  ✓ Keep the head up and the back straight during the downward and upward movements.

  ✓ Alternate the lead foot on successive repetitions.

  ✓ Exhale throughout the upward movement.

Chest Exercises

❑ Dumbbell Bench Press:

- Joint action—shoulder horizontal flexion and elbow extension

- Prime-mover muscles—pectoralis major, anterior deltoid, and triceps

- Movement plane—transverse

- Movement path—linear

- Exercise technique—Lie face-up on flat bench with feet flat on floor. Hold dumbbells above chest with arms straight and palms facing away from head. Lower dumbbells downward to chest with upper arms at right angles to torso. Press dumbbells upward to starting position, and repeat.

- Technique tips:

  ✓ Keep the head and hips on the bench.

  ✓ Keep the feet on the floor.

  ✓ Lower and lift the dumbbells evenly.

  ✓ When positioned properly, the arms should move perpendicular to the floor.

  ✓ Exhale throughout the upward movement.

❏ Barbell Bench Press:

• Joint action—shoulder horizontal flexion and elbow extension

• Prime-mover muscles—pectoralis major, anterior deltoid, and triceps

• Movement plane—transverse

• Movement path—linear

• Exercise technique—Lie face-up on a flat bench with the feet flat on the floor. Grasp the barbell with a shoulder-width or wider grip, lift the barbell off the rack, and hold it directly over the chest, with the arms extended. Lower the barbell to the thickest part of the chest. Press the barbell upward to the starting position, and repeat.

• Technique tips:

✓ Keep the head and hips on the bench.

✓ Keep the feet on the floor.

✓ Lower and lift the barbell evenly.

✓ When positioned properly, the arms should move perpendicular to the floor.

✓ Exhale throughout the upward movement.

Note: This exercise should be performed with a spotter to assist the lifter, if needed.

❏ Dumbbell Incline Press:

- Joint action—shoulder horizontal flexion and elbow extension

- Prime-mover muscles—pectoralis major, anterior deltoid, and triceps

- Movement plane—transverse

- Movement path—linear

- Exercise technique—Sit on an incline bench with the feet flat on the floor. Hold a dumbbell in each hand directly over the upper chest, with the arms extended. Lower the dumbbells downward to the upper chest. Press the dumbbells upward to the starting position, and repeat.

- Technique tips:

  ✓ Keep the head and hips on the bench.

  ✓ Keep the feet on the floor.

  ✓ Lower and lift the dumbbells evenly.

  ✓ When positioned properly, the arms should move perpendicular to the floor.

  ✓ Exhale throughout the upward movement.

❏ Barbell Incline Press:

- Joint action—shoulder horizontal flexion and elbow extension
- Prime-mover muscles—pectoralis major, anterior deltoid, and triceps

- Movement plane—transverse

- Movement path—linear

- Exercise technique—Sit on an incline bench with the feet flat on the floor. Grasp the barbell with a shoulder-width or wider grip, lift the barbell off the rack, and hold it directly over the upper chest, with the arms extended. Lower the barbell downward to the upper chest. Press the barbell upward to the starting position, and repeat.

- Technique tips:

  ✓ Keep the head and hips on the bench.

  ✓ Keep the feet on the floor.

  ✓ Lower and lift the barbell evenly.

  ✓ When positioned properly, the arms move perpendicular to floor.

  ✓ Exhale throughout the upward movement.

  Note: This exercise should be performed with a spotter to assist the lifter, if needed.

❏ Dumbbell Chest Fly:

- Joint action—shoulder horizontal flexion

- Prime-mover muscles—pectoralis major and anterior deltoid

- Movement plane—transverse

- Movement path—rotary

- Exercise technique—Lie face-up on a flat bench with the feet flat on the floor. Hold the dumbbells above the chest, with the arms almost straight and the palms facing each other. Lower the dumbbells downward and outward until the upper arms are approximately parallel to the floor. Lift the dumbbells upward and inward to the starting position, and repeat.

- Technique tips:

  ✓ Keep the head and hips on the bench.

  ✓ Keep the feet on the floor.

  ✓ Keep the elbows bent throughout exercise.

  ✓ When positioned properly, the arms should move perpendicular to floor.

  ✓ Exhale throughout the upward movement.

❏ Dumbbell Incline Fly:

- Joint action—shoulder horizontal flexion

- Prime-mover muscles—pectoralis major and anterior deltoid

- Movement plane—transverse

- Movement path—rotary

- Exercise technique—Lie face-up on an incline bench, with the feet flat on the floor. Hold the dumbbells above the upper chest, with the palms facing each other. Lower the dumbbells downward and outward until the upper arms are approximately parallel to the floor. Lift the dumbbells upward and inward to the starting position, and repeat.

- Technique tips:

  ✓ Keep the head on the bench.

  ✓ Keep the feet on the floor.

  ✓ Keep the elbows bent throughout the exercise.

  ✓ When positioned properly, the arms should move perpendicular to the floor.

  ✓ Exhale throughout the upward movement.

❏ Bar Dip:

- Joint action—shoulder flexion and elbow extension

- Prime-mover muscles—pectoralis major, anterior deltoid, and triceps

- Movement plane—sagittal

- Movement path—linear

- Exercise technique—Grip the dip bars and hold in a straight-arm support position. Lower the body until the elbows are bent 90 degrees. Press up slowly to a straight-arm support position, and repeat.

- Technique tips:

  ✓ Maintain an erect posture.

  ✓ Maintain a neutral head position.

  ✓ Exhale throughout the upward movement.

Upper Back Exercises

❏ Dumbbell Pullover:

- Joint action—shoulder extension

- Prime-mover muscles—latissimus dorsi, teres major, and triceps

- Movement plane—sagittal

- Movement path—rotary

- Exercise technique—Lie face-up on a flat bench and hold a dumbbell in both hands, with the arms extended above the chest. Lower the dumbbell slowly backward and downward behind the head as far as comfortable. Lift the dumbbell upward and forward to the starting position, and repeat.

- Technique tips:

  ✓ Keep the head and hips on the bench at all times.

  ✓ Keep the arms relatively straight during the downward and upward movements.

  ✓ Exhale throughout the upward movement.

❏ Dumbbell Bent Row:

- Joint action—shoulder extension and elbow flexion

- Prime-mover muscles—latissimus dorsi, teres major, posterior deltoid, rhomboids, trapezius, and biceps

- Movement plane—sagittal

- Movement path—linear

- Exercise technique—Place the left knee and left hand on a flat bench to support the back, which is parallel to the floor. Grasp a dumbbell with the right hand, with the arm extended. Pull the dumbbell upward to the chest. Return slowly to the starting position, and repeat. Change the leg and hand positions, and repeat the exercise, using the left arm to lift the dumbbell.

- Technique tips:

  ✓ Maintain a neutral head position.

  ✓ Maintain the back parallel to the floor.

  ✓ Having the elbow near the torso places a greater emphasis on the latissimus dorsi and teres major muscles.

  ✓ Having the elbow away from the torso places a greater emphasis on the posterior deltoid muscle.

  ✓ Exhale throughout the upward movement.

❑ Pulldown:

- Joint action—shoulder extension and elbow flexion

- Prime-mover muscles—latissimus dorsi, teres major, and biceps

- Movement plane—sagittal

- Movement path—linear

- Exercise technique—Adjust the seat to just reach the handles and secure the thighs under the restraining pads. Pull the handles downward below the chin. Return slowly to the starting position, and repeat.

- Technique tips:

  ✓ Maintain an erect posture.

  ✓ Maintain a neutral head position.

  ✓ Use a shoulder-width grip with the palms either toward the face or toward each other recommended.

  ✓ Exhale throughout the downward pulling movement.

❏ Chin-Up:

- Joint action—shoulder extension and elbow flexion

- Prime-mover muscles—latissimus dorsi, teres major, and biceps

- Movement plane—sagittal

- Movement path—linear

- Exercise technique—Grasp the chin bar and the lower body to a full-hanging position. Pull the body upward until the chin is above the chin bar. Return slowly to the full-hanging position, and repeat.

- Technique tips:

  ✓ Maintain an erect posture.

  ✓ Maintain a neutral head position.

  ✓ Use a shoulder-width grip with the palms facing toward the face for best results.

  ✓ Exhale throughout the upward movement.

Shoulder Exercises

❏ Dumbbell Press:

- Joint action—shoulder abduction and elbow extension

- Prime-mover muscles—deltoids, triceps, and upper trapezius

- Movement plane—frontal

- Movement path—linear

- Exercise technique—Stand with the feet shoulder-width apart, holding the dumbbells at shoulder level, with the palms facing forward. Press the dumbbells upward until the elbows are almost fully extended. Return slowly to the starting position, and repeat.

- Technique tips:

  ✓ Maintain an erect posture.

  ✓ Maintain a neutral head position.

  ✓ The dumbbells may be pressed overhead in an alternating manner, if desired.

  ✓ Exhale throughout the upward movement.

❏ Barbell Press:

- Joint action—shoulder abduction and elbow extension

- Prime-mover muscles—deltoids, triceps, and upper trapezius

- Movement plane—frontal

- Movement path—linear

- Exercise technique—Stand with the feet shoulder-width apart, holding a barbell at shoulder level, with the palms facing forward. Press the barbell upward until the elbows are almost fully extended. Return slowly to the starting position, and repeat.

- Technique tips:

  ✓ Maintain an erect posture.

  ✓ Maintain a neutral head position.

  ✓ Avoid bending backward during the pressing movement.

  ✓ Exhale throughout the upward movement.

❏ Dumbbell Lateral Raise:

• Joint action—shoulder abduction

• Prime-mover muscles—middle/anterior deltoid, and upper trapezius

• Movement plane—frontal

• Movement path—rotary

• Exercise technique—Stand with the feet shoulder-width apart, and hold the dumbbells in front of the torso with the elbows bent at 90 degrees. Lift the dumbbells upward until the arms are parallel to the floor by rotating the shoulder joint through 90 degrees of movement. Return slowly to the starting position, and repeat.

• Technique tips:

✓ Maintain an erect posture.

✓ Maintain a neutral head position.

✓ Maintain a 90-degree bend in the elbow joint throughout the upward and downward movements.

✓ Exhale throughout the upward movement.

❏ Dumbbell Reverse Fly:

- Joint action—shoulder horizontal extension

- Prime-mover muscles—rear deltoids, latissimus dorsi, teres major, rhomboids, and middle trapezius

- Movement plane—transverse

- Movement path—rotary

- Exercise technique—Lie face-down on a flat bench, with a dumbbell in each hand, and the arms hanging downward. With a slight bend in the elbows, lift the arms upward as far as possible. Return slowly to the starting position, and repeat.

- Technique tips:

  ✓ Maintain a neutral head position.

  ✓ Bend the arms slightly during the upward and downward movements.

  ✓ Exhale throughout the upward movement.

❏ Barbell Upright Row:

- Joint action—shoulder abduction and elbow flexion

- Prime-mover muscles—middle/anterior deltoids, biceps, and upper trapezius

- Movement plane—frontal

- Movement path—linear

- Exercise technique—Stand with the feet shoulder-width apart and hold a barbell, using a close, overhand grip. Lift the barbell directly upward to the chin, leading with the elbows. Return slowly to the starting position, and repeat.

- Technique tips:

  ✓ Maintain an erect posture.

  ✓ Maintain a neutral head position.

  ✓ Keep the barbell close to the torso during the upward and downward movements.

  ✓ Exhale throughout the upward movement.

Arm Exercises

❏ Dumbbell Standing Curl:

- Joint action—elbow flexion

- Prime-mover muscles—biceps

- Movement plane—sagittal

- Movement path—rotary

- Exercise technique—Stand with the feet shoulder-width apart and hold a dumbbell in each hand beside the hips, with the palms facing forward. Curl the dumbbells upward to the shoulders. Return slowly to the starting position, and repeat.

- Technique tips:

  ✓ Maintain an erect posture.

  ✓ Maintain a neutral head position.

  ✓ Keep the elbows against the sides throughout the upward and downward movements.

  ✓ Keep the palms facing forward throughout the upward and downward movements.

  ✓ Exhale throughout the upward movement.

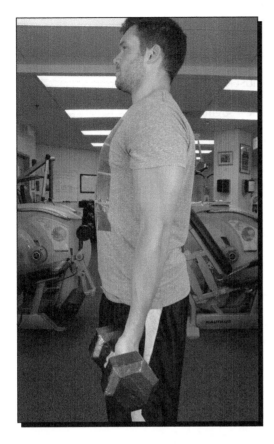

❏ Barbell Curl:

- Joint action—elbow flexion

- Prime-mover muscles—biceps

- Movement plane—sagittal

- Movement path—rotary

- Exercise technique—Stand with the feet shoulder-width apart and grasp the bar using an underhand grip, with the elbows extended. Curl the barbell upward to the shoulders. Return slowly to the starting position, and repeat.

- Technique tips:

  ✓ Maintain an erect posture.

  ✓ Maintain a neutral head position.

  ✓ Keep the elbows against the sides throughout the upward and downward movements.

  ✓ Exhale throughout the upward movement.

❏ Dumbbell Seated Curl:

- Joint action—elbow flexion

- Prime-mover muscles—biceps

- Movement plane—sagittal

- Movement path—rotary

- Exercise technique—Sit on a flat bench and hold a dumbbell in each hand, with the arms straight and the palms facing forward. Curl the dumbbells upward to the shoulders. Return slowly to the starting position, and repeat.

- Technique tips:

  ✓ Maintain an erect posture.

  ✓ Maintain a neutral head position.

  ✓ Keep the elbows against the sides throughout the upward and downward movements.

  ✓ Keep the palms facing forward throughout the upward and downward movements.

  ✓ Exhale throughout the upward movement.

BUILDING STRENGTH & STAMINA

❏ Dumbbell Incline Curl:

- Joint action—elbow flexion

- Prime-mover muscles—biceps

- Movement plane—sagittal

- Movement path—rotary

- Exercise technique—Sit on an incline bench and hold a dumbbell in each hand, with the arms straight and the palms facing forward. Curl the dumbbells upward the to shoulders. Return slowly to the starting position, and repeat.

- Technique tips:

  ✓ Maintain a neutral head position.

  ✓ Keep the palms facing forward throughout the upward and downward movements.

  ✓ Exhale throughout the upward movement.

BUILDING STRENGTH & STAMINA

❏ Barbell Preacher Curl:

- Joint action—elbow flexion

- Prime-mover muscles—biceps

- Movement plane—sagittal

- Movement path—rotary

- Exercise technique—Sit on a flat bench with the upper arms on a preacher pad, and the palms facing forward. Curl the barbell upward until the biceps are fully contracted. Return slowly to the starting position, and repeat.

- Technique tips:

  ✓ Maintain an erect posture.

  ✓ Maintain a neutral head position.

  ✓ It is not necessary to fully extend the elbows between repetitions.

  ✓ Exhale throughout the upward movement.

❏ Dumbbell Concentration Curl:

- Joint action—elbow flexion

- Prime-mover muscles—biceps

- Movement plane—sagittal

- Movement path—rotary

- Exercise technique—Sit on a flat bench with the legs apart, a dumbbell in right hand, the right elbow against the right inner thigh, and the palms facing away from the thigh. Keeping the elbow stationary, curl the dumbbell upward to the chin. Return slowly to the starting position, and repeat. Switch sides and repeat with the left arm.

- Technique tips:

  ✓ Lean slightly forward and place the non-lifting forearm on the same-side thigh for torso support.

  ✓ Maintain a neutral head position.

  ✓ Exhale throughout the upward movement.

❏ Triceps Pressdown:

- Joint action—elbow extension

- Prime-mover muscles—triceps

- Movement plane—sagittal

- Movement path—rotary

- Exercise technique—Stand with the feet shoulder-width apart in front of a pressdown cable. Grasp the V-bar with an overhand grip, with the elbows against the sides, and hold it at chest level. Push the V-bar downward until the elbows are fully extended. Return slowly to the starting position, and repeat.

- Technique tips:

  ✓ Maintain an erect posture.

  ✓ Maintain a neutral head position.

  ✓ Return the V-bar to a point no higher than chest level between repetitions.

  ✓ Exhale throughout the downward pushing movement.

❏ Dumbbell Overhead Triceps Extension:

- Joint action—elbow extension

- Prime-mover muscles—triceps

- Movement plane—sagittal

- Movement path—rotary

- Exercise technique—Stand with the feet shoulder-width apart, grasp the dumbbell with both hands, and hold it, with the arms extended overhead. Lower the dumbbell behind the head until the elbows are fully flexed. Extend the arms upward until the elbows are fully extended, and repeat.

- Technique tips:

  ✓ Maintain an erect posture.

  ✓ Maintain a neutral head position.

  ✓ Keep the upper arms perpendicular to the floor throughout the downward and upward movements.

  ✓ Exhale throughout the upward movement.

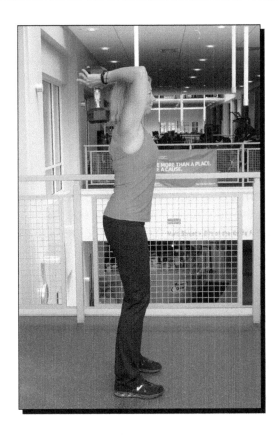

❏ Dumbbell Lying Triceps Extension:

- Joint action—elbow extension

- Prime-mover muscles—triceps

- Movement plane—sagittal

- Movement path—rotary

- Exercise technique—Lie face-up on a flat bench and hold a dumbbell in each hand, with the arms extended directly above the chest. Keeping the elbows stationary, lower the dumbbells downward beside the head. Lift the dumbbells upward to the starting position by extending the elbows, and repeat.

- Technique tips:

  ✓ Maintain a neutral head position.

  ✓ Keep the head, back, and hips on the bench.

  ✓ Keep the upper arms perpendicular to the floor throughout the downward and upward movements.

  ✓ Exhale throughout the upward movement.

❏ Dumbbell Triceps Kickback:

- Joint action—elbow extension

- Prime-mover muscles—triceps

- Movement plane—sagittal

- Movement path—rotary

- Exercise technique—Place the left knee and left hand on a flat bench to support the back, which is parallel to the floor. Hold a dumbbell in the right hand, with the elbow bent at 90 degrees and pressed against the hip. Lift the dumbbell backward and upward until the elbow is fully extended. Return slowly to the starting position, and repeat.

- Technique tips:

  ✓ Maintain a neutral head position.

  ✓ Keep the back parallel to the floor throughout the exercise.

  ✓ Keep the elbow firmly pressed against the hip throughout the upward and downward movements.

  ✓ Exhale throughout the upward movement.

Midsection Exercises

❏ Trunk Curl:

- Joint action—trunk flexion

- Prime-mover muscles—rectus abdominis

- Movement plane—sagittal

- Movement path—rotary

- Exercise technique—Lie face-up with the knees flexed, the feet flat on the floor, and the hands clasped loosely behind the head. Lift the shoulders off the floor about 30 degrees until the abdominal muscles are fully contracted. Return slowly to the starting position, and repeat.

- Technique tips:

  ✓ Maintain a neutral head position.

  ✓ The lower back should be pressed against the floor at the end of each upward curling movement.

  ✓ Exhale throughout the upward movement.

❑ Trunk Curl Tower (Bodyweight Training):

- Joint action—trunk flexion and hip flexion

- Prime-mover muscles—rectus abdominis and hip flexors

- Movement plane—sagittal

- Movement path—rotary

- Exercise technique—Lie face-up with the legs comfortably straight and vertical. Lift the shoulders off the floor about 30 degrees until the abdominal muscles are fully contracted and bring the knees to the elbows by flexing the hips. Return slowly to the starting position, and repeat.

- Technique tips:

  ✓ Maintain a neutral head position.

  ✓ The lower back should be pressed against the floor at the end of each upward curling movement.

  ✓ The legs should remain as straight as possible throughout the exercise.

  ✓ Exhale throughout the upward movement.

❏ Twisting Knee-Lift Trunk Curl (Bodyweight Training):

- Joint action—trunk flexion, trunk rotation, hip flexion and extension, and knee flexion and extension

- Prime-mover muscles—rectus abdominis, obliques, hip flexors and extensors, and knee flexors and extensors

- Movement plane—sagittal

- Movement path—rotary and linear

- Exercise technique—Lie face-up, clasping the hands loosely behind the head, holding the trunk-curl position, with the lower back pressed against the floor. Lift both feet a few inches off the floor and alternately bring the knees backward and forward. Alternately twist the torso from side to side, attempting to touch the right elbow to the left knee and the left elbow to the right knee.

- Technique tips:

  ✓ Maintain a neutral head position throughout the trunk twisting movements.

  ✓ Keep the lower back pressed against the floor throughout the exercise.

  ✓ Fully extend the knees in the forward leg movements.

  ✓ Breathe continuously throughout the exercise.

❏ Hanging Knee Lift—Legs Straight (Bodyweight Training):

- Joint action—hip flexion

- Prime-mover muscles—rectus femoris, iliacus, psoas, and rectus abdominis

- Movement plane—sagittal

- Movement path—rotary

- Exercise technique—Place the forearms on the pads and the grip handles, with the body supported in a vertical position. Lift both legs upwards, with the knees straight until the thighs are parallel to the floor. Return slowly to the starting position, and repeat.

- Technique tips:

  ✓ Maintain an erect posture.

  ✓ Maintain a neutral head position.

  ✓ Exhale throughout the lifting movement.

❏ Trunk Extension (Bodyweight Training):

- Joint action—trunk extension

- Prime-mover muscles—erector spinae

- Movement plane—sagittal

- Movement path—rotary

- Exercise technique—Lie face-down on the floor, with the hands folded under the chin. Raise the chest off floor, about 30 degrees, until the low back muscles are fully contracted. Return slowly to the starting position, and repeat.

- Technique tips:

  ✓ Maintain a neutral head position.

  ✓ Keep the hips and feet on the floor at all times, securing the feet under a sturdy anchor object, if necessary.

  ✓ Exhale throughout the upward movement.

Neck Exercise

❏ Barbell Shoulder Shrug:

- Joint action—shoulder elevation

- Prime-mover muscles—upper trapezius

- Movement path—rotary

- Exercise technique—Stand with the feet shoulder-width apart and hold a barbell, using an overhand grip, with the arms fully extended. Keeping the arms straight, lift the barbell upward a few inches by elevating the shoulders toward the head. Return slowly to the starting position, and repeat.

- Technique tips:

   ✓ Maintain an erect posture.

   ✓ Maintain a neutral head position.

   ✓ Keep the arms straight throughout the upward and downward movements.

   ✓ Exhale throughout the upward movement.

Total Body Exercise

❏ Hang Power Clean:

- Joint action—hip extension, knee extension, trunk extension, shoulder elevation, shoulder abduction, and elbow flexion

- Prime-mover muscles—hamstrings, gluteals, quadriceps, erector spinae, upper trapezius, anterior/middle deltoids and biceps

- Movement plane—sagittal

- Movement path—linear

- Exercise technique—Hold an Olympic barbell, using a shoulder-width, overhand grip. Assume partial squat position, with the hips flexed, the knees flexed, the back straight, and the arms straight. Explosively extend the hips and knees and shrug the shoulders to produce an upward movement/momentum in the barbell. Quickly drop downward, while concurrently pulling the arms upward, flexing the elbows, and catching the barbell at the shoulders, with the elbows pointed forward. Return the barbell to the starting position, and repeat.

- Technique tips:

  ✓ Keep the head up throughout the exercise.

  ✓ Keep the back straight throughout the exercise.

  ✓ Lead the arm pull with the elbows.

  ✓ Catch the barbell, with the upper arms almost parallel to the floor.

CHAPTER 6:
Strength Training Programs: Basic, Circuit, Advanced

Minerva Studio/iStock/Thinkstock

The previous chapter provided an overview of weight stack machine and free-weight exercises for all of the major muscle groups of the body. Due to the large number of resistance exercises and the different muscular impact of linear and rotary actions, it is important to develop a progressive strength training program that begins with a few key exercises and eventually evolves into a comprehensive muscular workout.

The first section of this chapter presents a sample basic strength training program, with week-by-week progressions for adding resistance exercises and selecting appropriate weightloads through the first two-months of training. The second section of this chapter provides sample circuit strength training protocols for workouts that concurrently promote both muscular strength and cardiovascular endurance. The third section of this chapter addresses a variety of advanced strength training muscle-building techniques, cumulatively referred to as high-intensity strength training.

It should be noted that the sample strength training programs are simply examples and may be modified according to physical abilities and personal preferences. Nonetheless, all of the recommended programs are based on research studies that have demonstrated them to be safe, effective, and efficient means for achieving the desired strength training objectives.

BASIC STRENGTH TRAINING PROGRAM

Individuals who are just beginning to strength train should start with a few basic resistance training exercises, and then gradually increase the number of exercises in their workout regimen as their muscles become better conditioned. This approach not only establishes a solid base of support in the major muscle groups, it also permits progressive strength development. Individuals should also incorporate different strength exercises in their training regimen as their muscles become accustomed to their standard training routine. This prevents boredom, as well as enhances the training effect by emphasizing different motor units and muscle fibers.

Although an exercise facility may not have all of the equipment in this basic protocol, participants should employ this sample two-month training program as a guide for achieving better strength fitness. As necessary, they can adapt the program to their needs and interests, as well as the available equipment. This program is a proven, highly effective, and efficient means of muscular conditioning. It is important to note that individuals may repeat a week of recommended training, if they do not feel ready for the next training progression.

The sample two-month strength training program utilizes machine exercises. For individuals who prefer free-weight training, suggested exercises for the eight weeks of progressive strength training are presented at the end of this chapter.

Month #1

Because this phase is an individual's first month of serious and sensible strength exercise, they must begin slowly to maximize positive muscle responses and to prevent overdoing it. If a person adheres to the recommended exercise program, they should make excellent progress, without experiencing any training setbacks. This month of training is detailed on a week-by-week basis. Participants should be sure to use the first and last two to three minutes of each session for warming up and cooling down.

❏ Month 1, Week 1:

Participants should begin their training by performing exercises on those machines that enable individuals to do basic strength exercises that address a number of the key muscle areas of the body—the leg press machine, the chest press machine, and the seated row machine. These three machines incorporate six out of the 12 major muscle groups.

Because all of these exercises are linear in nature, i.e., involving pushing or pulling in a straight line, they address more than one muscle group at the same time. By design, these exercises involve familiar movements that are important for daily activities and sport performance. The leg press strengthens the quadriceps, hamstrings, and gluteal muscles. The chest press strengthens the pectoralis major and triceps muscles, and the seated row stresses the latissimus dorsi and biceps muscles.

An individual should perform one set of 8 to 12 repetitions of each exercise. When they can complete 12 repetitions of a particular exercise, they should increase their training resistance by about 5 percent. It should be noted that the suggested starting weight loads for these exercises are based on age and gender (see Table 6-1). The actual starting weight loads must be determined by personal trial, beginning with light resistance and adding weight until the lifter is in the 8- to 12-repetition range. If a person cannot complete eight repetitions of a particular exercise, they should reduce the level of resistance in that exercise to prevent overstressing their muscles and joints.

❏ Month 1, Week 2:

During the second week of training, an individual should incorporate two additional exercises to their exercise regimen—the low back machine and the abdominal machine. Table 6-2 lists the recommended exercise order and shows the major muscle groups that these five exercises address.

Exercise order	Training sets	Training repetitions	Training speed*
1. Leg press	1	8-12	3/3
2. Chest press	1	8-12	3/3
3. Seated row	1	8-12	3/3
*number of seconds (up/down)			

Major muscle group	Machine	Age	Leg press*	Chest press*	Seated row*
1. Quadriceps	Leg press	**20-29**			
2. Hamstrings	Leg press	Males	150.0	65.0	85.0
3. Hip adductors	-	Females	100.0	40.0	55.0
4. Hip abductors	-	**30-39**			
5. Pectoralis major	Chest press	Males	137.5	60.0	80.0
6. Latissimus dorsi	Seated row	Females	92.5	37.5	52.5
7. Deltoids	-	**40-49**			
8. Biceps	Seated row	Males	125.0	55.0	75.0
9. Triceps	Chest press	Females	85.0	35.0	50.0
10. Low back	-	**50-59**			
11. Abdominals	-	Males	112.5	50.0	70.0
12. Neck	-	Females	77.5	32.5	47.5
		60-69			
		Males	100.0	45.0	65.0
		Females	70.0	30.0	45.0
		70-79			
		Males	87.5	40.0	50.0
		Females	62.5	27.5	42.5
*Weight load in pounds					

Table 6-1. Training program for month 1, week 1

The low back and abdominal exercises are rotary in nature (i.e., moving in an arc around a rotational axis) and, as indicated by their designated names, target the low back and abdominal muscles. Participants should perform one set of 8 to 12 repetitions of each exercise. When a person can perform 12 repetitions of a particular exercise, they should increase their training resistance in that exercise by about 5 percent. Because low back problems and midsection weaknesses are common, individuals should begin doing these exercises with less than the standard starting weight loads. It is always better to begin too light and then add resistance later, than to begin too heavy and risk suffering an injury.

Exercise order	Training sets	Training repetitions	Training speed*
1. Leg press	1	8-12	3/3
2. Chest press	1	8-12	3/3
3. Seated row	1	8-12	3/3
4. Low back**			
5. Abdominal**			
*Number of seconds (up/down)			
** New exercises this week			

Major muscle group	Machine	Age	Abdominal exercise	Low back exercise
1. Quadriceps	Leg press	**20-29**		
2. Hamstrings	Leg press	Males	70.0	70.0
3. Hip adductors	-	Females	50.0	45.0
4. Hip abductors	-	**30-39**		
5. Pectoralis major	Chest press	Males	65.0	65.0
6. Latissimus dorsi	Seated row	Females	47.5	42.5
7. Deltoids	-	**40-49**		
8. Biceps	Seated row	Males	60.0	60.0
9. Triceps	Chest press	Females	45.0	40.0
10. Low back	Low back	**50-59**		
11. Abdominals	Abdominal	Males	55.0	55.0
12. Neck	-	Females	42.5	37.5
		60-69		
		Males	50.0	50.0
		Females	40.0	35.0
		70-79		
		Males	45.0	45.0
		Females	37.5	42.5
*Weight load in pounds				

Table 6-2. Training program for month 1, week 2

❏ Month 1, Week 3:

The third week is a good time to add two new leg exercises—hip adduction and hip abduction. The recommended machine order and the major muscle groups addressed by this program are listed in Table 6-3.

Exercise order	Training sets	Training repetitions	Training speed*
1. Leg press	1	8-12	3/3
2. Hip adductor**	1	8-12	3/3
3. Hip abductor**	1	8-12	3/3
4. Chest press	1	8-12	3/3
5. Seated row	1	8-12	3/3
6. Low back	1	8-12	3/3
7. Abdominal	1	8-12	3/3

*Number of seconds (up/down)
** New exercises this week

Major muscle group	Machine	Age	Hip abductor exercise*	Hip adductor exercise*
1. Quadriceps	Leg press	**20-29**		
2. Hamstrings	Leg press	Males	70.0	80.0
3. Hip adductors	Hip adductor	Females	45.0	55.0
4. Hip abductors	Hip abductor	**30-39**		
5. Pectoralis major	Chest press	Males	65.0	75.0
6. Latissimus dorsi	Seated row	Females	42.5	52.5
7. Deltoids	-	**40-49**		
8. Biceps	Seated row	Males	60.0	70.0
9. Triceps	Chest press	Females	40.0	50.0
10. Low back	Low back	**50-59**		
11. Abdominals	Abdominal	Males	55.0	65.0
12. Neck	-	Females	37.5	47.5
		60-69		
		Males	50.0	60.0
		Females	35.0	45.0
		70-79		
		Males	45.0	55.0
		Females	32.5	42.5

*Weight load in pounds

Table 6-3. Training program for month 1, week 3

The hip adduction exercise works the inner thigh muscles, while the hip abduction exercise targets the outer thigh muscles. Both exercises are rotary activities that strengthen the muscles responsible for lateral-movement activities, such as skating, skiing, tennis, and basketball.

An individual should perform one set of 8 to 12 repetitions of each exercise. When they can perform 12 repetitions of a particular exercise, they should increase their training resistance in that exercise by about 5 percent. Table 6-3 lists typical starting weight loads for these new leg exercises, based on age and gender.

❑   Month 1, Week 4:

During the fourth week of training, a person can add another upper-body exercise, as well as a machine exercise that addresses the neck muscles. The recommended additions are the overhead press machine, a linear exercise that employs the deltoids and the triceps, and the 4-way neck machine, typically utilized to develop the flexor and extensor muscles of the neck. Table 6-4 lists the recommended exercise order and shows the major muscle groups addressed by these nine exercises. As can be seen, at this point, an individual is now working all of the major muscle groups.

As with the other three phases of the initial month of training, an individual should perform one set of 8 to 12 repetitions of each exercise. Similarly, when they can do 12 repetitions of a particular exercise, they should increase their training resistance in that exercise by about 5 percent. Typical starting weight loads for the overhead press exercise, the neck flexion exercise, and the neck extension exercise based on age and gender are listed in Table 6-4.

Month #2

At this point, individuals who have stuck to the recommended regimen should be congratulated for completing their first month of progressive strength training. During the second month of training, they may add several more exercises to round out their strength workouts. These exercises are designed to provide a comprehensive program of muscle conditioning, within relatively brief training sessions. Similar to the first month, this month of training is also detailed on a week-by-week basis.

❑   Month 2, Week 1:

As individuals begin their second month of training, they should add two strength exercises that target the upper arm muscles—the biceps curl and the triceps extension. The biceps curl machine provides rotary exercise for the biceps muscles, while the triceps extension machine provides rotary exercise for the triceps muscles. Both machines offer full-range strength training for their respective muscle groups. Table 6-5 lists the recommended exercise order for this phase of training. These 11 machines address all of the major muscle groups with more direct training for the muscles of the upper arm.

Similar to the phases of training previously reviewed, an individual should perform one set of 8 to 12 repetitions of each exercise. When they can complete 12 repetitions of a particular exercise, they should increase their training resistance for that exercise by about 5 percent. Table 6-5 shows typical starting weight loads for these new exercises, based on age and gender.

Exercise order	Training sets	Training repetitions	Training speed*
1. Leg press	1	8-12	3/3
2. Hip adductor	1	8-12	3/3
3. Hip abductor	1	8-12	3/3
4. Chest press	1	8-12	3/3
5. Seated row	1	8-12	3/3
6. Overhead press**	1	8-12	3/3
7. Low back	1	8-12	3/3
8. Abdominal	1	8-12	3/3
9. 4-way neck**	1	8-12	3/3
*Number of seconds (up/down)			
**New exercises this week			

Major muscle group	Machine	Age	Overhead press*	Neck flexion*	Neck extension*
1. Quadriceps	Leg press	**20-29**			
2. Hamstrings	Leg press	Males	50.0	45.0	50.0
3. Hip adductors	Hip adductor	Females	35.0	40.0	35.0
4. Hip abductors	Hip abductor	**30-39**			
5. Pectoralis major	Chest press	Males	47.5	42.0	47.5
6. Latissimus dorsi	Seated row	Females	32.5	27.5	32.5
7. Deltoids	Overhead press	**40-49**			
8. Biceps	Seated row	Males	45.0	40.0	45.0
9. Triceps	Chest press	Females	30.0	25.0	30.0
10. Low back	Low back	**50-59**			
11. Abdominals	Abdominal	Males	42.5	37.5	42.5
12. Neck	4-way neck	Females	27.5	22.5	27.5
		60-69			
		Males	40.0	35.0	40.0
		Females	25.0	20.0	25.0
		70-79			
		Males	37.5	32.5	37.5
		Females	20.0	20.0	22.5
*Weight load in pounds					

Table 6-4. Training program for month 1, week 4

Exercise order	Training sets	Training repetitions	Training speed*
1. Leg press	1	8-12	3/3
2. Hip adductor	1	8-12	3/3
3. Hip abductor	1	8-12	3/3
4. Chest press	1	8-12	3/3
5. Seated row	1	8-12	3/3
6. Overhead press	1	8-12	3/3
7. Biceps curl**	1	8-12	3/3
8. Triceps extension**	1	8-12	3/3
9. Low back	1	8-12	3/3
10. Abdominal	1	8-12	3/3
11. 4-way neck	1	8-12	3/3

*Number of seconds (up/down)
**New exercises this week

Major muscle group	Machine	Age	Biceps curl*	Triceps extension*
1. Quadriceps	Leg press	**20-29**		
2. Hamstrings	Leg press	Males	60.0	60.0
3. Hip adductors	Hip adductor	Females	32.5	32.5
4. Hip abductors	Hip abductor	**30-39**		
5. Pectoralis major	Chest press	Males	55.0	55.0
6. Latissimus dorsi	Seated row	Females	30.0	30.0
7. Deltoids	Overhead press	**40-49**		
8. Biceps	Seated row	Males	50.0	50.0
	Biceps curl	Females	27.5	27.5
9. Triceps	Chest press	**50-59**		
	Overhead press	Males	45.0	45.0
	Triceps extension	Females	25.0	25.0
10. Low back	Low back	**60-69**		
11. Abdominals	Abdominal	Males	40.0	40.0
12. Neck	4-way neck	Females	22.5	22.5
		70-79		
		Males	35.0	35.0
		Females	20.0	20.0

*Weight load in pounds

Table 6-5. Training program for month 2, week 1

❏ Month 2, Week 2:

This week, two specific machines to exercise can be added to the training regimen to exercise the thigh muscles—the leg extension machine for the quadriceps and the leg curl machine for the hamstrings. Both machines provide rotary movement and full-range exercise for the largest muscle groups of the body (quadriceps and hamstrings). The recommended exercise order and the major muscles involved in these exercises are detailed in Table 6-6.

Exercise order	Training sets	Training repetitions	Training speed*
1. Leg extension**	1	8-12	3/3
2. Seated leg curl**	1	8-12	3/3
3. Leg press	1	8-12	3/3
4. Hip adductor	1	8-12	3/3
5. Hip abductor	1	8-12	3/3
6. Chest press	1	8-12	3/3
7. Seated row	1	8-12	3/3
8. Overhead press	1	8-12	3/3
9. Biceps curl	1	8-12	3/3
10. Triceps extension	1	8-12	3/3
11. Low back	1	8-12	3/3
12. Abdominal	1	8-12	3/3
13. 4-way neck	1	8-12	3/3
*Number of seconds (up/down) **New exercises this week			

Major muscle group	Machine	Age	Leg extension*	Seated leg curl*
1. Quadriceps	Leg press	**20-29**		
	Leg extension	Males	70.0	70.0
2. Hamstrings	Leg press	Females	42.5	42.5
	Seated leg curl	**30-39**		
3. Hip adductors	Hip adductor	Males	65.0	65.0
4. Hip abductors	Hip abductor	Females	40.0	40.0
5. Pectoralis major	Chest press	**40-49**		
6. Latissimus dorsi	Seated row	Males	60.0	60.0
7. Deltoids	Overhead press	Females	37.5	37.5
8. Biceps	Seated row	**50-59**		
	Biceps curl	Males	55.0	55.0
9. Triceps	Chest press	Females	35.0	35.0
	Overhead press	**60-69**		
	Triceps extension	Males	50.0	50.0
10. Low back	Low back	Females	32.5	32.5
11. Abdominals	Abdominal	**70-79**		
12. Neck	4-way neck	Males	45.0	45.0
		Females	30.0	30.0
*Weight load in pounds				

Table 6-6. Training program for month 2, week 2

As before, individuals engaged in this phase of training should perform one set of each exercise, beginning with a level of resistance that permits doing at least eight repetitions, and subsequently increasing the weight load by about 5 percent, when the person can complete 12 repetitions. The usual starting weight loads for the leg extension and leg curl machines are shown in Table 6-6.

❏ Month 2, Week 3:

At this point in their training program, individuals may benefit from (and enjoy) performing two bodyweight exercises—chin-ups and bar-dips on the weight-assisted chin/dip machine. The chin-up is a linear exercise that involves the latissimus dorsi and biceps muscles, whereas the bar-dip is a linear exercise that works the pectoralis major and triceps muscles. The recommended exercise order and the muscle groups utilized in each exercise are detailed in Table 6-7.

Individuals should complete one set of each exercise, starting with a counterbalance weight load that enables them to perform eight repetitions of a particular exercise. When they are capable of performing 12 repetitions of a given exercise, they should reduce the level of resistance for that exercise by approximately 5 percent. It should be noted that on the weight-assisted bar-dip and chin-up exercises, decreasing the counterbalance weight load actually increases the level of training resistance (enabling a person to use a larger percentage of their bodyweight). The typical beginning weight loads for weight-assisted chin-ups and bar-dips are shown in Table 6-7.

❏ Month 2, Week 4:

As individuals approach the completion of their second training month, they can substitute more specific exercise for the pectoralis major, latissimus dorsi, and deltoid muscles. For example, the pec dec machine can replace the chest press, the super pullover can be substituted for the seated row, and the lateral raise can be exchanged for the overhead press. Arguably, the new exercises are able to better isolate the target torso muscles (pectoralis major, latissimus dorsi, and deltoids) without involving the arm muscles (triceps, biceps). Table 6-8 lists the recommended exercise order and the major muscle groups addressed in this program.

Individuals should complete one set of each exercise, using a resistance that enables them to perform at least eight repetitions. Subsequently, they should increase the weight load by 5 percent when they can do 12 repetitions of that exercise. Table 6-8 outlines the usual beginning weight loads for the pec dec, super pullover, and lateral raise exercises, based on age and gender.

❏ Conclusion of Two-Month Training Program:

After completing eight weeks of progressive strength and endurance workouts with a variety of resistance exercises, individuals should have a reasonably high level of confidence and competence in their training ability. They have succeeded in the most challenging phase of their muscle conditioning program.

At this point, the participants can continue their current strength training protocol or periodically change the exercises that they do to enhance the effectiveness of their efforts, as well as possibly heighten their level of motivation. They may also choose to perform fewer exercises or more exercises, depending

Exercise order	Training sets	Training repetitions	Training speed*
1. Leg extension	1	8-12	3/3
2. Seated leg curl	1	8-12	3/3
3. Leg press	1	8-12	3/3
4. Hip adductor	1	8-12	3/3
5. Hip abductor	1	8-12	3/3
6. Chest press	1	8-12	3/3
7. Seated row	1	8-12	3/3
8. Overhead press	1	8-12	3/3
9. Biceps curl	1	8-12	3/3
10. Triceps extension	1	8-12	3/3
11. Low back	1	8-12	3/3
12. Abdominal	1	8-12	3/3
13. 4-way neck	1	8-12	3/3
14. Chin/dip**	1	8-12	3/3

*Number of seconds (up/down)
**New exercises this week

Major muscle group	Machine	Age	Chin-up exercise*	Bar-dip exercise*
1. Quadriceps	Leg press	**20-29**		
	Leg extension	Males	40.0	40.0
2. Hamstrings	Leg press	Females	55.0	55.0
	Seated leg curl	**30-39**		
3. Hip adductors	Hip adductor	Males	45.0	45.0
4. Hip abductors	Hip abductor	Females	60.0	60.0
5. Pectoralis major	Chest press	**40-49**		
	Weight-assisted chin/dip	Males	50.0	50.0
6. Latissimus dorsi	Super pullover	Females	65.0	65.0
	Weight-assisted chin/dip	**50-59**		
7. Deltoids	Overhead press	Males	55.0	55.0
8. Biceps	Biceps curl	Females	70.0	70.0
	Weight-assisted chin/dip	**60-69**		
9. Triceps	Triceps extension	Males	60.0	60.0
	Weight-assisted chin/dip	Females	75.0	75.0
10. Low back	Low back	**70-79**		
11. Abdominals	Abdominal	Males	65.0	65.0
12. Neck	4-way neck	Females	80.0	80.0

*Weight load in pounds

Table 6-7. Training program for month 2, week 3

Exercise order	Training sets	Training repetitions	Training speed*
1. Leg extension	1	8-12	3/3
2. Seated leg curl	1	8-12	3/3
3. Leg press	1	8-12	3/3
4. Hip adductor	1	8-12	3/3
5. Hip abductor	1	8-12	3/3
6. Pec dec**	1	8-12	3/3
7. Super pullover**	1	8-12	3/3
8. Lateral raise	1	8-12	3/3
9. Biceps curl	1	8-12	3/3
10. Triceps extension	1	8-12	3/3
11. Low back	1	8-12	3/3
12. Abdominal	1	8-12	3/3
13. 4-way neck	1	8-12	3/3
14. Chin/dip	1	8-12	3/3

*Number of seconds (up/down)
**New exercises this week

Major muscle group	Machine	Age	Pec dec exercise*	Super pullover*	Lateral raise*
1. Quadriceps	Leg press	**20-29**			
	Leg extension	Males	60.0	65.0	55.0
2. Hamstrings	Leg press	Females	37.5	40.0	35.0
	Seated leg curl	**30-39**			
3. Hip adductors	Hip adductor	Males	57.5	62.5	52.5
4. Hip abductors	Hip abductor	Females	35.0	37.5	32.5
5. Pectoralis major	Pec dec	**40-49**			
	Weight-assisted chin/dip	Males	55.0	62.5	50.0
6. Latissimus dorsi	Super pullover	Females	32.5	35.0	30.0
	Weight-assisted chin/dip	**50-59**			
7. Deltoids	Lateral raise	Males	52.5	57.5	47.5
8. Biceps	Seated row	Females	30.0	32.5	27.5
	Biceps curl	**60-69**			
	Weight-assisted chin/dip	Males	50.0	55.0	45.0
9. Triceps	Triceps extension	Females	27.5	30.0	25.0
	Weight-assisted chin/dip	**70-79**			
10. Low back	Low back	Males	47.5	52.5	42.5
11. Abdominals	Abdominal	Females	25.0	27.5	22.5
12. Neck	4-way neck				

*Weight load in pounds

Table 6-8. Training program for month 2, week 4

on their training objectives and time availability. The underlying key is for them to remember to address the major muscle groups in their exercise regimen and to work the opposing muscles for comprehensive conditioning and muscle balance. In addition, they need to be sure to increase the level of exercise resistance for an exercise whenever they are able to perform 12 repetitions in good form of that exercise.

They also have other possible options. For example, they could alternate endurance exercises with the strength exercises in their training protocol. The critical point is to remember to apply the basic training principles to all of their aerobic efforts.

Free Weight Training

Table 6-9 details the recommended free weight exercises for an initial two-month training period. Similar to the progression featuring machine-based exercises, individuals begin by performing three basic exercises and then systematically add and substitute new exercises each week of their training. The exercise selection and training sequence essentially parallels the recommended machine-based strength training program. As before, an exercise resistance level should be employed for each exercise that permits 8 to 12 properly performed repetitions to be done. When 12 repetitions of a particular exercise can be completed, the weight load for that exercise should be increased by approximately 5 percent.

❑ Summary:

After two months of engaging in a sensible and progressive strength and endurance exercise program, individuals should notice major improvements in their muscular and cardiovascular fitness, as well as in their level of body composition and physical appearance. At that point, they can either continue with these programs indefinitely, or may change their exercise protocols periodically as they keep on with their training.

Circuit Training Programs

As discussed in Chapter 4, circuit strength training is a time-efficient way to train, in which a series of exercises for different muscle groups is performed in a specific sequence. Each exercise is performed for one set of 10 to 15 repetitions, with quick transitions (10 to 15 seconds) between successive training stations. Each resistance exercise is typically performed for 60 seconds, which provides a productive anaerobic training bout for increasing muscular strength. Completing the entire training session may take between 10 to 40 minutes, depending on the number of exercises and circuits performed. This training method provides an effective aerobic training experience for improving cardiovascular endurance.

Standard strength training programs involve doing three sets of each exercise, with a two- to three-minute recovery period between sets. Assuming one minute to perform each exercise set, a 10-exercise workout would therefore take between 90 minutes (two-minute rests) and two hours (three-minute rests). While it is necessary to provide recovery time between exercise sets for the same muscle

Week	Exercises	
1	Barbell squat*	
	Barbell bench press*	
	Dumbbell bent row*	
2	Barbell squat	Trunk extension*
	Barbell bench press	Trunk curl*
	Dumbbell bent row	
3	Barbell squat	Dumbbell press*
	Barbell bench press	Trunk extension
	Dumbbell bent row	Trunk curl
4	Barbell squat	Barbell curl*
	Barbell bench press	Triceps pressdown*
	Dumbbell bent row	Trunk extension
	Dumbbell press	Trunk curl
5	Barbell squat	Barbell curl
	Dumbbell lunge*	Triceps pressdown
	Barbell bench press	Barbell shoulder shrug*
	Pullover*	Trunk extension
	Dumbbell press	Trunk curl
6	Barbell squat	Dumbbell overhead triceps extension*
	Dumbbell lunge	Barbell shoulder shrug
	Barbell incline press*	Trunk extension
	Pulldown*	Trunk curl
	Dumbbell lateral raise*	Chin-up*
	Dumbbell preacher curl*	Bar dip*
7	Barbell squat	Dumbbell preacher curl
	Dumbbell lunge	Dumbbell overhead triceps extension
	Dumbbell bench fly*	Dumbbell shoulder shrug
	Barbell incline press	Trunk extension
	Dumbbell pullover*	Twisting knee-lift trunk curl*
	Pulldown	Chin-up
	Dumbbell lateral raise	Bar dip
8	Barbell squat	Dumbbell preacher curl
	Dumbbell lunge	Dumbbell triceps kickback*
	Dumbbell step-up*	Dumbbell shoulder shrug
	Dumbbell bench fly	Trunk extension
	Dumbbell pullover	Twisting knee-lift trunk curl
	Pulldown	Chin-up
	Dumbbell lateral raise	Bar dip

*New exercises this week

Table 6-9. Recommended program of free weight training for the first two months

groups, circuit training greatly reduces the duration of the rest periods by working different muscle groups at successive exercise stations. Given one minute to perform each exercise set and 15 seconds between each exercise, a 10-exercise workout would therefore require about 12 ½ minutes for one set of each exercise, 25 minutes for two sets of each exercise, and 37 ½ minutes for three sets of each exercise.

Most circuit strength training programs take about 15 to 20 minutes for completion and involve only resistance exercises. Table 6-10 presents a sample resistance exercise-only circuit strength training program that alternates opposing muscles from larger-to-smaller groups. Table 6-11 presents a sample resistance exercise-only circuit strength training program that sequences lower-body, upper-body, and midsection muscles groups. Other circuit training programs alternate resistance exercises with aerobic activity, such as the research protocol that the author and his colleagues conducted with the United States Air Force. The combined resistance and aerobic circuit that produced excellent results in the Air Force study is detailed in Table 6-11.

Station	Exercise	Target muscles
1	Leg extension	Quadriceps
2	Leg curl	Hamstrings
3	Hip adduction	Hip adductors
4	Hip abduction	Hip abductors
5	Leg press	Quadriceps, hamstrings, gluteals
6	Chest cross	Pectoralis major
7	Pullover	Latissimus dorsi
8	Lateral raise	Deltoids
9	Biceps curl	Biceps
10	Triceps extension	Triceps
11	Low back	Erector spinae
12	Abdominal	Rectus abdominis

Note: The time allotted to perform each exercise is 60 seconds. As such, the total time to complete one entire circuit is approximately 15 minutes.

Table 6-10. Sample circuit strength training program alternating opposing muscle groups from larger-to-smaller groups

All of these circuit training programs are designed for one-minute bouts of activity at each exercise station, with no more than 15 seconds of transition time between successive exercises. For example, individuals who adhere to the Air Force circuit strength training program would perform one minute of leg presses, followed as quickly as possible by one minute of stationary cycling, then one minute of leg curls, followed as quickly as possible by one minute of stationary cycling, and so on, until they have completed both the 10 resistance exercises and the 10 bouts of stationary cycling.

Station	Exercise	Target muscles
1	Leg extension	Quadriceps
2	Chest cross	Pectoralis major
3	Leg curl	Hamstrings
4	Pullover	Latissimus dorsi
5	Hip adduction	Hip adductors
6	Lateral raise	Deltoids
7	Hip abduction	Hip abductors
8	Biceps curl	Biceps
9	Leg press	Quadriceps, hamstrings, gluteals
10	Triceps extension	Triceps
11	Low back	Erector spinae
12	Abdominal	Rectus abdominis

Note: The time allotted to perform each exercise is 60 seconds. The total time to complete one entire circuit is approximately 15 minutes.

Table 6-11. Sample circuit strength training program alternating lower-body, upper-body, and midsection muscle groups

Circuit strength training is a time-efficient means for concurrently attaining relatively high levels of muscular and cardiovascular fitness. The resistance exercise-only protocols presented in Tables 6-10 and 6-11 place greater emphasis on muscular strength, whereas the focus of resistance exercise plus aerobic activity protocol presented in Table 6-12 is on cardiovascular endurance.

Advanced Strength Training Programs

Once individuals reach a relatively high level of muscular fitness, they are likely to encounter a temporary training plateau. That is, they are working just as hard but not making the strength gains they once did. Although such a lack of progress may be discouraging, it is simply a sign that they should change some aspect of their exercise program.

Because everyone has different genetic potential for muscular development, they should approach advanced training in a sensible manner. The three best approaches for overcoming strength plateaus are to choose new exercises, change the workout protocol, or increase the training intensity.

❏ Choose New Exercises:
One fundamentally sound recommendation for achieving further strength gains is to select new training exercises. For example, if a person is not progressing in the bench press exercise, that individual could simply substitute the incline press exercise. While the slightly different movement pattern of the incline press still targets the pectoralis major muscles, it activates different motor units and muscle fibers. As a result, additional stimuli for strength development are produced.

Station	Exercise	Target muscles
1	Leg press	Quadriceps, hamstrings, gluteals
2	Cycle	Cardiovascular system
3	Leg curl	Hamstrings
4	Cycle	Cardiovascular system
5	Leg extension	Quadriceps
6	Cycle	Cardiovascular system
7	Chest press	Pectoralis major, triceps
8	Cycle	Cardiovascular system
9	Seated Row	Latissimus dorsi, biceps
10	Cycle	Cardiovascular system
11	Shoulder press	Deltoids, triceps
12	Cycle	Cardiovascular system
13	Lat pull down	Latissimus dorsi, biceps
14	Cycle	Cardiovascular system
15	Triceps press	Triceps
16	Cycle	Cardiovascular system
17	Biceps curl	Biceps
18	Cycle	Cardiovascular system
19	Abdominal crunch	Rectus abdominis
20	Cycle	Cardiovascular system

Note: The time allotted to perform each exercise is 60 seconds. The total time to complete the entire circuit is approximately 25 minutes.

Table 6-12. Sample circuit strength training program alternating resistance exercise stations and stationary cycling stations

Periodically changing training exercises is also an excellent means of preventing boredom, as well as address strength plateaus. It should be noted, however, that a person should stay with a given exercise protocol long enough to maximize muscle response. As such, an individual should spend at least one month with a specific exercise program to allow the muscles time to adapt to the new training stimulus.

❏   Change Workout Protocol:

In addition to choosing new training exercises, to deal with a training plateau, a person could also systematically vary their workout procedures. This approach, referred to as periodization, involves changing the exercise resistance and repetitions scheme. For example, during the first month of training, an individual may complete 12 to 16 repetitions with relatively light resistance. During the second month, that person's training regimen may involve doing 8 to 12 repetitions with moderate weight loads. In contrast, the third month may encompass performing four to eight repetitions with relatively heavy resistance.

Periodically changing the resistance-repetitions relationship varies the muscle fiber activation pattern and provides a new stimulus for strength development. The key is to be sure to give each training program enough time to be productive. For continuity purposes, the person should try to not change their strength training protocol more often than every four weeks.

❏   Increase Training Intensity:

Two other ways to make workouts more demanding is either to increase the training volume by performing more exercises for each major muscle group or to complete more sets of each exercise. Competitive bodybuilders have traditionally taken the latter option, training two to four hours a day, six days a week. Recently, however, because of time limitations and overtraining injuries, a number of strength training enthusiasts have taken a different approach to performing advanced workouts—a method referred to as high-intensity strength training. Involving time-efficient exercise procedures, this training technique produced excellent results for people of various ages and abilities, including champion bodybuilders and professional football teams.

The basic premise of high-intensity strength training is that a person can exercise hard or can exercise long, but an individual can't exercise really hard for very long. The key to effective high-intensity strength training is to put more effort into each exercise set, rather than to put more exercise sets into the workout. This type of training emphasizes the exercise intensity, instead of the exercise duration. The key is to keep in mind that more demanding exercise sessions require more time for tissue recovery and muscle building. As such, for best results, a person should not perform high-intensity strength training more than twice a week.

Considering the differences between multiple-set and high-intensity strength training can help clarify why many strength exercises prefer high-intensity training. Because the motor unit activation pattern is essentially the same for a specific exercise, doing repeat sets fatigues the same muscle fibers again and again, rather than stimulating additional muscle fibers. For example, if an individual performs 10 leg extensions to temporary muscle fatigue with 75 percent of their maximum resistance, about 25 percent of the quadriceps muscle fibers are fatigued and stimulated. If that person rests two minutes and repeats this procedure (i.e., the multiple-set protocol), the same 25 percent of the quadriceps muscle fibers are again fatigued and stimulated.

In contrast, if a person hypothetically performs 10 leg extensions to temporary muscle fatigue, with 75 percent of their maximum resistance, similar to the multiple-set protocol, 25 percent of the quadriceps muscle fibers will again be fatigued and stimulated. Instead of stopping and resting, however, that individual immediately reduces the resistance by 10 to 20 percent and completes a few additional repetitions. Performing a few post-fatigue repetitions with a reduced resistance fatigues and stimulates more muscle fibers, which elicits an even greater strength-building effect. In other words, when a person reduces the weight load and performs an extended exercise set, two progressive levels of muscle fatigue are experienced. As a result, an enhanced stimulus for muscle development is imparted.

Extending the Exercise Set

There are three standard high-intensity procedures for extending the exercise set and enhancing the strength-building stimulus: breakdown training, assisted training, and pre-exhaustion training.

❏ Breakdown Training:

One means of fatiguing or stimulating more muscle fibers is to perform a few additional repetitions with slightly less resistance upon reaching temporary muscle fatigue. This high-intensity exercise technique is typically referred to as breakdown training, because the resistance to accommodate the momentarily reduced level of muscle strength is broken down.

As a general rule, breakdown training is fairly straightforward. Once individuals reach temporary muscle fatigue with their standard exercise weight load (about 8 to 12 repetitions), they then quickly reduce the level of resistance by approximately 10 to 20 percent. Doing so should permit them to complete about two to four additional repetitions, thereby enabling them to reach a second level of muscle fatigue and stimulus within the anaerobic energy system (less than 90 seconds). For example, a person may perform 10 lateral raises to fatigue, using 10-pound dumbbells. In breakdown training, at that point, they then quickly exchange these for eight-pound dumbbells and complete four more repetitions of the exercise to achieve a second level of muscle fatigue.

In 1997, Westcott and his colleagues examined the effects of breakdown training on strength development in beginning exercisers. In this study, all 45 subjects performed standard strength training (one set of 8 to 12 repetitions to fatigue) on 11 weight stack machines for the first four weeks of the study. During the second four weeks, half of the subjects continued their standard training, while the other half performed breakdown training on two of the machines (seated leg curl and abdominal). The participants who performed breakdown training experienced 40 percent more strength development during the eight-week exercise period than their standard training counterparts. Individuals in the standard training group achieved an average 18-pound improvement in these two exercises, while the breakdown training subjects attained an average 25-pound strength gain.

Because breakdown training reduces the resistance at the point of muscle fatigue, it is a safe exercise technique, as well as an effective one, for beginning participants. In order to determine if breakdown training can produce further improvement in advanced exercisers, Westcott and his colleagues conducted another study with 11 well-trained men and women. After just six weeks of breakdown training, the subjects in this investigation increased their average exercise resistance by 14 pounds. In addition, they performed 1.5 more chin-ups and 2.5 more bar dips after breakdown training, even though they did not practice these exercises during the period of the study. In other words, breakdown training produced significant improvements in both weight-stack and body weight exercises in previously plateaued participants.

❑ Assisted Training:

Assisted training is another high-intensity training procedure for fatiguing and stimulating more muscle fibers by extending the exercise set. Similar to breakdown training, assisted training allows individuals to complete a few additional repetitions with reduced resistance when they reach temporary muscle fatigue. In assisted training, however, the weight load remains the same for post-fatigue repetitions. In this form of training, the assistant helps the lifter raise the weight load, but allows the individual to lower the weight load on their own. This technique works well, because muscles are about 40 percent stronger in lowering movements (negative muscle actions) than in lifting movements (positive muscle actions).

Nonetheless, as a person further fatigues the target muscles, the lowering movements become increasingly more difficult. As such, the extended exercise set should be ended at the point where an individual can no longer control the lowering movement. When this type of training is performed properly, this juncture typically occurs within two to four assisted repetitions, enabling the lifter to reach both concentric and eccentric muscle fatigue within the anaerobic energy system (under 90 seconds).

In 1998, Westcott and his colleagues studied the effects of assisted training on strength gains in beginning exercisers. In this investigation, all 42 subjects performed standard strength training (one set of 8 to 12 repetitions to fatigue) on 11 weight stack machines for the first four weeks of the study. During the next four weeks, half of the subjects continued their standard training, while the other half performed assisted training on two of the machines (seated leg curl and abdominal). The participants who performed assisted training experienced 45 percent greater strength gains during the eight-week exercise period than their standard training counterparts. The standard training subjects achieved an average 20-pound strength improvement in these two exercises, while the assisted training participants attained an average 29-pound strength gain.

Similar to breakdown training, assisted training reduces the resistance at the point of muscle fatigue, which makes it a safe and productive exercise procedure for beginning participants. To determine if assisted training can further enhance strength development in advanced exercisers, Westcott and his colleagues conducted another study with 15 well-conditioned men and women. After five weeks of assisted training, the subjects in this investigation increased their average exercise resistance by 11 pounds. They also performed 1.4 more chin-ups and 4.5 more bar dips after assisted training, even though they did not practice these exercises during the period of the study. In other words, assisted training produced significant improvements in both weight-stack and bodyweight exercises in previously plateaued participants.

❑ Pre-Exhaustion Training:

A third method of extending the exercise set in a high-intensity manner is pre-exhaustion training. If individuals like to do more than one set of an exercise for the targeted muscle group, they should definitely try the pre-exhaustion procedure. Pre-exhaustion training begins with a rotary (single-joint) exercise to fatigue the target muscle, followed immediately by a linear (multiple-joint) exercise that elicits fresh assisting muscles to further fatigue the target muscle.

The first set of rotary exercise should generate muscle fatigue within 60 seconds (about 10 repetitions), and the follow-up set of linear exercise should produce muscle fatigue within 30 seconds (about five repetitions). As such, the successive exercises for the same target muscle should provide two progressive levels of muscle stimulus within the anaerobic energy system (90 seconds).

For example, when an individual performs two set of 10 bench presses with the same resistance, the same pectoralis major muscle fibers are activated twice. While this procedure increases the exercise duration, it does not necessarily increase the exercise intensity. In other words, a person works the same muscle fibers more, rather than engage more muscle fibers.

In contrast, in pre-exhaustion training, a person performs a set of chest crosses (10 repetitions), followed immediately by a set of bench presses (five repetitions). The chest cross is a rotary exercise that targets the pectoralis major muscles. When the target muscles fatigue, an individual can no longer continue this exercise. On the other hand, if an individual then immediately performs a bench press, a linear exercise that uses both the pre-fatigued pectoralis major muscles and the fresh triceps muscles, the target muscle (pectoralis major) can be pushed to a deeper level of fatigue and stimulus (see Figures 6-1a and 6-1b).

Figure 6-1a

Figure 6-1b

Antonio_Diaz/iStock/Thinkstock

In essence, the different movement patterns of the chest cross and the bench press activate different muscle fibers. In turn, assistance from the fresh triceps muscle permits the fatigued pectoralis major to do even more work for better strength-building benefits. Table 6-13 presents several pairs of rotary and linear exercises that provide pre-exhaustion training for most of the major muscle groups.

Extending the Exercise Repetition— Slow Training

Slow training is a form of high-intensity training that produces a greater strength stimulus by extending each repetition. By performing each repetition more slowly, the role of momentum is reduced. The technique also enhances both muscle tension and muscle force production.

Muscle group	Rotary exercise	Linear exercise
Quadriceps	Leg extension	Leg press
Hamstrings	Leg curl	Leg press
Pectoralis major	Chest cross	Chest press
Latissimus dorsi	Pullover	Lat pulldown
Deltoids	Lateral raise	Overhead press
Biceps	Biceps curl	Assisted chin-up
Triceps	Triceps extension	Assisted bar dip

Table 6-13. Examples of pre-exhaustion exercises

The standard slow training method, an approach developed in 1982 by Ken Hutchins and referred to as Super Slow exercise, advocates utilizing a 10-second lifting movement (positive muscle action) and a four-second lowering movement (negative muscle action) for a 14-second repetition. The training regimen recommends performing four to six repetitions of each exercise to fatigue the target muscles within the anaerobic energy system (4 X 14 seconds = 56 seconds; 6 X 14 seconds = 84 seconds).

When doing slow-speed strength exercise, it is important to be sure to breathe continuously throughout every repetition. Participants should never hold their breath. In spite of being tough, tensive, and tedious to perform, slow training has been found to be a productive procedure for increasing muscle strength in both beginning and advanced exercisers. For example, in one study, conducted by Westcott and his colleagues in 2001, 147 subjects were divided into a standard training group (8 to 12 repetitions at seven seconds each) and a slow- training group (four to six repetitions at 14 seconds each). The slow-training participants gained 50 percent more strength than the standard training subjects (25.5 pounds versus 17.0 pounds) over the two-month training period.

Comparison of High-Intensity and Standard Training

A 1995 study by Westcott and his colleagues examined the effects of various high-intensity techniques and standard training on advanced exercisers whose strength had plateaued. In this investigation, the 22 subjects performed some exercises with standard training (one set of 8 to 12 repetitions, two seconds lifting and four seconds lowering) and other exercises with various high-intensity training techniques. These routines included breakdown training (three post-fatigue reps with reduced resistance), assisted training (three post-fatigue reps with manual assistance), slow positive-emphasis training (10 seconds lifting and four seconds lowering), and a slow negative-emphasis training (four seconds lifting and 10 seconds lowering).

All of the exercise procedures produced significant improvements in muscle strength over the six-week training period, including standard training supervised by an instructor (see Figure 6-2). Apparently, working with an instructor encourages better training technique and elicits greater exercise effort. Even so, each of the high-intensity training techniques produced a higher level of strength gain than standard training.

Combined High-Intensity Training Program

Arguably, the most successful system of high-intensity strength training is a six-week program that includes all of the advanced techniques. As presented in Table 6-14, the experienced exercisers performed breakdown training during the first week, assisted training during the second week, slow positive-emphasis training during the third week, slow negative-emphasis training during the fourth week, pre-exhaustion training during the fifth week, and their preferred high-intensity training technique during the final week. The subjects worked all of the major muscle groups in 30-minute sessions on Mondays and Fridays, with an instructor involved. The 48 subjects increased their exercise weight loads by 17.8 pounds, added 2.5 pounds of lean (muscle) weight, and lost 3.3 pounds of fat weight. Descriptions of these high intensity training techniques are presented in Table 6-15.

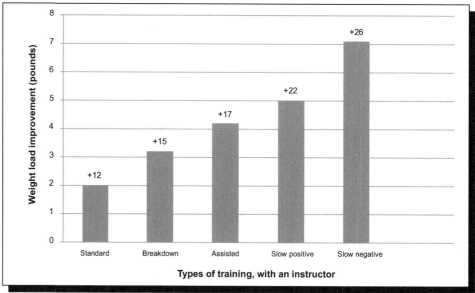

Figure 6-2. Strength improvements for previous plateaued individuals after six weeks of training using different exercise techniques

Week	Exercise technique
1	Breakdown training
2	Assisted training
3	Pre-exhaustion training
4	Slow-positive emphasis training
5	Slow-negative emphasis training
6	Personal preference training technique

Table 6-14. Combined technique high-intensity strength training program components

Table 6-15 provides brief descriptions of the basic high-intensity strength training protocols. Table 6-16 presents a sample high-intensity strength training protocol, using breakdown training for lower-body exercises and assisted training for upper-body exercises. Table 6-17 details a sample high-intensity strength training protocol using pre-exhaustion techniques. Table 6-18 offers a model for high-intensity strength training, utilizing slow-positive repetitions for lower-body exercises and slow-negative repetitions for upper-body exercises.

One of the most interesting studies conducted in 2001 by Westcott and his colleagues for the United States Navy, compared a 20-minute per session high-intensity strength training program with a 60-minute per session boot-camp exercise program. In his research, both groups trained twice a week for a period of five weeks. The high-intensity training consisted of a pre-exhaustion protocol and assisted repetitions, whereas the boot-camp training involved bodyweight exercises, such as push-ups and sit-ups.

Training Procedure	**Exercise Example**
❏ Breakdown training: At completion of the exercise set, reduce your resistance about 10 to 20 percent and perform a few post-fatigue repetitions.	Complete 10 to 12 leg extensions to fatigue with 100 lbs. Immediately drop the weight load to 85 lbs. and perform 2 to 4 additional repetitions to push the quadriceps muscles to a deeper level of fatigue.
❏ Assisted training: At completion of the exercise set, have your helper provide manual assistance on the lifting phase of a few post-fatigue repetitions.	Complete 10 to 12 leg curls to fatigue with 80 lbs. Immediately perform 2 to 4 additional repetitions with manual assistance on the lifting phase to push the hamstring muscles to a deeper level of fatigue.
❏ Pre-exhaustion training: At completion of the first (rotary movement) exercise set, perform a second (linear movement) exercise set for the same target muscle group without resting between the successive exercises.	Complete 8 to 10 lateral raises to fatigue with 60 lbs. Immediately perform four to six overhead presses to push the deltoid muscles to a deeper level of fatigue.
❏ Slow positive-emphasis training: Perform fewer repetitions at a slower speed. Taking 10 seconds for each concentric muscle action and four seconds for each eccentric muscle action.	Complete four to six bicep curls, taking 10 seconds for each lifting movement and four seconds for each lowering movement.
❏ Slow negative-emphasis training: Perform fewer repetitions at a slower speed, taking four seconds for each concentric muscle action and 10 seconds for each eccentric muscle action.	Complete four to six triceps extensions, taking four seconds for each lifting movement and 10 seconds for each lowering movement.

Table 6-15. Brief descriptions of basic high-intensity strength training protocols

Exercise	Pre-fatigue resistance and repetitions	Post- fatigue resistance and repetitions
Leg extensions	100 lb. X 10-12 reps	85 lb. X 2-4 reps
Leg curl	80 lb. X 10-12 reps	70 lb. X 2-4 reps
Hip adduction	120 lb. X 10-12 reps	100 lb. X 2-4 reps
Hip abduction	100 lb. X 10-12 reps	85 lb. X 2-4 reps
Leg press	200 lb. X 10-12 reps	170 lb. X 2-4 reps
Chest cross	90 lb. X 10-12 reps	2-4 assisted reps
Super pullover	110 lb. X 10-12 reps	2-4 assisted reps
Lateral raise	75 lb. X 10-12 reps	2-4 assisted reps
Biceps curl	65 lb. X 10-12 reps	2-4 assisted reps
Triceps extension	65 lb. X 10-12 reps	2-4 assisted reps
Abdominal curl	105 lb. X 10-12 reps	2-4 assisted reps
Low back extension	115 lb. X 10-12 reps	no post-fatigue reps
Neck flexion	75 lb. X 10-12 reps	no post-fatigue reps
Neck extension	60 lb. X 10-12 reps	no post-fatigue reps

Table 6-16. Sample high-intensity strength training protocol, using breakdown training for lower-body exercises and assisted training for upper-body exercises

Exercise	First (rotary exercise resistance and repetitions)	Second (linear exercise resistance and repetitions)
❏ Leg extension Leg press	100 lb. X 8-10 reps	180 lb. X 4-5 reps
❏ Leg curl Leg press	80 lb. x 8-10 reps	150 lb. X 4-5 reps
❏ Chest cross Chest press	90 lb. X 8-10 reps	140 lb. X 4-5 reps
❏ Pullover Compound row	110 lb. X 8-10 reps	150 lb. X 4-5 reps
❏ Lateral raise Overhead press	75 lb. X 8-10 reps	100 lb. X 4-5 reps
❏ Biceps curl Weight-assisted chin-up	65 lb. X 8-10 reps	40 lb. X 4-5 reps
❏ Triceps extension Weight-assisted bar dip	65 lb. X 8-10 reps	40 lb. X 4-5 reps

Table 6-17. Sample high-intensity strength training protocol using pre-exhaustion training for major muscle groups

Exercise	Resistance and repetitions	Lifting speed (seconds)	Lowering speed (seconds)
Leg extension	80 lb. X 4-6 reps	10	4
Seated leg curl	70 lb. X 4-6 reps	10	4
Leg press	175 lb. X 4-6 reps	10	4
Chest press	130 lb. X 4-6 reps	4	10
Lat pulldown	145 lb. X 4-6 reps	4	10
Overhead press	90 lb. X 4-6 reps	4	10
Biceps curl	55 lb. X 4-6 reps	4	10
Triceps extension	55 lb. X 4-6 reps	4	10
Abdominal curl	95 lb. X 4-6 reps	4	10
Low back extension	100 lb. X 4-6 reps	4	10

Table 6-18. Sample high-intensity strength training protocol using slow-positive training for lower-body exercises and slow-negative training for upper-body exercises

Comparison Between High-Intensity and Boot-Camp Training

All 34 previously trained participants improved their strength performance in the two assessment exercises (chin-ups and bar dips), even though neither group practiced these exercises during the period the study was held. The high-intensity trainees, however, attained significantly more improvement in their ability to perform chin-ups and bar dips, as well as a large increase in their performance on weight-stack exercises. Furthermore, psychological surveys completed before and after the five-week exercise programs showed no indications of burnout among the high-intensity trainees. Accordingly, it was concluded that the relative brief high-intensity strength training protocol is an effective and efficient alternative to the relative long-and-redundant boot-camp training procedures.

❏ Summary:

On reaching a point where they encounter a strength plateau, individuals may continue to attain muscle development by choosing new exercises, changing workout protocols, or increasing training intensity. The latter approach has produced excellent results for exercise enthusiasts at all levels of strength fitness.

High-intensity strength training typically involves extending the exercise set (as in breakdown, assisted, and pre-exhaustion procedures) or extending the exercise repetition (as in slow-speed training). In addition to being extremely effective, high-intensity strength training is also very time-efficient. Participants typically train only 30 minutes each session and perform just two workouts a week. While this type of high-effort exercise training produces a greater strength-building stimulus than standard training, it requires more time for muscle remodeling between training sessions.

References

1. Westcott WL. (1995). High-intensity strength training. *IDEA Personal Trainer.* 6: 7,9.
2. Westcott WL. (1997). Strength training 201. *Fitness Management.* 13(7): 33-35.
3. Westcott WL. (1998). High intensities improve body composition. *ACE Certified News.* 4(2): 1-3.
4. Westcott WL, Annesi J, D'Arpino T, Burak B. (2001). Boot camp vs. high-intensity training. *Fitness Management.* 17(7): 46-49.
5. Westcott WL, Winett R, Anderson E, et al. (2001). Effects of regular and slow speed resistance training on muscle strength. *J. Sports Med. Phys. Fit.* 41: 154-158.

CHAPTER 7:
Endurance Training Benefits and Guidelines

A number of individuals tend to avoid endurance exercise, often because they have had previous unpleasant experiences with long and laborious training sessions. Fortunately, individuals can achieve relatively high levels of cardiovascular fitness by participating in programs with reasonable training durations and a variety of interesting workout protocols, such as interval training, cross training, and fartlek training. Furthermore, different modes of exercise equipment can add pep to their endurance endeavors. Even if their workouts become relatively challenging, they will find that the results are well worth the time and effort that they expend.

Benefits of Endurance Exercise

Properly performed endurance training has a number of physiological benefits. Unfortunately, some fitness enthusiasts have done too much aerobic exercise and, as a result, have suffered the consequences of various overuse injuries. When individuals properly balance their endurance training programs, however, they should achieve an enhanced level of both aerobic fitness and enhanced cardiovascular health, as well as injury-free exercise experiences.

In reality, the best approach to endurance exercise is performing enough aerobic activity to promote cardiovascular benefits, but not so much to cause musculoskeletal overuse-related problems. The following well-documented reasons help clarify why endurance exercise is so important to a healthy lifestyle.

❑ Physical Capacity:
The most obvious outcome of regular endurance exercise is the ability to do more aerobic activity that is physically demanding for longer periods of time. In reality, individuals who are out of shape may find it difficult at first to complete even five minutes of relatively light aerobic activity. On the other hand, as a person gradually increases the activity demands that the body must handle, the individual's body makes positive physiological adaptations that enable that person to exercise at a faster pace for a longer duration. As such, achieving a greater capacity for walking, running, cycling, skating, rowing, and stepping can make endurance exercise a worthwhile endeavor.

❑ Cardiovascular Health:
Heart disease accounts for almost half of all deaths in the United States and a substantial percentage of deaths elsewhere. According to the Harvard Health Letter, many people are concerned about their cardiovascular health. One of the best ways to avoid cardiovascular illness is to develop and maintain a high level of aerobic fitness. Sedentary people have about twice the risk of heart disease as physically active people. In reality, inactivity increases a person's risk of heart disease just as much as high blood pressure, high blood cholesterol, or cigarette smoking. On the other hand, even if an individual has one or more of these risk factors, being in good physical condition can significantly reduce the risk of a heart attack, as depicted in Figure 7-1. Perhaps even more important, people in poor physical condition have more than three times the risk of death from heart disease and other causes as do individuals with high fitness levels.

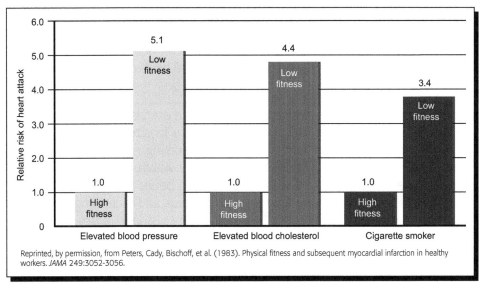

Figure 7-1

To improve their cardiovascular fitness, individuals need to perform at least 20 minutes of aerobic activity on two or three nonconsecutive days a week. All factors considered, such a time commitment it reasonable, given the concomitant opportunity to enjoy a more active lifestyle and to achieve an enhanced level of cardiovascular health.

❏ Cardiovascular Function:

A number of cardiovascular benefits result from engaging in regular endurance exercise. These positive physiological changes take place in the heart, the circulatory system, and the blood (see Table 7-1). Endurance exercise increases the heart's stroke volume, making the heart a stronger pump, i.e., it is able to pump more blood every time it beats. Endurance exercise also decreases the heart rate, i.e., it beats less frequently. A slower heart rate allows the heart to rest longer and to fill more completely with blood between beats.

❏ The heart becomes a stronger pump:
  • Stroke volume increases (heart pumps more blood each beat).
  • Heart rate decreases (heart beats less frequently).
  • Cardiac output increases (pumping capacity improves).
❏ The circulatory system becomes more efficient in function:
  • Size of blood vessels increases (more blood-carrying capacity).
  • Number of blood vessels increases (better blood distribution).
  • Tone of blood vessels increases (better blood control).
❏ The blood becomes a better transporter:
  • Blood volume increase (more transporting capacity).
  • Number and mass of red blood cells increase (more oxygen-carrying capacity).
  • Platelet stickiness decreases (reduced risk of blood clots).

Data from Fox, S.M., J.P. Naughton, and P.A. Gorman. 1972. Physical activity and cardiovascular health. *Modern Concepts of Cardiovascular Health* 41:20.

Table 7-1. Benefits of cardiovascular adaptations to regular endurance exercise

After several weeks of engaging in regular endurance exercise, an individual should experience a reduced resting heart rate. When the fact that an untrained heart beats about 75 times per minute and a trained heart beats about 55 times per minute is considered, the difference is almost 30,000 beats per day. In other words, the trained heart has a lot less wear and tear on the body's most important muscle.

The circulatory system responds to endurance exercise by becoming more efficient in blood delivery. Blood vessels increase in size, number, and tone. Larger blood vessels carry more blood to the working muscles, including the heart. More blood vessels distribute blood better within the working muscles, including the heart. Toned blood vessels respond better to the body's physical demands, reducing the blood flow to inactive areas and increasing blood flow to the working muscles, as needed. These circulatory system changes may reduce resting blood pressure, as well as enhance cardiovascular function.

Endurance exercise also changes a person's blood for the better. First, regular aerobic activity increases blood volume, expanding its transporting capacity. Second, it expands the number and size of the red blood cells, enhancing the blood's oxygen-carrying capacity. Third, endurance exercise decreases stickiness among blood platelets, reducing the risk of blood clots.

Although a number of other cardiovascular improvements can result from aerobic activity, learning about these key benefits should hopefully motivate people to engage in endurance training. Exercise that makes the heart a stronger pump, the circulatory system more efficient, and the blood a better transporter is certainly worth the time and effort.

Health Benefits

Statistics indicate that everyone is at risk when it comes to cardiovascular disease. Arguably, then, everyone should make some degree of effort to improve their chances of experiencing good health and achieving long life. The most significant coronary risk factors include high blood pressure, high blood cholesterol, cigarette smoking, obesity, glucose intolerance, and psychological stress. Fortunately, regular endurance exercise may help in all of these areas.

❏ High Blood Pressure:
Regular endurance exercise effectively reduces both systolic and diastolic blood pressure. This factor is true for endurance exercise alone, as well as in combination with strength training.

❏ High Blood Cholesterol:
Elevated blood cholesterol levels may be lowered by regular endurance training. More importantly, endurance exercise has consistently resulted in better ratios of good cholesterol (HDL) to bad cholesterol (LDL), which, in turn, will lead to more desirable lipid profiles.

❏ Smoking:
Although aerobic activity does not automatically cause a person to stop smoking, it may influence their smoking behavior. At least one study has demonstrated

that people who exercise are less likely to smoke than those who don't exercise. Smoking and endurance activity are certainly incompatible behaviors, especially if a person exercises regularly.

❏ Obesity:

More than one-third of adult Americans are classified as overweight, while another one third are classified as obese. In addition to being a cardiovascular risk factor itself, obesity is closely associated with other related-health problems, such as diabetes. Although dieting can reduce body fat, it also has the undesirable effect of decreasing the level of lean tissue. In fact, several studies document the fact that the most desirable fat loss and body composition changes result when dieting is combined with exercise.

As discussed previously, the optimal body composition results can be achieved by performing both strength and endurance exercise, an outcome confirmed by a study conducted by Westcott in 1993. In Westcott's research, after eight weeks of strength and endurance training, more than 300 of the adult exercise program participants averaged three pounds more muscle and 8.5 pounds less fat, for an 11.5-pound improvement in body composition. Without a doubt, the fact that regular endurance exercise burns a relatively high level of calories and can play a significant role in reducing body fat.

❏ Glucose Intolerance:

Glucose intolerance is associated with insulin resistance in the tissues of the body, a situation that may lead to type 2 diabetes and heart disease. Fortunately, type 2 diabetes responds favorably to endurance training. Exercise sessions appear to decrease insulin resistance and increase glucose utilization, which collectively lessen the risk of glucose intolerance problems.

❏ Psychological Stress:

Psychological stress has been determined to be a contributing factor to cardiovascular risk. Although research has not definitively proven the positive effects of endurance exercise on psychological stress, most physiologists, psychologists, and fitness enthusiasts agree that physical activity is often influential in reducing the tensions created by daily living.

Lifestyle Benefits

Individuals should notice some important lifestyle benefits from regular aerobic activity, including improved sleep, digestion, and elimination. In addition, people who engage in endurance training often report higher levels of energy, not only for performing their exercise sessions, but also for doing other physical activities of daily living, such as gardening, golf, tennis, cycling, and skiing.

Because the heart functions as the fuel pump for the body, a well-conditioned cardiovascular system enhances the energy supply to the muscles. This factor helps the muscles work better and longer, with less effort and faster recovery. When a person combines strength and endurance exercise, the improvements in both muscular and cardiovascular fitness make a remarkable difference in an individual's level of physical capacity. Arguably, a person may wonder how they were able to function adequately before they became fit.

Endurance Training Options

A number of training activities are available for possible inclusion in a workout program. The most popular indoor endurance exercises include treadmill walking and jogging, stationary cycling, stepping, and rowing. Outside the workout room, running, bicycling, swimming, hiking, and kayaking are among the favorite endurance activities.

In addition to a variety of exercise activities, an individual can choose from four different endurance training methods. The first and most common exercise procedure is steady pace training. The second and most productive exercise procedure is interval training. The third and most comprehensive exercise practice is cross-training. The fourth and most individualized exercise procedure is known as fartlek training.

❏ Steady Pace Training:

Most people prefer steady pace training as a possible training method, because it involves a consistent and comfortable exercise effort. For instance, a person may find it relatively convenient to walk at a specific speed, such as 3.5 miles per hour. This approach facilitates a steady heart rate response at a given training level for safe and effective endurance exercise sessions. Walking at this pace may (or may not) raise an individual's heart rate to the appropriate range for cardiovascular conditioning. As the person becomes more fit, however, they may need to increase their pace to four miles per hour to produce the same training effect.

Steady pace training should not be either too easy or too difficult. It should be vigorous enough to stimulate the cardiovascular system, but not so strenuous that it is uncomfortable or unpleasant. As a rule, if an individual is able to converse in relatively short sentences during steady pace training, they are probably exercising at the appropriate (i.e., moderate) effort level.

❏ Interval Training:

Interval training divides an endurance exercise session into harder and easier segments. For example, a person may be able to pedal a recumbent cycle at 75 watts for 30 minutes, but would like to improve to 100 watts for 30 minutes. One option for that individual would be to alternate harder and easier three-minute segments for the entire 30-minute training period. For example, that person's training session could begin by performing three minutes at 50 watts (lower-effort interval), followed by three minutes at 100 watts (higher-effort interval)—an interval training protocol that would be continued for the entire 30-minute exercise session.

Although an individual's total exercise time is the same, the effort put into the workout and the benefits gained will be greater in the interval training session. This situation occurs because the higher-effort at 100-watt segments place greater demands on the body's cardiovascular system, while the lower effort 50-watt segments provide recovery, enabling a person to maintain a desirable overall heart rate response throughout the entire workout. As such, interval training provides better cardiovascular conditioning, while preparing the body to perform at higher levels of exercise intensity.

Another physiological advantage of interval training is that it provides more than one cardiovascular stimulus per training session. Each high-effort training interval has a positive impact on the stroke volume of the heart, a factor that helps develop a greater blood pumping capacity for enhanced aerobic fitness.

A psychological advantage of interval training is related to the harder-than-normal training level. Although the high-effort segments may be relatively brief, doing them demonstrates greater performance potential, making the usual training level seem considerably less demanding by comparison.

The concept of interval training is fairly simple. This type of protocol, however, provides several options that can be employed to personalize each exercise session. As such, a number of interval training variations are possible, as an individual progresses to higher levels of cardiovascular fitness, including:

- Increase the exercise effort required during the harder intervals.
- Increase the exercise effort required during the easier intervals.
- Increase the duration of the harder intervals.
- Decrease the duration of the easier intervals.
- Increase the number of hard and easy intervals that can be completed during a training session.

❏ Cross-Training:

Cross-training is another way to incorporate endurance exercise into a person's workout regimen. While interval training alternates harder and easier segments of the same exercise, cross-training combines two or more endurance exercise activities. For example, a 30-minute cross-training session may include 10 minutes of jogging, 10 minutes of cycling, and 10 minutes of rowing. An individual may do cross-training exercise at a moderate pace or use higher- and lower-effort intervals throughout the workout. As such, a number of endurance athletes cross-train during their off-season to maintain their cardiovascular fitness and avoid overuse injuries.

The advantages of cross-training are twofold. Psychologically, by frequently changing the exercises, a person is less likely to experience boredom during the training sessions. Physiologically, the cardiovascular system receives a training stimulus throughout the entire exercise session, just as long as the individual performs each activity with at least a moderate level of effort. Furthermore, by using different muscle groups in different activities, the general conditioning effect is increased and the risk of overuse injuries is decreased. For example, jogging emphasizes the hamstring muscles, cycling engages the quadriceps muscles, and rowing utilizes both the lower-body and the upper-body muscles.

If an individual prefers to spend an entire exercise session on a single activity, they can apply cross-training on a week-by-week basis. For example, an individual may perform 30 minutes of jogging on Monday, 30 minutes of cycling on Wednesday, and 30 minutes of rowing on Friday. Once again, by including three types of endurance exercise, the exerciser alternates the use of different muscle groups, thereby reducing the risk of overuse injuries. The benefits to the cardiovascular system are similar for each aerobic activity as long as the individual adheres to the basic training principles attendant to engaging in endurance exercise.

❑ Fartlek Training:

Fartlek is a Swedish term that means speed play. Fartlek training involves an exercise program with periods of faster-paced activity that are interspersed with periods of slower-paced activity. In contrast to interval training, however, fartlek exercise is more impulsive, or playful, in nature. As such, whenever an exerciser feels like picking up the pace, they do so, for as long as they desire. For example, the individual may row at a moderate pace for a few minutes, then row very fast for several seconds, and then row easily for a couple of minutes before again rowing at a powerful pace. A person does not time the various segments of their training session, but simply exercises as they feel throughout their entire workout, without any attempt at regimentation.

Cardiovascular Training Design

Although endurance exercise can provide a number of physical benefits, an individual must train within certain parameters to maximize cardiovascular conditioning. Because the effectiveness of endurance exercise methods varies considerably, training principles developed and advocated by the American College of Sports Medicine are recommended. These widely adopted exercise guidelines provide a solid framework for enhancing endurance fitness safely and productively. All factors considered, for maximum cardiovascular benefit, a person should engage in a variety of aerobic activities that utilize large muscle groups, can be maintained continuously, and are rhythmic in nature.

❑ Exercise Selection and Order:

In reality, a number of aerobic activities meet the criteria of continuous large muscle, including walking, jogging, running, cycling, cross-country skiing, aerobic dancing, rope skipping, rowing, stepping, swimming, in-line skating, and endurance sports, such as soccer and basketball.

Most people partake in one endurance activity at a time during a particular activity period, such as a five-mile run or a 15-mile bicycle ride. Arguably, however, given the relatively high rate of overuse injuries, single-exercise endurance training is not recommended. All factors considered, cross-training, with two or more aerobic activities, is a better alternative, because it provides more comprehensive conditioning, has a lower risk of overuse injuries, and tends to be more engaging. As previously noted, common cross-training exercises include cycling, running, stepping, and rowing, as well as other combinations of endurance activities that complement each other.

An individual should not worry about a specific order for performing cross-training activities. Except for triathletes, who swim first, cycle second, and run third, the exercise order is a matter of personal preference. Each aerobic activity produces about the same benefits for a person's cardiovascular system, but utilizes different muscle groups. For example, swimming emphasizes the upper-body muscles, and cycling and running work the leg muscles, while rowing targets both the upper-body and lower-body muscle groups.

Although outdoor activities, such as walking and cycling, are attractive options, they may not be the best choices for everyone. Safe outdoor walking or cycling requires sidewalks, bike paths, or roads with minimal traffic to avoid accidents. Weather and surface conditions, such as rain, snow, or ice, can interfere with your outdoor exercise program. For a variety of exercise- control factors, beginners who are overweight or otherwise out of shape often will find well-designed endurance equipment more appropriate. Such equipment not only provides structural stability and training consistency, it also offers precise exercise conditions that can be repeated or changed progressively each workout.

If an individual is unfit, for a number of reasons, recumbent cycling is one of the best activities that they can select to initiate their endurance training program (see Figure 7-2). First, the recumbent cycle supports the exerciser's back and body weight, eliminating weight-bearing forces that could overstress weak muscles and joints. Second, the recumbent cycle places the body in a more horizontal position, which enhances blood circulation and cardiovascular function. Third, the recumbent cycle provides electronic resistance that can be adjusted to any fitness level, rather than involving bodyweight resistance (e.g., running or stepping), which may be too much for a person's present level of physical conditioning.

Jupiterimages/Stockbyte/Thinkstock

Figure 7-2

From working out on a recumbent cycle, an individual can then progress to upright cycling, which is similar to recumbent cycling, except for the body position (see Figure 7-3). Upright cycling requires greater postural control and a little more cardiovascular effort. It also provides electronic resistance that can be precisely and progressively increased as the individual's fitness level improves.

Figure 7-3

The next recommended endurance training activity is treadmill walking (see Figure 7-4). This mode of exercise is one of the most natural and least stressful weight-bearing exercises available. Because walking is mostly a horizontal movement, exercising on a treadmill at an appropriate pace is not too demanding on the muscular or cardiovascular systems of the body. Exercisers also have several options for increasing the intensity level while working out on the treadmill, for example, raising the treadmill, walking faster, or progressing to jogging as their aerobic condition improves.

Figure 7-4

Stepping (see Figure 7-5) is more demanding than cycling and walking, because its vertical movement pattern lifts your body weight directly against the force of gravity with every step you take. All factors considered, an individual should develop at least a moderate level of cardiovascular conditioning before they add stepping to their exercise regimen.

Figure 7-5

Perhaps the most comprehensive and challenging piece of endurance equipment is the rowing machine (see Figure 7-6). Rowing requires sequential activation of the leg, lower back, upper back, and arm muscles in a coordinated and controlled movement pattern. Although an exerciser's bodyweight is supported, rowing is a more advanced form of aerobic activity, one that is better suited to well-conditioned individuals.

Figure 7-6

It should be noted that individuals can perform the activity they choose at various effort levels. For example, they may do a low-effort walk on a flat treadmill or a high-effort run on an inclined treadmill. Obviously, they can train longer at a slower pace than they can at a faster pace. The point to remember is that the keys to achieving cardiovascular fitness are adhering to the basic endurance training principles and exercising the large muscle groups in continuous and rhythmic movement patterns.

❏ Exercise Frequency:

Although endurance exercise affects the muscular system of the body, its primary purpose is cardiovascular conditioning. In order to improve their cardiovascular fitness, an individual should perform at least two aerobic workouts a week. In fact, three weekly training sessions are recommended. It is important to remember, however, that more is not necessarily better. As such, three sessions a week produces almost the same health-related results as five weekly workouts. This factor can be encouraging news for busy people. It is also important to note that training more than three to five days a week increases a person's risk of injury without adding cardiovascular benefits.

❏ Exercise Duration:

Short bursts of exercise can enhance muscular strength, while longer periods of continuous activity are necessary to improve cardiovascular endurance. For example, each set of strength exercise requires about one minute, but a productive session of endurance activity should take between 20 and 60 minutes.

Strength training is relatively high-intensity, low-duration exercise, whereas endurance training is relatively low-intensity, high-duration exercise. Within certain limits, endurance exercise may also vary considerably in intensity and duration. For example, 30 minutes of running at 12 calories per minute and 60 minutes of walking at six calories per minute are different aerobic activities that require approximately the same amount of energy. When the total work an individual does is about equal, shorter sessions of faster-paced endurance e exercise and longer sessions of slower-paced endurance exercise will provide similar improvements in cardiovascular fitness.

In general, individuals should begin with slower-paced aerobic activities that are well within their fitness ability and that place less stress on their body. As such, they should start with just a few minutes of endurance exercise and gradually increase the duration of the activity in subsequent bouts of training. At some point in their training progression, the exercise pace may seem too easy, and the exercise duration may seem too long. When this situation occurs, they should gradually increase the exercise pace and decrease the exercise duration, until they reach a point where their training session is more satisfying. Soon, they'll be doing the same amount of work in much less time.

Although the duration of a workout is largely a matter of personal preference, it is important, according to the ACSM guidelines, to stay within the range of 20 to 60 minutes. Doing less than 20 minutes of aerobic activity may decrease the cardiovascular benefits of the training, while completing more than 60 minutes of endurance exercise may increase the risk of overuse injuries.

People who perform 20 to 30 minutes of aerobic activity are more likely to stay with their training programs, than those individuals who attempt to do 50- to 60-minute sessions. Furthermore, given time-pressured society, long training sessions seem more difficult to maintain on a regular basis. Many people find that 20 to 30 minutes of strength training combined with 20 to 30 minutes of endurance training creates a practical and productive program for improving overall physical fitness.

❏   Exercise Intensity:

Exercise intensity is the relative effort level at which a person performs aerobic activity. A simple means of rating exercise intensity is referred to as the "talk test." If an individual can talk normally while working out, their exercise effort is most likely relatively low. If, on the other hand, they are able to speak only in short sentences, their level of training effort is most likely moderate. If, on the other hand, they are not capable of carrying on a conversation at all, their exercise effort is definitely high.

Although the talk test provides a reasonable estimate of training intensity, it is clearly subjective in nature. For example, some people may rate a moderate effort as light, while others may consider a moderate effort to be heavy. For this reason, a person should employ a more objective method of determining their exercise effort, at least until they become familiar with the rating relationships involved in the talk test.

Because heart rate is closely related to training effort, heart rate monitoring is a more precise means of assessing an individual's level of exercise intensity. As a rule of thumb, a person's maximum heart rate can be estimated by subtracting their age from 220. For example, if an individual is 40 years old, their predicted maximum heart rate is about 180 beats per minute. In turn, if a person is 50 years old, their predicted maximum heart rate is about 170 beats per minute. As can be seen, a person's maximum heart rate decreases by approximately one beat per year throughout adult life. It should be noted that this situation is a normal part of the aging process and does not limit an individual's ability to achieve a high level of aerobic fitness. Table 7-2 lists predicted maximum heart rates for men and women between 20 and 90 years of age.

Maximum heart rate corresponds to an all-out exercise effort in which the heart is pumping as much oxygen-rich blood as possible to the working muscles. It is also important to note that a person can only train at maximum physical capacity for a very short time, and such intense exercise is not appropriate for cardiovascular conditioning. In general, an individual should train at about 70 percent of their maximum heart rate, although beginning exercisers may start at a lower level, e.g., around 60 percent. On the other hand, participants who are extremely fit may want to exercise at about 80 percent of their maximum heart rate.

Table 7-2 provides a list of appropriate age-related exercise heart rates. It is important to keep in mind that individuals should periodically monitor their heart rate during their training sessions to make sure that they are exercising within their target training zone.

Because it can be difficult for individuals to feel their pulse when they are exercising, they need to adopt a method of monitoring their heart rate that is both practical and viable. One realistic option is for them to simply pause for 10 seconds every 10 minutes during a workout. Then, they should place their fingers on one of their wrists and keep their eyes on the clock as they count every heartbeat for 10 seconds (Figure 7-7). Next, they should multiply the resultant pulse count by six to determine their training heart rate in beats per minute. For example, if they count 20 beats in 10 seconds, their exercise heart rate is about 120 beats per minute. It is also important to note that when exercising, if individuals take their pulse for more than 10 seconds, their heart rate may slow down so much that they will underestimate their actual training heart rate.

Age	60%	70%	80%	100%
20	120	140	160	200
25	117	136	156	195
30	114	133	152	190
35	111	129	148	185
40	108	126	144	180
45	105	122	140	175
50	102	119	136	170
55	99	115	132	165
60	96	112	128	160
65	93	108	124	155
70	90	105	120	150
75	87	101	116	145
80	84	98	112	140
85	81	94	108	135
90	78	91	104	130

Table 7-2. Predicted maximum age-related heart rates and selected percentages for training

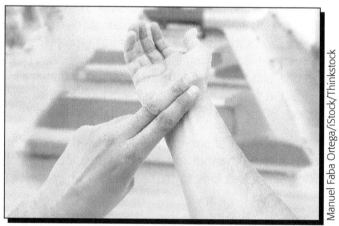

Manuel Faba Ortega/iStock/Thinkstock

Figure 7-7

As a person gains experience monitoring their exercise heart rate, they will correlate their heart rate response with their talking ability. In other words, over time, a person will develop the ability to closely estimate their exercise heart rate, based on their subjective assessment of the training effort. Nonetheless, an individual should periodically check their pulse during exercise, because factors other than activity level may affect their heart rate. For example, high heat or humidity, psychological stress, and physical illness make the heart work harder than usual at a given exercise pace.

As a person becomes more fit, that individual may decide to increase their exercise intensity and train at higher effort levels. The key, in that instance, is to be sure to avoid overtraining and risking overuse injuries. Unless the person is a competitive endurance athlete, they need not exercise harder than 80 percent of their maximum heart rate, because they do not achieve additional cardiovascular health benefits by training at higher heart rate levels. After an individual surpasses the beginning exercise level, they should typically train between 70 to 80 percent of their maximum heart rate for most practical purposes.

Warm-Ups and Cool-Downs

The main purpose of warm-ups and cool-downs is to provide a gradual progression from a condition of rest to a condition of expending a comparatively high level of physical effort and producing a relatively high level of energy. While children typically jump right into vigorous activity and stop suddenly without any apparent difficulties, a similar situation is not generally the case for adults and older adults. Their physical performance is enhanced, and their risk of injury is reduced, when they sandwich their training activity between progressive warm-ups and cool-downs.

Warm-ups may include a variety of calisthenics exercises, such as trunk curls, push-ups, and knee bends, as well as dynamic stretches, such as arm circles, knee lifts, and trunk twists. The major focus of the warm-up, however, should be on performing the same activity as the training exercise, beginning at a low intensity and gradually progressing to a moderate level of intensity. For example, if the workout is running interval quarter-miles, an appropriate warm-up would begin with easy jogging, progressing to easy running, then to moderate-effort striding, before proceeding to the higher-intensity quarter-mile intervals. In general, the higher the workout intensity, the longer the warm-up should be. Accordingly, five minutes of progressive warm-up activity may be sufficient prior to undertaking a three-mile training run, whereas 10 minutes of progressive warm-up activity may be advisable prior to doing quarter-mile intervals.

Cool-downs are essentially warm-ups in reverse. Rather than transitioning from rest to activity, cool-downs provide a gradual reduction from high physical effort and high energy production to a lower level of muscular and cardiovascular function. Cool-downs are especially essential for older adults and post-coronary patients, because suddenly stopping vigorous activity may result in reduced blood return to the heart, with accompanying cardiac stress and lightheadedness/fainting.

Basically, the cool-down should be characterized by progressive reductions in the training intensity, such as slowing from a fast running pace to a moderate running pace, followed by jogging and walking. After returning close to resting level (within 10 to 20 beats of normal resting heart rate), the muscles should still be warm from the prior activity session. This occasion is an excellent time to perform a few static stretching exercises that can enhance joint flexibility. As such, the static stretches should further reduce metabolism so that the body feels loose and relaxed, rather than tight and tense. Depending on the intensity and duration of the training session, as well as personal preferences, the cool-down period may be completed within 5 to 10 minutes.

Stretching

While most individuals agree that stretching exercises are useful for enhancing joint flexibility and overall physical fitness, they do not always find time for this essential part of their exercise program. If an individual does about 30 minutes of strength training and 30 minutes of endurance exercise each training session, there is often little room for adding stretching to their one-hour workout.

Although properly performed strength training alone improves joint flexibility, a person should still do stretching exercises. The key muscle-joint structures that should be addressed in a stretching program include the following:

- Calf muscles, which cross the ankle and knee joints
- Hamstring muscles, which cross the knee and hip joints
- Low-back muscles, which lie on both sides of the vertebral column
- Rotator cuff muscles, which surround the shoulder joints

Although some of these muscles are large and others are small, the basic stretching procedure is about the same. As such, a person should gradually stretch the target muscles until they feel comfortably lengthened, and then hold that position for at least 20 seconds. This gentle approach reduces the risk of overstretching and maintains the stretched position long enough to produce positive muscle adaptations. If an individual has the time, it may help to perform each stretch twice.

Another time-saving alternative is to stretch the muscles just worked immediately after each strength exercise. Research has shown almost 20 percent greater strength gains occur when a person combines their strength exercises and stretching. For example, the leg extension exercise may be followed by a 20-second stretch for the quadriceps muscles, the seated leg curl exercise may be followed by a 20-second stretch for the hamstring muscles, and so on.

❏ "Big Four" Stretches:

Although an individual may include additional exercises in their workout regimen if they'd like, the following "big four" recommended stretches are ideal for developing overall flexibility. When performed properly, these four stretches should enhance flexibility in the major muscle-joint structures of the body:

- Step stretch
- Figure-4 stretch
- Letter-T stretch
- Doorway stretch

Step Stretch

The step stretch targets the calf muscles in the lower leg. Because these muscles cross both the knee and ankle joints, the individual should keep their knee straight as they perform this exercise. The exerciser should stand with their right foot fully on the step and their left foot half on and half off the step. The person should place one hand on a handrail or a wall for balance. Then, the individual should gently shift their weight to their left foot and allow their left heel to slowly drop downward. As soon as their left calf muscles feel comfortably stretched, the exerciser should hold the position for at least 20 seconds. At that point, the individual should change foot positions and repeat the same procedure for their right calf muscles (see Figure 7-8).

Figure 7-8

Figure-4 Stretch

The figure-4 stretch resembles the number after which it is named. Although it actually addresses several muscles, the exerciser should feel the greatest stretch in the hamstrings at the back of the thighs (see Figure 7-9). The person should begin the stretch by sitting on the floor with their left leg straight and their right leg bent at the knee, so that their right foot touches their left thigh. At that point, the individual should slowly reach their left hand toward their left foot until their hamstrings feel comfortably stretched. Next, the person should grasp their foot, ankle, or lower leg and hold the stretched position for at least 20 seconds. The exerciser should then change leg positions and repeat the same procedure for the right hamstrings. As such, the individual should also feel some stretching effects in their calf, hip, lower back, and shoulder muscles as they do the figure-4 stretch.

Figure 7-9

Letter-T Stretch

As might be imagined, this stretch resembles the letter T. It is designed to stretch the lower back and hip muscles from a fully supported position (see Figure 7-10). To do the stretch, the exerciser should start by lying face-up on the floor, with their arms straight out to the sides in a T-position. At that point, the individual should slowly lift their left leg upward, and then cross it over so that their left foot is near their right hand. This stretched position should be held comfortably for at least 20 seconds. Finally, the exerciser should return to the starting position and repeat the same procedure with their right leg. As they carefully cross their leg over their body, the individual should do their best to keep the other leg straight.

Figure 7-10

Doorway Stretch

This two-part stretching exercise targets some of the rotator cuff muscles in the shoulder. Before beginning the doorway stretch, an exerciser may want to do some very slow arm circles to loosen up their shoulder joints. The first phase of the doorway stretch begins by standing in a doorway with the right arm across the body, grasping the left doorframe at about shoulder level (see Figure 7-11). The individual then gently turns their body to the right until their rear shoulder muscles feel comfortably stretched. This position should then be held for at least 20 seconds. The second phase of the doorway stretch is initiated by grasping the right doorframe with the right arm at about shoulder level. The exerciser should then gently turn their body to the left until the front shoulder muscles feel comfortably stretched. As before, this position should be held for a minimum of 20 seconds. Both stretches should be repeated with the left arm.

Figure 7-11

It should be noted that slow and controlled stretching is critical for safety and success. A lack of muscle tension and a relaxed sensation should characterize the stretching process. Against the urge to do otherwise, exercisers should always avoid trying too hard and stretching into the discomfort zone. The "big four" stretching sequence is an ideal way to conclude an individual's exercise sessions. The key for exercisers is to leave feeling invigorated, rather than exhausted.

❑ Summary:

Although individuals should not overdo endurance exercise, engaging in an appropriate amount of aerobic activity can provide many physiological benefits. Regular endurance exercise improves physical function, aerobic capacity, and cardiovascular health. Because the heart serves as the fuel pump for the body, a well-conditioned cardiovascular system enables the muscles to work better and longer, with less effort and faster recovery.

The key is for participants to adhere to the general principles of endurance exercise when they select their workout activities or determine their level of training frequency, duration, and intensity. To best condition the cardiovascular system, exercisers should be sure to choose aerobic activities that use the large muscle groups of the body, can be maintained for at least 20 minutes, and are rhythmic in nature. Cycling, walking, jogging, stepping, and rowing are all appropriate endurance training activities. As such, individuals should be sure to incorporate them into their exercise regimen in order of their physical demands.

As a rule, a person can safely train up to an hour, three to five days a week, although 20- to 30-minute segments are a more practical approach for most individuals. In general, endurance exercise should involve a moderate level of physical effort.

It is important to perform 5 to 10 minutes of warm-up and cool-down activity before and after endurance exercise workouts in order to safely and effectively transition the body between resting and exercising states. It is also recommended to perform a few static stretching exercises during the cool-down period to enhance joint flexibility, as well as to conclude the training session feeling loose and relaxed.

References

1. American College of Sports Medicine. (2013). *Guidelines for exercise testing and prescription*, 9th ed. Philadelphia: Lippincott, Williams and Wilkins.
2. Blaire SN, Kohl III HW, Paffenbarger Jr DG, et al. (1989). Physical fitness and all-case mortality: A prospective study of healthy men and women. *JAMA*. 262: 2395-2401.
3. Caspersen, CJ. (1987). Physical inactivity and coronary heart disease. *Phys Sportsmed*. 15:43-44.
4. Fox, SM, Naughton JP, Gorman PA. (1972). Physical activity and cardiovascular health. *Modern Conc. Cardio. Health*. 41:20.
5. Goldberg L, Elliot DL. (1985). The effect of physical activity on lipid and lipoprotein levels. Med. *Clinics N. Amer*. 69:41-55.
6. Harris KA, Holly RG. (1987). Physiological response to circuit weight training in borderline hypertensive subjects. *Med. Sci. Sports Exerc*. 19: 246-252.
7. Harvard Heart Letter. (1995). Data debunk myths about heart disease. 5 (June): 1-3.
8. Hedley AA, Ogden CL, Johnson CL, et al. (2004). Obesity among U.S. children, adolescents, and adults. (1999-2002). *JAMA*. 291:2847-2850.
9. Peters RK, Cady LD Jr., Bischoff DP, et al. (1983). Physical fitness and subsequent myocardial infarction in healthy workers. *JAMA*. 249:3052-3056.
10. Porcari JP. (1994). Fat-burning exercise: Fit or farce. *Fit. Manage*. 10:40-41.
11. Pollock ML, Gettman LR, Milesis MD, et al. (1977). Effects of frequency and duration of training on attrition and incidence of injury. *Med. Sci. Sports. Exerc*. 9:31-36.
12. Pomerleau O, Scherzer H, Grunberg N, et al. (1987). The effects of acute exercise on subsequent cigarette smoking. *J Behav. Med*. 10:117-127.
13. Powell KE, Thompson PD, Caspersen CJ, et al. (1987). Physical activity and the incidence of coronary heart disease. *Ann. Rev. Pub. Health*. 8:253-287.
14. Rippe JM. (1992). The exercise exchange program. New York: Simon & Schuster.
15. Seals DR, Hagberg JM. (1984). The effect of exercise training on human hypertension: A review. *Med. Sci. Sports Exerc*. 16:207-215.
16. Sharkey BJ. (1990). *Physiology of fitness*. 3d ed. Champaign, IL: Human Kinetics.
17. Westcott WL. (1993). Strength training and blood pressure response. *Nautilus*. 2 (Fall):8-9.
18. Westcott WL. (1993). Weight gain and weight loss. *Nautilus*. 3 (Winter):8-9.
19. Westcott WL, LaRosa Loud R. (2000). Stretching for strength. *Fitness Management*. 16 (7):44-46.
20. Wilmore JH, Costill DL. (1994). Physiology of sport and exercise. Champaign, IL: *Human Kinetics*.
21. Zuti WB, Golding L. (1976). Comparing diet and exercise as weight reduction tools. *Phys. Sportmed*. 4:59-62.

CHAPTER 8
Endurance Training Equipment and Exercise Performance

Properly performing endurance exercise involves more than just getting on a piece of aerobic equipment and working out as hard as a person can for as long as they can. As with strength training, an individual should be fully familiar with each machine's features and requirements before beginning their exercise program.

The fitness industry offers many types of endurance exercise equipment. Furthermore, within each category, there are many variations in design, function, and performance. This chapter presents the proper procedures for using four of the most popular endurance training machines—upright and recumbent cycles, treadmills, steppers, and rowers. Regardless, however, of what piece of endurance exercise equipment is used, it is essential that participants closely adhere to the general guidelines for safe and successful endurance training.

General Training Guidelines

No single method of using an exercise cycle, treadmill, stepper, or rowing machine exists. As noted previously, a number of general guidelines for safe and productive training apply to all types of endurance training equipment.

For example, individuals should check with their personal physician before beginning a cardiovascular exercise regimen. Participants may also want to consult with a certified personal trainer professional exercise instructor if they exercise at a fitness facility or with a health/fitness professional if they work out at home.

It is important that individuals dress appropriately for exercise. Doing so will not only enhance their level of performance, it will also reduce their risk of suffering an injury. First and foremost, wearing proper footwear is essential, especially for weight-bearing activities, such as walking, jogging, and stepping. As such, exercisers should wear supportive, well-cushioned athletic shoes that fit loosely around the toes and snugly around the heels.

Because exercise produces heat, a person's clothing should allow heat transfer from the body to the environment. Ordinarily, an individual should wear light athletic clothing, such as a t-shirt and shorts. On the other hand, if the person tends to feel cool in the first few minutes of exercise, that individual should wear an athletic suit or sweatshirt that they can easily remove as they warm up and begin to perspire. Participants should be careful not to overdress, because doing so can prevent perspiration from evaporating. When a person is exercising vigorously, the evaporation of perspiration from the skin is absolutely critical for releasing body heat.

It is also important for an individual to stay well hydrated throughout the exercise session. As such, an exerciser should drink plenty of fluids—preferably water—before each workout. To replace water while exercising, exercisers should frequently drink water, that is, hopefully, conveniently available. Because participants tend to lose more water than they typically consume during exercise, they need to be sure to continue consuming fluids after their workout. Fruit juices and sports drinks can be substituted for water. As a rule, exercisers should drink between six and eight glasses of fluids each day.

Individuals should be sure to begin each endurance training session with a progressive warm-up, work at a moderate effort level of intensity, train for a reasonable duration, stay within their target heart rate zone, and end with a gradual cool-down. It is also crucial that exercisers train on a regular basis, three or more days a week, unless they are ill or injured.

Monitoring their training progress can be an excellent motivator for individuals. As such, it is highly recommended that exercisers record the results of each of their exercise sessions in a training logbook. For each training bout, they should keep track of their exercise activity, intensity level, training duration, exercise heart rate, and other pertinent information. Periodically, they should review their logbook whenever it may be appropriate, for example, when they need an extra boost of exercise enthusiasm. In those situations, when they see how much they have improved, they'll realize how much their training investment has paid off. The logbook also provides valuable information to guide a person as the individual plans progressively more difficult workouts.

Endurance Training Machines and Procedures

Essentially, all types of aerobic activity can be effective for enhancing cardiovascular fitness and heart health. All aerobic exercise equipment, however, is not the same. Different endurance exercise equipment addresses different muscle groups, requires different physical performance, and elicits different physiological and psychological responses.

❏ Upright and Recumbent Cycles:
The most obvious difference between the more traditional upright cycle and the more recent recumbent cycle is body position. Upright cycles require a vertical posture. In contrast, recumbent cycles require a more horizontal exercise position. One advantage of the recumbent cycle is the level of back and neck support provided. Another benefit of the horizontal position is enhanced blood flow from the legs back to the heart. At the same effort level, the heart rate stays slightly lower during recumbent cycling than during upright cycling. Both recumbent and upright cycling stress the quadriceps and the hamstrings by placing fairly equal emphasis on knee extension and hip extension. Upright cycles, with moving handles, add an upper-body aspect to each exercise session.

Well-designed exercise cycles offer a wide range of training levels to accommodate various fitness abilities. They also provide several exercise program options, ranging from steady-pace training to interval training. Whatever protocol is selected, exercisers should remember that each training session should begin with a progressive warm-up and finish with a gradual cool-down.

The following steps should be adhered to when using upright or recumbent cycles:
• Adjust the seat so that the knees are slightly bent when the feet are in the extended pedal positions (see Figures 8-1a and 8-1b). Slide each foot as far into the pedal strap as is comfortable, with the ball of the foot over the pedal pivot point. Make sure that the hips are fully supported by the seat. If using a recumbent cycle, place the hands across the lap or on the side handles, and rest the back comfortably against the seat back.

- Turn on the exercise monitor and select an appropriate training profile. Some people may prefer a program with a progressive warm-up, a gradual cool-down, and a constant training level in between. Other individuals may prefer an interval training program that alternates periods of lower-effort and higher-effort cycling (e.g., 30 seconds low and 30 seconds high).

- Adjust the effort level to the exerciser's current fitness ability. On 9-level machines, the first three tiers are recommended for beginners; the next three for intermediate exercisers; and the final three for advanced participants.

- Adjust the exercise time according to the individual's fitness level. If the exerciser is a beginner, they should stay in the range of 10 minutes. If the individual considers themselves moderately fit, they should exercise for 10 to 20 minutes. If they're in pretty good shape, they should train for 20 to 30 minutes. For whatever reason, some competitive athletes may wish to exercise longer. On the other hand, if their primary purpose is cardiovascular fitness, they don't need to cycle more than 30 minutes per session.

- Keep the pedaling speed at approximately 20 miles per hour, or about 80 pedal revolutions per minute. If the bike has a pacer, participants should do their best to stay with the pacer throughout the exercise program.

Figure 8-1a

Figure 8-1b

After completing the course, exercisers should be sure to cool down with a slower, but still continuous, pedaling action, and then walk around to conclude the cool-down.

Motor-Driven Treadmills

There are two basic types of treadmills—those that are self-propelled and those that are motor-driven. Although considerably more expensive, motor-driven treadmills are clearly superior in design, function, and durability. Good motor-driven treadmills have enough horsepower to maintain the desired speed and to keep the track from slipping. The track should be strong and stable to maximize exercise performance, yet cushioned and resilient to minimize stress on the feet, legs, and lower back. Sturdy handrails and convenient control buttons are a must for training safety.

The two major program variables in treadmill training are speed and inclination. Well-designed treadmills provide walking and running speeds between 2 and 10 miles per hour. This feature accommodates the individual who walks at a 30-minute-mile pace, as well as the person who runs at a six-minute-mile pace.

The greater the treadmill inclination, the greater the exercise effort at a given training speed. For example, if an individual prefers not to run, that person can make their walking workout more challenging by increasing the treadmill inclination. For most practical purposes, treadmills should incline up to 10 degrees.

Treadmill walking and running should begin and end with slower-paced warm-up and cool-down segments. The actual conditioning session may consist of steady-pace activity or interval exercise, depending on how the exerciser changes the treadmill speed and inclination.

Before individuals begin to exercise on a treadmill, they should attach the safety clip to their shirt, and note where the handlebars and stop button are located in case they lose their balance. The following guidelines should be adhered to when using a motorized treadmill:

- Straddle the track with the feet on the solid side frames, place one hand on the handlebar, and touch the power button with the other hand. Push the incline button to make sure the treadmill is at zero degrees and completely level. If the treadmill offers preprogrammed exercise protocols, select the desired workout.

- Touch the start button and the track should begin moving slowly. While holding the handrail, place one foot gently on the track and stride with one leg to feel the movement speed. When comfortable, place both feet on the moving track and walk naturally, while still holding the handrail.

- When the exerciser feels confident, they should let go of the handrail, first with one hand and then the other, and walk naturally. Be sure to stay on the front portion of the track to keep close to the handrail and controls, and to reduce the risk of drifting off the back of the track. It is important to note that exercise posture greatly influences a person's treadmill performance. Try to walk or run "tall," with normal stride length and natural arm action (see Figure 8-2). Avoid short, choppy steps and allow the arms to move smoothly in coordination with the legs. In other words, the right arm and left leg should move forward and backward together, as should the left arm and right leg. Focus the eyes forward, rather than downward. Keep the shoulders and hips square, without allowing the torso to swing side-to-side or to shift forward or backward.

- If and when the exerciser wants to walk faster, press the speed button to quicken the pace. The individual should be sure to increase the miles per hour gradually as they progress to their desired training speed. Once the exerciser reaches four miles per hour, they are walking at a relatively fast 15-minute-mile pace. To further increase the effort, the exerciser can either raise the grade slightly so that they are walking uphill, or can increase the speed at which they are running. Every treadmill training session should include warming up and cooling down for a few minutes at a slow speed and low grade. For the actual training phase, a moderate effort level should be chosen by selecting a track speed and elevation that raises the heart rate to about 75 percent of maximum.

• If the exerciser is not in good condition, the training duration should be kept around 10 minutes. Individuals who are moderately fit should do about 10 to 20 minutes on the treadmill. Very fit exercisers should work out for 20 to 30 minutes.

• As the individual prepares to finish the exercise session, they should gradually reduce the speed and grade to the lowest levels, grasp the handrail, and touch the stop switch. The track should not be dismounted until it has stopped moving completely.

Figure 8-2

If at any time exercisers feel uncomfortable, off balance, or out of control, they should immediately touch the stop button, and the track will stop gently, but quickly. As an alternative to engaging in a steady-pace program, a variety of interval training workouts can be performed. For example, the individual could do two minutes at a slower than normal pace, followed by two minutes at a faster than normal pace, alternated throughout the exercise session. Whatever training program is performed, the exerciser should be sure to advance the controls one unit at a time, since the track speed and elevation changes are electronically delayed.

Steppers

Initially introduced as actual stairclimbing machines with revolving staircases, stepping is an effective vertical-movement endurance exercise that places high demands on the cardiovascular system. In that regard, a 1995 study conducted by Westcott found that stepping produces higher heart-rate responses than cycling, treadmill walking, and jogging, when these activities were performed at the same effort level (see Table 8-1). This outcome occurs because stepping requires lifting the body weight vertically, which uses more energy than most other endurance exercises. The participants in this research study rated stepping higher than other aerobic activities for both muscular and cardiovascular effort, which may make it more appropriate for intermediate exercisers than for beginners (see Table 8-2). Similar to other types of endurance exercise machines, exercisers may select a steady pace step program or a more challenging interval training program.

Exercise time (minutes)	Cycle		Stepper		Treadmill		Skate Machine	
	HR	BP	HR	BP	HR	BP	HR	BP
4	96	133/76	110	137/74	92	129/74	103	131/71
8	130	153/74	140	148/74	123	143/71	116	145/75
12	138	161/77	143	155/76	126	149/74	127	154/75
16	140	159/76	150	156/72	135	154/73	128	151/76
20	109	135/75	124	135/74	99	134/73	109	135/74
Mean	123	148/76	133	146/74	115	142/73	117	144/74

Test subjects averaged 42 years old, with a target heart rate range of 107 to 160 beats per minute.

Table 8-1. Heart rate and blood pressure responses on endurance machines

	Cycle	Stepper	Treadmill	Skate machine
Muscular effort	3.3	4.4	2.8	4.1
Cardiovascular effort	3.8	4.6	3.8	3.5
Coordination required	2.2	3.3	2.8	4.6
Overall fitness benefit	3.8	4.4	3.9	3.7
Exercise satisfaction	3.8	4.2	3.6	3.7

1 = low, 5 = high

Table 8-2. Rating of exercise factors on endurance machines

Step machines fall into two general categories based on their movement mechanics. Independent steppers have separated foot pedals that work independently of each other. As such, neither foot pedal influences the action of the other. Dependent steppers have connected foot pedals that work in a coordinated manner. In other words, as the left foot pedal moves upward, the right foot pedal moves downward, and vice versa. Since the foot pedal arrangement has little effect on the cardiovascular benefits or energy requirements of stepping, the choice between independent or dependent step machines is largely a matter of personal preference.

Muscle involvement in stepping is closely related to the individual's exercise technique. The quadriceps and hamstrings provide most of the movement force. The calf muscles of the lower leg are also involved, particularly if the exerciser performs much of the stepping action on the toes.

A person may inadvertently involve the muscles of their upper body if they do not use appropriate stepping posture. Proper stepping form requires a fairly upright posture, using the hands for balance, rather than for body support (see Figure 8-3). When working out, the individual should avoid leaning forward and unnecessarily stressing the wrists and lower back, which is not the intent of stepping exercise. As with walking and running, the exerciser should strive to keep the head up and the back straight while stepping.

Serghei Starus/iStock/Thinkstock

Figure 8-3

The depth of the steps should be moderate and comfortable. Just as there is no set stride length for walking and running, there is no set step depth for stepping. Relatively shallow stepping may decrease muscular work, while relatively deep stepping may increase the risk of injury. A moderate stepping action provides the exerciser with a reasonable range of movement, effectively involving the leg muscles, while still maintaining level hips and shoulders.

Because stepping is a demanding physical activity, it is essential to spend the first few minutes warming up and the last few minutes cooling down during each exercise session. The actual workout may consist of either a steady stepping cadence or a series of high-effort and low-effort intervals. The key for the exerciser is to be sure to maintain proper form and to remain within their target heart rate zone at all times.

The following guidelines should be adhered to when using a step machine:

- Step on the pedals and record the body weight, according to the computer prompts.
- Choose an exercise program that has built-in warm-up and cool-down phases, with an appropriate steady-state or interval training program in between. If the exerciser's current level of fitness is low, they should train at a minimal effort level (i.e., 1, 2, or 3 on a 9-point intensity scale). On the other hand, if the individual's present fitness level is moderate, that person should train at a middle-of-the-road effort level (i.e., 4, 5, or 6 on a 9-point scale). In contrast, if a person's current fitness level is relatively high, they can try exercising at a top-tier effort level (i.e., 7, 8, or 9 on a 9-point scale). As a person exercises, the workout can be made harder or easier by adjusting the intensity and pace controls.
- Select an appropriate exercise duration. Beginners should start with up to 10 minutes of exercise, intermediate exercisers may train for 10 to 20 minutes, and advanced exercisers for 20 to 30 minutes.
- Take medium steps, while maintaining level hips and shoulders.
- After the main phase of the exercise session is completed, dismount the stepper and walk for a few minutes to finish the cool-down.

Rowing Machines

Rowing machines come in various shapes, sizes, and resistance modes. Arguably, the most realistic rowers are those that employ revolving paddles and air resistance. On the other hand, hydraulic and electric models also provide similar cardiovascular benefits.

Although people sometimes think of rowing as an upper-body activity, this exercise uses the legs and lower back, as well as the upper back and arms. The first movement in the rowing stroke is a simultaneous extension of the knees and hips, a leg-pushing action that uses the quadriceps, hamstrings, and gluteal muscles. This maneuver is followed by trunk extension produced by the erector spinae muscles in the lower back. The final action in the rowing stroke is the arm pull, accomplished primarily by the latissimus dorsi, rhomboids, and trapezius muscles of the upper back and the biceps muscles of the arms.

All of the rowing movements should be performed smoothly and sequentially, with a firm, but relaxed, hand grip, an upright head, and a moderate range of trunk extension. Exercisers should not approach a horizontal torso position while rowing, since such a situation can place excessive stress on the lower back. On the return movement, individuals should reverse the muscular actions to come forward quickly, gently, and easily in preparation for the next pull.

To facilitate these successive and coordinated body movements, well-designed rowing machines should be structurally stable and operationally smooth. There should be no sticking points or rough spots in the pulling movement, and the return action should be easy to perform.

The rowing action will vary according to the stroke employed, which, in turn, is dependent on the length of the exerciser's arms and legs, as well as their training technique. Whatever cadence is utilized in the rowing exercise, the key to cardiovascular conditioning is the individual's heart rate response to the training effort. Exercisers should try to work within their training heart rate range, i.e., they should be able to converse in relatively short sentences during their rowing workout.

The following guidelines should be adhered to when exercising on a rowing machine:
- Sit on the moving seat and secure the feet to the footpads.
- Grip the handle comfortably, with the knees, hips, and trunk flexed.
- Push the body backward by extending the knees, hips, and trunk, and pull the handle to the midsection (see Figure 8-4).
- Return to the starting position as smoothly as possible.
- Begin with easy strokes, until the exerciser is warmed up, and then progressively increase the exercise effort.
- Pulling harder or faster increases the exercise resistance and training intensity.
- Finish the rowing workout with a few minutes of lower-effort strokes to cool down gradually.
- Beginning rowers should strive for up to 10 minutes of continuous exercise, intermediate rowers should train for 20 to 20 minutes, and advanced rowers may complete 20 to 30 minutes at a relatively vigorous pace.

Figure 8-4

Equipment Selection

The most important consideration when choosing endurance exercise equipment is personal preference. If the person is a lively individual, then they may enjoy the unencumbered feeling of running on a treadmill. If, on the other hand, they are overweight or out of shape, the supportive structure of a recumbent or upright cycle may make more sense as their basic training mode.

Of course, equipment availability may also play a major role in a person's choice of aerobic activity. If an individual has access to cycles, treadmills, steppers, and rowers, then a cross-training program may make their workouts more enjoyable. By performing a combination of endurance exercises each workout or by changing aerobic activities every training session, the level of both personal motivation and physical conditioning may be increased.

The key is for an individual to choose the modes of endurance exercise that they like best. If a person prefers a lower-intensity training experience, recumbent or upright cycling may be best for the majority of their endurance workouts. If an individual likes more rhythmic forms of aerobic activity, the rowing machine may be the most appropriate piece of exercise equipment for them. If an exerciser is already in relatively good shape and wants a high-intensity workout that provides the most training benefit in the least amount of time, they should try stepping. On the other hand, if a person prefers an activity that combines both rhythm and intensity, treadmill walking and running are good choices.

❏ Summary:

Similar to all modes of activity, individuals should approach endurance exercise sensibly. Without question, a "no gain without pain" attitude may do more harm than good. Before beginning their training regimen, exercisers should familiarize themselves with the guidelines reviewed at the beginning of this chapter.

In reality, a person has a number of choices of endurance exercise, each of which effectively conditions the cardiovascular system. Accordingly, the choice of exercise equipment is largely a matter of personal preference and physical condition.

Well-designed aerobic exercise equipment is scientifically sound, permits gradual warming up and cooling down, provides a variety of training levels and programs, displays performance feedback, offers user-friendly operation, and keeps the risk of injury to a minimum. It is also crucial to keep in mind that individuals should always workout on an exercise machine, exactly as directed by the manufacturer of the device. Furthermore, exercisers should always adhere to the endurance training principles detailed in this chapter.

References

1. Westcott WL. (1991). Comparison of upright and recumbent cycling exercise. *Amer. Fit. Quart.* 10 (October):36-38.
2. Westcott WL. (1995). From the world of research: The skate machine. *Amer. Fit. Quart.* 13:20-21.

CHAPTER 9
Endurance Training Programs:
Basic, Interval, Circuit, Cross-Training

This chapter reviews several sample endurance training programs that employ various exercise protocols. These exercise protocols are applicable to essentially all types of aerobic activities, including walking, jogging, running, upright cycling, recumbent cycling, rowing, stepping, swimming, and elliptical training. It is important to keep in mind that these suggested programs are only examples, and may be modified according to a person's current fitness level and time availability.

Basic Endurance Training Program

The basic endurance training program produces a trapezoid pattern of exercise effort, whether evaluated by heart rate response or perceived physical exertion. This training session should begin with a progressive warm-up segment, followed by a relatively steady-state of endurance exercise, and concluded with a gradual cool-down period.

For example, a 60-year-old man or woman has an estimated maximum heart rate of 160 beats per minute (220 − 60 = 160). Assuming a target heart rate training range of 70 to 80 percent of maximum, the steady-state portion of the exercise session should maintain a heart rate between 112 and 128 beats per minute. (160 x 0.7 = 112; 160 x 0.8 = 128). Assuming a resting heart rate of 70 beats per minute, the warm-up segment should gradually increase the heart rate from about 70 beats per minute to about 115 beats per minute. Conversely, the cool-down period should gradually decrease the heart rate from about 125 beats per minute to about 80 beats per minute.

The American College of Sports Medicine recommends a minimum of 20 minutes of continuous exercise for an effective endurance workout. For example, a four-minute warm-up segment may gradually increase the heart rate from 70 to 115 beats per minute, the 20-minute steady-state portion may maintain the heart rate between 115 and 120 beats per minute, and the four-minute cool-down period may gradually decrease the heart rate from 120 to 80 beats per minute.

Assuming a treadmill walking workout, the first four minutes may see increases in the track speed from 2.0 mph, to 2.5 mph, to 3.0 mph, to 3.5 mph in one-minute increments. As such, the 20-minute aerobic conditioning (steady-state) portion may be maintained at 4.0 mph, with a slight increase in heart rate during the latter part of the workout due to cumulative fatigue. The last four minutes may be the warm-up in reverse, gradually reducing the track speed to 3.5 mph, to 3.0 mph, to 2.5 mph, to 2.0 mph. As the cardiovascular system becomes better conditioned, the individual can either increase the treadmill speed or add an incline to keep the exercise heart rate in the desired training range.

Interval Endurance Training Program

As discussed in Chapter 7, interval endurance training offers physiological and psychological advantages over basic (steady-state) endurance training. In essence, interval endurance training divides the exercise portion of the workout into higher- and lower-effort intervals that alternate between the high and low limits of the target heart rate range.

Given the same 60-year-old individual from the previous example, this training session again has three distinct exercise components. First, there is a progressive four-minute warm-up segment, followed by a 20-minute interval protocol, and concluded with a four-minute cool-down period. The major difference is that the basic endurance training program maintains a constant exercise intensity, whereas the interval endurance training program provides undulating intensities. This example uses equal intervals of two minutes each, with the higher-intensity segments eliciting heart rates near the top of the heart rate training zone (128 beats per minute) and the lower-intensity segments eliciting heart rates near the bottom of the training zone (112 beats per minute).

Assuming a recumbent cycling workout, the first four minutes may see an increase in the cycling resistance from 25 watts to 50 watts, to 75 watts, to 100 watts. The 20-minute aerobic conditioning portion may alternate two-minute intervals at 125 watts with two-minute intervals at 75 watts (five intervals at each intensity level). The last four minutes may be the warm-up in reverse, gradually reducing the cycling resistance from 100 watts to 75 watts, to 50 watts, to 25 watts. Although the average interval training intensity is 100 watts, the 125-watt segments provide an enhanced exercise effect, and the 75-watt segments enable an active recovery within the target heart rate range. As the cardiovascular system becomes better conditioned, the exerciser may increase the intensity of the high-effort intervals to keep the exercise heart rate in the desired training range.

Circuit Endurance Training Program

The circuit endurance training program also offers physiological and psychological advantages over basic endurance training programs. Circuit endurance training typically involves three or more aerobic activity stations at which the participants work for one to three minutes each, before quickly transitioning to the next station. Circuit endurance training programs may be performed on exercise equipment (e.g., treadmills, recumbent cycles, step machines, upright cycles, rowers, elliptical machines, etc.), or with bodyweight activities (e.g., jumping jacks, pushups, squat jumps, sit-ups, rope skipping, burpees, etc.).

As a general rule, circuit endurance training on aerobic equipment would have longer exercise periods (e.g., three minutes per station), and circuit endurance training with body weight activities would have shorter exercise periods (e.g., one minute per station). The key to effective circuit endurance training is to make very brief transitions between successive exercise stations.

Due to the variety of activities, circuit endurance training involves a number of muscle groups, a factor that reduces the risk of overuse injuries. Similarly, by frequently changing the mode of exercising, there tends to be less likelihood of boredom during a circuit endurance training program.

To better understand the underlying application of circuit training, a relatively fit 30-year-old male or female who wants to do a challenging aerobic activity session that can be performed with bodyweight exercises could be considered. This individual may do each exercise in the endurance training circuit for two minutes, with as little transition time as possible between stations. The five-station circuit (i.e., jumping jacks, push-ups, squat jumps, sit-ups, and rope skipping) takes about 10 minutes for completion and will be repeated once for a total exercise time of 20 minutes. Jogging in place for three or four minutes may serve as both the warm-up and the cool-down activity.

Assuming a maximum heart rate of 190 beats per minutes (200 − 30 = 190) and a target heart rate training range of 70 to 80 percent of maximum, this individual should maintain an exercise heart rate between 133 and 152 beats per minute (190 x 0.7 = 13; 190 x 08 = 152). During this type of training session, however, it may be more practical to adjust the exercise intensity, according to the rating of perceived exertion. The effort level should be about seven (out of 10) during the first few exercise stations and will most likely increase to eight and nine (out of 10) as the body experiences the cumulative effects of a fatiguing workout. If the exercise effort is too low, the activity performance pace may be increased. On the other hand, if the exercise effort is too high, the pace at which the activity is performed may be decreased.

Cross-Training Endurance Exercise Program

Cross-training is similar to circuit endurance training in a few respects. For example, both training programs involve more than one exercise activity, which provides physiological and psychological advantages compared to the basic endurance training program. By performing a variety of aerobic activities, cross-training reduces the risk of overuse injuries and lessens the likelihood of exercise boredom or burn-out.

The major difference between circuit endurance training and cross-training is the duration that each exercise is performed. Whereas circuit endurance training exercises are typically performed for one to three minutes each, cross-training aerobic activities are generally done for 5 to 10 minutes each. Cross-training workouts typically involve two to four aerobic activities that emphasize different major muscles groups. For example, a 20-minute cross-training workout could be comprised of 10 minutes of treadmill jogging that emphasizes the hamstrings muscles and 10 minutes of upright cycling that emphasizes the quadriceps muscles. Another example of a cross-training workout might be a 20-minute cross-training workout that would consist of five minutes each of treadmill jogging, upright cycling, rowing, and stepping.

The following hypothetical example illustrates the underlying concepts in developing a cross-training workout—a relatively fit 30-year-old engages in a cross-training workout (jogging, cycling, rowing, stepping), within a target heart rate range of 133 to 152 beats per minutes. Making relatively quick transitions between the different aerobic activities should enable the participant to maintain a fairly consistent heart rate response (approximately 145 beats per minute), as well as a rating of perceived exertion around eight (out of 10) throughout the 20-minute training session. The four-minute warm-up should be performed on the first aerobic exercise machine (treadmill), and the four-minute cool-down should be completed on the final aerobic exercise machine (stepper).

Due to the relatively brief exercise periods (five minutes) on each machine, a basic (steady-state) training protocol is recommended for the cross-training program. If the exerciser prefers, however, each training bout could be performed in intervals (e.g., 30 seconds of higher-effort training alternated with 30 seconds of lower-effort training).

Cross-training endurance exercise regimens may be conducted on a weekly basis, as well as on a daily basis. For example, instead of doing three different exercises during a single training session, a person could do different exercises on three different days. In a similar vein, an individual could perform a running workout on Mondays, a cycling workout on Wednesdays, and a rowing workout on Fridays.

❏   Summary:
Safe and effective endurance exercise experiences involve three primary keys: a progressive warm-up; a 20-minute (or longer) training period within the target heart-rate range; and a gradual cool-down. Exercising in this manner provides the essential stimulus for increasing cardiovascular fitness and reduces the risk of overtraining. With regard to aerobic endurance training, four time-tested aerobic activity programs exist—basic (steady-state) endurance training protocols; interval endurance training protocols; circuit endurance training programs; and cross-training endurance exercise protocols.

CHAPTER 10
Strength Training and Protein Intake

Most fitness professionals are fully aware of the general guidelines for healthy eating. The most recent recommendations from the United States Department of Agriculture (see Figure 10-1) call for approximately 40 to 50 percent of daily food intake to be eaten from vegetables and fruits, about 15 to 20 percent from lean meats, about 15 to 20 percent from low fat dairy products, and about 15 to 20 percent from grains, with vegetable oils and nuts as the major sources for healthy fats.

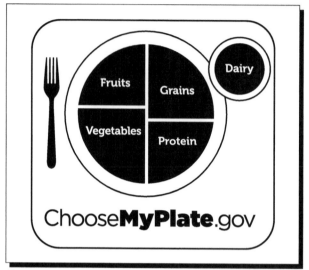

Figure 10-1

It is also widely recommended that every individual drinks between six and eight (eight-ounce) glasses of water daily. This factor is especially important for people who perform strength exercise, as muscle tissue is approximately 75 percent water. The remaining 25 percent of muscle tissue consists mostly of proteins that comprise the protein filaments that are responsible for muscle contraction. Accordingly, obtaining a sufficient amount of protein is essential for optimizing muscle and strength development.

Protein Recommendations

A common misconception exists that most Americans eat plenty of protein in their daily meals and snacks. In fact, this assumption is not necessarily true for a relatively large percentage of the population. As such, a substantial number of people over age 50 do not obtain sufficient daily protein to maintain their muscle mass, even if they perform regular resistance exercise.

According to leading nutrition researcher Dr. Wayne Campbell, individuals aged 50 and older who eat the recommended daily allowance (RDA) for protein (approximately 0.4 grams of protein per pound of body weight) will lose muscle mass, whether or not they strength train. In fact, in order to maintain their muscle mass, adults over age 50 must perform resistance exercise and eat at least 25 percent more daily protein than the RDA (about 0.5 grams of protein per pound of bodyweight). For people beyond their fifth decade of life who want to build muscle, Dr. Campbell's research indicates that they must perform resistance exercise and eat at least 50 percent more daily protein than the RDA (approximately 0.6 grams per pound of body weight).

Recent research conducted by Westcott and his colleagues has revealed excellent muscle-building results with a combination of sensible strength training and a daily protein intake of about 0.7 grams per pound of ideal body weight. For example, a person whose ideal body weight is 150 pounds should consume approximately 105 grams of protein every day.

Research on Resistance Exercise and Higher Protein Intake

In fact, a well-designed program of resistance exercise and higher protein intake can concurrently increase muscle mass and reduce fat weight. The authenticity of this factor was confirmed by the aforementioned research conducted by Westcott, a 10-week study that involved 121 men and women between 20 and 86 years of age. In Westcott's investigation, one study group performed a basic strength training program of nine resistance machine exercises, interspersed with three five-minute bouts of recumbent cycling, without any dietary changes. Another study group did the same strength training protocol, but increased their daily protein intake to 0.7 grams per pound of ideal bodyweight. A third study group performed the same strength training protocol, increased their daily protein intake to 0.7 grams per pound of ideal bodyweight, and reduced their daily calorie intake (1,200 to 1,500 calories/day for women and 1,500 to 1,800 calories/ day for men).

After 10 weeks of training, the exercise participants who increased their daily protein intake, without caloric restriction, added 2.5 times more lean (muscle) weight than the exercise participants who did not change their daily diets (2.8 lbs. versus 1.1 lbs.). Just as impressive, the exercise participants who increased their daily protein intake and decreased their daily consumption of calories added 1.5 times more lean (muscle) weight than the exercise participants who did not change their daily diets (1.7 lbs. versus 1.1 lbs.), even though they concurrently lost 7.1 pounds of fat weight. These research results indicated that a daily protein intake of 0.7 grams per pound of ideal bodyweight is effective for enhancing muscle gain in strength trainers who are eating a normal diet, as well as in those individuals who are eating a reduced calorie diet.

These findings are important, because most diet programs result in both fat loss and muscle loss. In fact, approximately one-third of the weight lost through typical diet plans is lean (muscle). Muscle loss leads to a metabolic slowdown, which makes it somewhat difficult to avoid weight regain.

In essence, when muscle mass is reduced, the body burns fewer calories, similar to changing from an eight-cylinder engine to a six-cylinder engine. Consequently, when a successful dieter returns to normal eating behavior, the caloric intake that previously maintained body weight is now too high for the slower metabolism, and the unused calories are converted into fat storage. This is the major reason that more than 90 percent of dieters regain all of the weight they lost within one year after completing their diet program.

Fortunately, dieters who perform regular resistance exercise and eat more protein may not experience muscle loss and a metabolic slowdown. In fact, as indicated previously, research reveals that people who combine a reasonable caloric restriction with strength training and higher protein intake can concurrently lose fat and gain muscle.

Post-Exercise Protein Supplementation

The resistance exercise plus protein program appears to be especially effective for improving body composition, when extra protein is consumed right after the strength training session. In another study conducted by Westcott in 2009, 46 participants performed a six-month program of strength and endurance exercise (11 resistance machine exercises and 20 minutes of stationary cycling). Half of the participants consumed a protein/carbohydrate shake (24 grams of protein and 36 grams of carbohydrate) immediately after each training session.

At the end of the study, the exercisers who did not take extra protein added 3.9 pounds of lean (muscle) mass and lost 4.9 pounds of fat weight. However, the exercisers who consumed the post-exercise protein/carbohydrate shakes added 5.5 pounds of lean (muscle) weight and lost 9.0 pounds of fat weight. Similar to the other study cited in the previous section, the participants who augmented their strength training with additional protein gained more muscle and lost more fat than the participants who did not take the post-exercise protein/carbohydrate shakes.

Research also indicates that supplemental protein may enhance the effects of resistance exercise on bone mineral density. In a study conducted by Westcott in 2011, 52 participants were divided into three groups: a control group, a strength training group, and a strength training plus supplemental protein group. Over the course of the nine-month program, the control group experienced a 1-percent decrease in bone mineral density, the strength training group experienced no change in bone mineral density, and the strength training plus supplemental protein group experienced a 1-percent increase in bone mineral density.

The resistance exercise program was the same for both strength training groups, and consisted of 12 weightstack machines performed for one set of 8 to 12 repetitions each workout. The strength training plus supplemental protein group consumed a shake immediately after each exercise session. The shake contained 24 grams of protein and 36 grams of carbohydrate. In addition, this group took a daily vitamin/mineral complex that contained 500 mg of calcium and 1,200 IU of vitamin D throughout the course of the study.

Whereas the strength training program appeared to prevent bone loss (no change in bone mineral density versus a 1-percent decrease for control subjects), the strength training plus supplemental protein program actually increased bone mineral density by 1 percent over the nine-month training period.

In addition, the strength training plus supplemental protein group experienced significantly greater increases in lean (muscle) weight than the strength training group (5.2 lbs. versus 3.9 lbs.). Once again, post exercise protein supplementation seemed to enhance the effects of standard resistance exercise on muscle development, and also had a positive impact on bone health.

Based on a recent review of protein supplementation following resistance training sessions conducted by Westcott and LaRosa Loud, it would appear that consuming pre- and/or post-exercise protein is an effective means for enhancing muscle strength and size. As such, it is important to realize that adults who do not strength train lose 3 to 8 percent of their muscle mass every decade after age 30, and 5 to 10 percent of their muscle mass every decade after age 50. As discussed in Chapter 1, muscle loss leads to metabolic slow-down, which results in fat gain with associate physiological problems and degenerative diseases, such as diabetes, cardiovascular complications, and certain types of cancer. On the other hand, a number of strength training studies have shown that one-pound-per-month increase in lean (muscle) weight occurs during the first three to six months of regular resistance exercise.

It is also crucial to understand that muscle remodeling and rebuilding may be attained by men and women of all ages, including individuals in their 80s and 90s. The stimulus for increasing muscle mass is sensible strength training, with progressive increments in the exercise resistance. The American Council on Exercise recommends a 5-percent increase in the training load, once an individual is able to perform the maximum number of prescribed exercise repetitions (e.g., 12 repetitions in an 8 to 12 repetition training protocol).

As such, a number of studies have shown that significantly greater gains in muscle size and strength may be attained when appropriate amounts of protein are ingested within one hour before and after the training session. Basically, resistance exercise increases both muscle protein breakdown and muscle protein synthesis. For several hours after strength training, however, the rate of muscle protein breakdown exceeds the rate of muscle protein synthesis. Consuming supplemental protein in close time proximity to resistance exercise enhances muscle protein synthesis and facilitates a net positive protein balance that is essential for muscle development.

In a classic study conducted by Cribb and Hayes in 2006, previously trained males (average age 22 years) performed four sessions of resistance exercise each week for a period of 10 weeks. The study participants performed mostly free-weight, multiple-muscle exercises at a high training intensity. All of the subjects consumed one gram of a protein/carbohydrate supplement for every kilogram of body weight. For example, a 100 kilogram (220 pound) male's supplement portion would be 100 grams, containing about 47 grams of protein and 43 grams of carbohydrate.

Half of the 17 subjects took the supplement just before and just after their weight workouts. The other half took the supplement on their strength training days in the morning (at least five hours before their weight workouts) and in the evening (at least five hours after their weight workouts).

Following the 10-week strength training program, the study participants who consumed the supplemental protein immediately before and after their workouts experienced significantly better results than the study participants who consumed the supplemental protein five hours before and five hours after their workouts. With respect to muscle development, the training group that ingested extra protein at the time of their workouts gained 2.8 kilograms of lean (muscle) weight, compared to 1.5 kilograms of lean (muscle) weight for the other training group. With respect to strength development, the training group that ingested extra protein at the time of their workouts experienced greater increases in bench press performance (12.2 kilograms versus 9.0 kilograms) and in squat performance (20.4 kilograms versus 16.1 kilograms) than the other training group. Furthermore, the participants who consumed extra protein at the time of their workouts attained greater increases in muscle protein content and muscle fiber cross-sectional size in both type 2a and type 2x fibers than the participants in the other training group.

Subsequently, the positive findings from the research conducted by Cribb and Hayes prompted several other investigations of pre/post strength training protein supplementation. Most of these studies showed impressive increases in muscle strength and mass with smaller doses of protein than those used in the Cribb and Hayes study. For example, two studies conducted in 2008 and 2011 by Westcott and colleagues revealed greater gains in lean (muscle) weight (5.5 lbs. versus 3.9 lbs. and 5.2 versus 3.9 lbs., respectively) in those strength trainers who consumed a post-training shake that contained 24 grams of protein and 36 grams of carbohydrate.

In their 2013 review of the available research on post-exercise protein supplementation, Westcott and LaRosa Loud recommended a sliding scale of pre- and post-strength training protein consumption, based on a person's ideal (healthy) bodyweight. The amounts of supplemental protein they suggest represent the averages of several research studies and are equally applicable for men and women (see Table 10-1).

Ideal Bodyweight		Protein Supplementation
Kilograms	Pounds	Grams
50	110	18–22
60	132	22–26
70	154	26–30
80	176	30–34
90	198	34–38
100	220	38–42

Source: Westcott, WL and LaRosa Loud, R. Enhancing resistance training results with protein/carbohydrate supplementation. *ACSM's Health & Fitness Journal*, Vol. 17, No. 2, 2013, page 13.

Table 10-1. Recommended pre or post exercise protein consumption based on ideal body weights

In fact, some research evidence exists that indicates that there may be a ceiling effect for the amount of protein consumed after a strength training session. In a 2009 study by Moore and associates, young men consumed different amounts of whole egg protein after a lower-body strength workout (0, 5, 10, 20, and 40 grams). Ten grams of post-exercise protein produced greater muscle protein synthesis than five grams, while 20 grams of post-exercise protein produced greater muscle protein synthesis than 10 grams. Forty grams of post-exercise protein, however, did not increase muscle protein synthesis more than the 20 gram supplement. Based on these findings, it could be assumed that young men, who process protein efficiently and effectively, may maximize the rate of post-exercise protein synthesis by consuming at least 20 grams of protein after their strength training session.

On the other side of the coin, there is research evidence that older adults, who do not process protein as efficiently or effectively, may need more than 15 grams of post-exercise protein to simulate the desired levels of muscle protein synthesis. In fact, as research from Arizona State University indicates, men and women in their 60s process less than half of the protein they consume compared to men and women in their 30s. Apparently, the body's ability to assimilate amino acids from ingested protein declines with age.

According to renowned nutrition researcher Dr. Douglas Paddon-Jones, older adults (over age 60) need to eat more than 15 grams of protein at a meal or snack in order for the amino acids assimilation process to be activated. For example, an older adult who eats a regular yogurt (approximately 10 grams of protein) for a mid-afternoon snack may not experience significant amino acid assimilation due to the inability to process relatively small amounts of protein. Consuming a Greek yogurt snack, however, with approximately 20 grams of protein, should be sufficient to stimulate muscle protein synthesis.

Based on the reduced protein processing ability of older adults, Baechle and Westcott have recommended specific daily protein consumption guidelines for resistance-trained men and women in their 50s, 60s, and 70s in order to optimize protein synthesis and muscle building (see Table 10-2).

Age ranges in years	Recommended daily protein intake	Percent increase for strength trainers	Recommended daily protein intake for strength trainers
50-59	Men: 56 grams	Men: 50%	Men: 85 grams
	Women: 46 grams	Women: 50%	Women: 70 grams
60-69	Men: 56 grams	Men: 60%	Men: 90 grams
	Women: 46 grams	Women: 60%	Women: 75 grams
70-79	Men: 56 grams	Men: 70%	Men: 95 grams
	Women: 46 grams	Women: 70%	Women: 80 grams

Table 10-2. Recommended daily protein intake for men and women over age 50 who perform resistance exercise

In fact, an upper limit may exist on the amount of protein that can contribute to muscle tissue remodeling and rebuilding following a single meal or snack. One study indicated that approximately 30 grams of ingested protein may be utilized for muscle protein synthesis at a given time, and that additional protein intake may be used for other purposes (energy production, energy storage). Accordingly, it is recommended that adults attain significant amounts of protein (at least 20 to 30 grams) at various times throughout the day (breakfast, lunch, dinner, snacks) to optimize their level of muscle protein synthesis. Table 10-3 presents common foods and serving sizes that contain between 20 and 30 grams of dietary protein.

Food	Amount	Protein Content
Almonds	1 cup	24 grams
Beef (lean)	4 ounces	28 grams
Chicken (white meat)	4 ounces	28 grams
Eggs	4 eggs	24 grams
Milk (low fat)	3 cups	24 grams
Peanut butter	8 tablespoons	28 grams
Salmon	4 ounces	28 grams
Tuna	4 ounces	28 grams
Turkey (white meat)	4 ounces	28 grams
Yogurt (Greek)	1 cup	20 grams

Table 10-3. Foods and serving sizes that provide between 20 and 30 grams of protein

While a number of physiological benefits may be attained by eating more protein-rich foods and performing regular strength training, it is advisable to drink more water (or other healthy fluids) to accommodate the digestive processes associated with additional protein consumption. A sensible recommendation is to drink about eight eight-ounce glasses of water on a daily basis.

❑ Summary:

The research reviewed in this chapter indicates that men and women who perform regular resistance exercise should consume approximately 0.7 grams of protein for every pound of ideal bodyweight. Studies have shown that this level of protein intake, in combination with regular strength training, significantly increases muscle mass and strength, significantly decreases fat weight, and increases bone mineral density. Research also supports the consumption of supplementary protein in close time proximity to resistance training sessions for maintaining a positive post-exercise protein balance that enhances muscle protein synthesis, strength development, and muscle hypertrophy.

It appears that there may be an upper limit of 20 to 30 grams of protein ingested at a given time for use in muscle protein synthesis. Consequently, eating 20 to 30 grams of protein at meals and snacks throughout the day may be more productive with regard to muscle development than a person consuming most of their daily protein during the evening meal. An increase in protein intake should be accompanied by an increase in water (fluid) intake, totaling approximately eight eight-ounce glasses each day.

References

1. Baechle T, Westcott WL. (2010). Fitness Professional's Guide to Strength Training Older Adults. Champaign, Ill.: *Human Kinetics.*
2. Ballor D, Poehlman E. (1994). Exercise training enhances fat-free mass preservation during diet-induced weight loss: a meta analytic finding. *Intern. J. Obesity.* 18: 35-40.
3. Biolo G, Maggi SP, Williams BD, et al. (1995). Increased rates of muscle protein turnover and amino acid transport after resistance exercise in humans. *Am. J. Physiol.* 268: E514-20.
4. Brehm B, Keller B. (1990). Diet and exercise factors that influence weight and fat loss. *IDEA Today.* 8: 33-46.
5. Campbell W, Crim MC, Young VR, Evans WJ. (1994). Increased energy requirements and changes in body composition with resistance training in older adults. *Am. J. Clin. Nutr.* 60: 402-407.
6. Campbell W, Trappe T, Wolfe R, Evans W. (2001). The recommended dietary allowance for protein may not be adequate for older people to maintain skeletal muscle. J. Gerontol. A: Biol. *Sci. Med. Sci.* 56: M373-M380.
7. Cribb P, Hayes A. (2006). Effect of supplement timing on skeletal muscle hypertrophy. Med. *Sci. Sports. Exerc.* 38(11): 1918-1925.
8. Elliot T, Cree M, Sanford A, et al. (2006). Milk ingestion stimulates net muscle protein synthesis following resistance exercise. Med. *Sci. Sports. Exerc.* 38(4): 667-674.
9. Fiatarone MA, Mrks E, Ryan N, et al. (1990). High-intensity strength training in nonagenarians. *JAMA.* 263(22): 3029-3034.
10. Flack KD, Davy KP, Huber MAW, et al. (2011). Aging, resistance training, and diabetes prevention. *J. Aging Res.* 2011: 127315.
11. Hartman JW, Tang JE, Wilkinson SB, et al. (2007). Consumption of fat-free fluid milk after resistance exercise promotes greater lean mass accretion than does consumption of soy or carbohydrate in young, novice, male weightlifters. *Am. J. Clin. Nutr.* 86(2): 373-381.
12. Josse A, Tang J, Tarnopolsky M, Phillips S. (2010). Body composition and strength changes in women with milk and resistance exercise. *Med. Sci. Sports Exerc.* 42(6): 1122-1130.
13. Katsanos, CS, Kobayashi, H, Sheffield-Moore, M, et al. (2005). Aging is associated with diminished accretion of muscle proteins after the ingestion of a small bolus of essential amino acids. *Am. J. Clin. Nutr.* 82(5): 1065-1073.
14. Mann T, Tomiyama A, Westling E, et al. (2007). Medicare's search for effective obesity treatment; diets are not the answer. *Am. Psych.* 62(3): 220-233.
15. Moore DR, Robinson MJ, Fry JL, et al. (2009). Ingested protein dose response of muscle and albumin protein synthesis after resistance exercise in young men. *Am. J. Clin. Nutr.* 89: 161-168.
16. Poole C, Wilborn C, Taylor L, Kerksick C. (2010). The role of post-exercise nutrient administration n muscle protein synthesis and glycogen syntheses. *J. Sports Sci. Med.* 9: 354-363.
17. Pratley R, Nicklas , Rubin M, et al. (1994). Strength training increases resting metabolic rate and norepinephrine levels in health 50- to 65-year-old men. *J. Appl. Physiol.* 76: 133-137.
18. Schardt D. (2007). Saving muscle: How to stay strong and healthy as you age. *Nutr. Action Health Let.* 34(3): 3-8.
19. Schardt D. (2011). Staying strong: How exercise and diet can help preserve your muscles. *Nutr. Action Health Let.* 38(3): 1-6.

20. Symons TB, Sheffield-Moore, M, Wolfe RR, Paddon-Jones, D. (2009). A moderate serving of high-quality protein maximally stimulates skeletal muscle protein synthesis in young and elderly subjects. *J. Am. Diet. Assoc.* 109: 1582-1586.

21. Westcott WL. (2012). Resistance training is medicine: Effects of strength training on health. Curr. *Sports Med. Reports.* 11(4); 209-216.

22. Westcott WL. (2014). In Bryant C, Merrill S, Green D, editors. *ACE Personal Trainer Manual.* 5th ed. American Council on Exercise. pgs. 326-390.

23. Westcott WL, Apovain CM, Puhala K, et al. (2013). Nutrition programs enhance exercise effects on body composition and resting blood pressure. *Phys. Sports Med.* 41(3): 85-91.

24. Westcott WL, LaRosa Loud R. (2013). Enhancing resistance training results with protein/carbohydrate supplementation. *ACSM's Health Fit. J.* 17(2): 10-15.

25. Westcott WL, Martin W, LaRosa Loud R, Stoddard S. (2008). Protein supplementation and body composition changes. *Fitness Manage.* 24(5): 50-53.

26. Westcott WL, Varghese J, DiNubile N, et al. (2011). Exercise and nutrition more effective than exercise alone for increasing lean weight and reducing resting blood pressure. *J. Exerc. Physiol.* 14(4): 120-133.

27. Westcott WL, Winett RA, Annesi JJ, et al. (2009). Prescribing physical activity: Applying the ACSM protocols for exercise type, intensity, and duration across 3 training frequencies. *Phys. Sports. Med.* 37(2): 51-58.

ABOUT THE AUTHOR

Wayne L. Westcott, Ph.D., is a professor of exercise science at Quincy College in Quincy, Massachusetts. Dr. Westcott has been a strength training consultant for numerous organizations, including the U.S. Navy, the U.S. Air Force, the American Council on Exercise, the YMCA of the USA, General Motors, and Nautilus. He has authored 28 books/textbooks, and more than 75 peer-reviewed research/academic papers.

Dr. Westcott has also served as an editorial advisor, reviewer, writer, and columnist for a number of publications, including *The Physician and Sportsmedicine, ACSM's Health & Fitness Journal, ACSM's Certified News, Fitness Management, Prevention, Men's Health*, and *Shape*. Furthermore, he has been a keynote speaker for national meetings of the American College of Sports Medicine, the American College of Nutrition, the National Intramural and Recreational Sports Association, and a repeat presenter at the Harvard Medical School International Conference on Preventing Obesity.

In addition, Dr. Westcott has received the Roberts-Gulick Memorial Award from the YMCA Association of Professional Directors, the Healthy American Fitness Leader Award from the President's Council on Physical Fitness and Sports, the Marla Richmond Memorial Education Award from the Medical Fitness Association, and the Alumni Recognition Award from the Pennsylvania State University.